69

Is the Holocaust Unique?

Is the Holocaust Unique?

PERSPECTIVES ON
COMPARATIVE GENOCIDE

edited, with an Introduction by
Alan S. Rosenbaum

with a Foreword by
Israel W. Charny

Westview Press
A Member of Perseus Books, L.L.C.

Copyright © 1998 by Westview Press, A Member of Perseus Books, L.L.C.

Published in 1996 in the United States of America by Westview Press, Inc., 5500 Central Avenue, Boulder, Colorado 80301-2877, and in the United Kingdom by Westview Press, 12 Hid's Copse Road, Cumnor Hill, Oxford OX2 9JJ

Library of Congress Cataloging-in-Publication Data
Is the Holocaust unique? : perspectives on comparative genocide /
    edited with an introduction by Alan S. Rosenbaum ; with a foreword
    by Israel W. Charny.
        p.   cm.
    Includes bibliographical references and index.
    ISBN 0-8133-2641-9 (hc). — ISBN 0-8133-2642-7 (pb)
    1. Holocaust, Jewish (1939–1945)—Historiography.   2. Genocide.
I. Rosenbaum, Alan S.
D804.348.I8   1996
940.53'18'072—dc20   96-33949
                                                                      CIP

The paper used in this publication meets the requirements of the American National Standard for Permanence of Paper for Printed Library Materials Z39.48-1984.

10   9   8   7   6   5   4   3

I dedicate this volume to my own children
Emily and Marc, Jascha and Libby
and
to the younger generations who are inheriting
a world not of their design but one
summoning their most courageous impulses against
the rising tides of intolerance, hatred,
and attempts at genocide.

"The only thing necessary for the triumph of
evil is for good men to do nothing."
Attributed to Edmund Burke (1729–1797)

Contents

Foreword

ISRAEL W. CHARNY

I am stunned and upset by this book and very grateful to its editor, Alan Rosenbaum, for creating it.

It is, as I will attempt to explain, a daring compilation of contemporary academic thinking about the Holocaust in a comparative perspective, so that in the process it also concerns, and in some cases also presents, important new information about other cases of genocide, including the following:

- the genocide of the Romani, or Gypsies, in the very same process of the Holocaust (which Ian Hancock correctly argues "deserves acknowledgment far beyond that which it now receives," especially by the Jewish establishment);
- the Armenian genocide, both in its own monumental right and then also as a prototype of genocide that many scholars see as the precursor, and in a sense also as a facilitator, of the Holocaust;
- too-little-known information about the genocides of so many indigenous peoples—the native Americans;
- genocide in Nigeria-Biafra;
- the ethnic cleansing and genocide that occurred in the former Yugoslavia throughout the first half of the 1990s;
- a stunning historical analysis of the Atlantic slave trade that argues—the first time for me as a genocide scholar—for its constituting genocide;
- the Ukrainian famine genocide;
- and more, making it clear to all people that genocide has been, is, and will continue to be the fate of many different peoples—and one must be careful that even legitimate considerations of the uniqueness of a given genocide (such as the archetypal event of the Holocaust) not blind us to the enormity of the problem of mass murders of many different peoples, especially toward our collective future on this planet.

This book is so daring, I now add, that in my opinion it includes several chapters and substantial sections of chapters that should never have been accepted for publication by a responsible editor *save for his intention to show the difficult truth of the jingoistic/ideological wars (above and beyond a healthy diversity of ideas and emphases) that are going on in Holocaust and genocide studies.* For, along with the devotion and scholarly skills of an increasing number of researchers unearthing more knowledge of the Holocaust and other genocides, there is a disquieting pattern of claims of the "incomparable uniqueness" of the Holocaust and a good deal of political power used in many places in academia, museums, and communities to back up these claims by pushing down and out nonadherents.

No less disturbing, many of the counterclaims—however justified in epistemological and moral intent to place the genocides of *all* peoples on the same level of tragedy and evil—go on to minimize the horror of the Holocaust and display a nasty lack of reverence for the victims of the Holocaust. And though such counterclaims correctly try to pull the Holocaust back into a comparative perspective and prove that the Holocaust was not uniquely more punishing, cruel, and betraying of human civilization than all other cases of genocide, they introduce serious factual distortions regarding the history of the Holocaust (e.g., the preposterous claim that Jews had it *easier* than victims in other genocides because the Nazi death machinery was so efficient). Yet at times the treatment of the subject of the Holocaust takes on the semblance of a competitive or prestige issue for academicians, progressing to a point that deeply violates reverence for the Holocaust, both as an enormous specific tragedy and as a watershed event in our century that has finally brought before our human civilization the denied subject of genocide as an all-too-frequent and, indeed, universal phenomenon.

❀   ❀   ❀

The central question in this book is whether it is possible to say, as one contributor says explicitly and several others say more guardedly, "Not all mass murders are genocide."

Can there be any case of mass murder which is not genocide? I do not believe so. Can there be any case of mass murder that is not with or without intention? with or without a plan to kill all the victim people? with or without a murder-enabling and camouflaging context of war against the victim nationality or against another people with whom the victims are or are not allied? with or without territorial, economic, or political motives? with or without religious, ethnic, or other historic enmity, memory, or cause for revenge for a previous genocide? that is even for "no reason"—other than the atavistic rotten cannibalism and sadistic cruelty that is, tragically, a serious part of human nature and potential?

In a presentation to the Raphael Lemkin Symposium on Genocide at Yale University Law School (see annotated references following this foreword), I proposed recognizing all cases of mass murder as genocide *and*, at the same time, subclassifying various cases of genocide into subgroups of similar events, so that we have a series of categories of types of genocide, with study and analysis of the differences and similarities in contexts, dynamics, methods, outcomes, possibilities for intervention, and so on. It is no different than a book about cancer diseases that kill; the various killer cancers are similar *and* different. We do not suffer competitions between different types of cancer as to which is to be celebrated as unique or worst.

I believe that all cases of genocide are similar and different, special and unique, and appropriately subject to comparative analysis.

For each person whose loved ones were killed in any genocide, for each people whose co-nationals were variously persecuted, tortured, driven into exile, and/or murdered, each genocide is inherently unique.

Moreover, each configuration of historical, political, military, societal, and psychological processes that define a given genocidal process is inherently unique.

I object to any statement that in any way minimizes the significance or sacredness of any people's losses, even when the understandable and legitimate purpose is to honor one's own people's tragedy, or even the specific tragedy of any other given people that one is respectfully researching or is committed to remembering.

I also object to scholars who transform the material of genocide scholarship predominantly into definitional arguments about what is or is not "genocide." I call this "definitionalism," or such an intense concern with establishing the boundaries of a definition that the reality of the phenomenon—in this case, human tragedy and infamy—is banished to a secondary position and no longer genuinely experienced.

Even more regrettable are those scholars who, patently, are more concerned with *their* ideas and with *their* political standing in academia or the community than with a commitment to all human lives.

❀ ❀ ❀

I recommend to the readers, and certainly to students who will be using this book in a university setting, that as one reads each chapter, ask the following questions about each scholar's work:

- *Does the author convey a genuine and unstinting concern with the tragedy and immorality of each and every genocide to which he refers in his comparative analysis?*
- *Does the author appear more concerned with perpetuating his own people's memory of their genocide than with a concern for all human lives?*
- *Does the author appear more involved with his own ideas and scholarship than with battling the evil of genocide?*
- *Does the author use all-or-none thinking and black-and-white argumentation to create diametrically opposed differences between different cases of genocide to the point where deaths in the one instance are claimed to be more terrible than in the other?*
- *Does the author utilize* post hoc *fallacious reasoning? The following are examples of such fallacies that will be found in contributions to this book:*

- *Most of the Armenians in Istanbul survived the Armenian genocide at the hands of the Turks; therefore, one cannot say the Turks intended or committed genocide, because genocide means the murder of an entire people.*
- *There is no evidence the Nazis planned to kill all the Jews outside of Europe; therefore, one cannot say they intended total annihilation of the Jewish people.*
- *When the Nazis faced defeat, many of them were willing to stop killing the Jews; hence, one cannot say they had been adherents to a pseudoreligious commitment to murder all the Jews.*

❀   ❀   ❀

This book is outstanding because it brings together in one volume the contentious and often unsavory Tower of Babel of scholars' voices in the field of Holocaust and genocide studies. In effect, editor Alan S. Rosenbaum has pitted the assembled scholars against one another in a grand gladiatorial coliseum, where he also lets us see many of the scholars in their naked reactions when they are consumed with proving something or other about their chosen genocide versus other genocides.

Rosenbaum himself is very clear in the Introduction that "the Holocaust is in many crucial aspects an unparalleled or singular event" but that this does not mean it is "unique" and, indeed, that the Holocaust is of great significance because it leads us to universal lessons about other "unqualified evil." It, therefore, can appear paradoxical that he has accepted for publication in his volume the following:

- A chapter that argues for the undisputed uniqueness of the Holocaust and utilizes the appearances of comparative analysis of other genocides to minimize every single one of them. One should note that in the penultimate version of this chapter, which served as the *final* version until just days before this volume went to press, statistical data about the Armenian genocide were presented that do not correspond to the press reports in *The New York Times* at the time of the genocide, to the published archives of U.S. diplomats, or to major historians such as Toynbee and Sachar, the purpose of the data being to minimize the fatalities in the genocide, and these data were also accompanied by a reference to a full-blown revisionist source, that is a known denier of that genocide. While the numerical details of this data will not, after all, be included in these pages, the skewed conclusion they support remains.
- A chapter that insists that state murder of 6 million Ukrainian people by starvation was never *intended* as murder but rather as a coercive political strategy with a necessary policy that overrode any concern for the dying; therefore, the whole process and the mass deaths by starvation did not constitute genocide.

- A chapter that—although correctly battling for recognition of all mass-murdered peoples as victims of an ugly universal process of genocide and courageously analyzing the relationship between denials of genocide and claims of uniqueness—insults and polarizes scholarship in the field no less than criticizes and corrects errors and contains some of the worst insults to the enormity of the Holocaust, including the illustration given earlier of reasoning that *since Nazis did not kill all the Jews, they did not intend to kill them all in the first place.*
- Chapters that contain many absolute assertions and interpretations of truth without humility or struggle and without references to alternative ideas.

The editor has clearly decided to allow all sides of the debate to speak in a wholly uncensored or even uncorrected way. One might disagree with this decision, but one can understand why he made it. Although the reader needs to be alerted to the fact that there are gross distortions courtesy of full-blown and irresponsible revisionists (there are others in addition to the case referred to earlier), there may not be any other way for the editor to give us a serious opportunity to see ourselves as we really are in the field of holocaust and genocide studies. I value what Rosenbaum has dared achieve for us, even as I, personally, don't like much of what I see. It seems to me that there are too many parts spun from the same cloth of all-or-nothing, ideologically driven thinking, prejudice, arrogance or degradation, and posturing for power—all elements that our true common enemy, the genocidal process, also builds on. For my soul and academic self, I believe holocaust and genocide studies should be dedicated to be a beacon of reverence and caring for *all* human life.

Jerusalem
August 1995

ANNOTATED REFERENCES TO SELECTED PUBLICATIONS WRITTEN BY ISRAEL W. CHARNY ON A "GENERIC" AND "HUMANISTIC" DEFINITION OF GENOCIDE

"Genocide: The Ultimate Human Rights Problem," *Social Issues Resource Series: Human Rights*, vol. 2, article 57 (1986), reprinted in *Social Education* 49(6) (1985): 448–452.

"The issue is the *wanton* murder of a group of human beings on the basis of any identity whatsoever that they share: national, ethnic, racial, religious, political, geographical, ideological. I reject out of hand that there can ever be any identity process that in itself will justify the murder of men, women and children 'because' they are anti some 'ism' or because their physical characteristics are high or low cheekboned, short or long eared, or green or orange colored" (*Social Education,* p. 448).

"Genocide and Mass Destruction: Doing Harm to Others as a Missing Dimension in Psychopathology," *Psychiatry* 49(2) (1986): 144–157.

A proposal to expand traditional mental health diagnosis from its usual emphasis on the harm people do to *themselves* and their own capacity to function, to include diagnosis of the harm people do to *other* human beings and their capacity to function.

"How to Avoid (Legally) Convictions for Crimes of Genocide (a One-Act Reading)," *Social Science Record* 24(2) (1987): 89–93.

A satire on a legal consultation pursued by the unholy alliance of Hitler, Stalin, Pol Pot, Talaal, and Idi Amin at the law offices of a top firm of international lawyers: Satan, Conformist, and Whore. The clients want to know how to protect themselves against possible international penalties for genocide. Their legal counsel propose that they be careful not to terminate a single victim people at one time but that they had best get their victim group when it is embedded within a larger population, for example, many Jews within the total population of New York City, and thus perhaps escape some of the pedantic stipulations in current genocide law.

Unpublished Typescript, Fiction. April 2018. Intergalactic Council for Protection of Ethnic and Planetary Human Rights and the Prevention of Genocide. *Internet on the Holocaust and Genocide, Special Double Issue 25/26 on the Seventy-Fifth Anniversary of the Armenian Genocide,* April 1990, pp. 13–14.

A satire about an interplanetary body in the future that rules the Holocaust qualifies only as *attempted genocide* and *humancide,* because in the final analysis it constituted only partial destruction of the Jewish people, many of whom survived, in contrast with *genocide,* which refers only to instances of actual total extinction of a people, and *planetcide,* which is the full extermination of an entire planet. The tiny country of Israel on Planet Earth votes against the proposal but loses, but the Armenians on Earth take revenge on Israel for past denials and minimization of their genocide by voting for the proposal.

"The Psychology of Denial of Known Genocides," in Israel W. Charny, ed., *Genocide: A Critical Bibliographic Review,* vol. 2 (London: Mansell Publishing, and New York: Facts on File, 1991), pp. 3–37.

A classification of different types of denial of known genocides and an analysis of the psychological dynamics of such denials, including to further incite violence, against the same and other victim peoples, in the future; humiliation of the victims and their survivors; "stealing" the record of history and rationality from human civilization—all further acts of aggression against humanity.

"Which Genocide Matters More? Learning to Care About Humanity," in *Genocide in the Twentieth Century: Critical Essays and Eyewitness Accounts,* ed. Samuel Totten, William S. Parsons, and Israel W. Charny (New York: Garland, 1995), pp. 535–542.

The concluding chapter of a book that, along with chapters that focus on a succession of genocides in the twentieth century, presents first-person accounts of genocides, creating an anthem of the voices of victims from a series of peoples in their common humanity. Usually, oral histories and first-person accounts appear in publications devoted to a single, specific people, and the voices of different peoples are rarely heard together.

"Toward a Generic Definition of Genocide," in *Genocide: Conceptual and Historical Dimensions,* ed. George Andreopoulos (Philadelphia: University of Pennsylvania Press, 1994), pp. 64–94 (presented at the Raphael Lemkin Symposium on Genocide, Yale University Law School, February 1991).

A proposal of a comprehensive classification of different forms of genocide, each category as a separate conceptual entity for legal and social science purposes, but all within a unifying generic concept of genocide as all cases of mass murder; so that no situation can arise where any form of mass murder can be denied recognition as *genocide.*

Preface

The reader should expect that the viewpoints expressed by some of the contributors to this collection are controversial and, despite their scholarly frame of reference, may occasion some challenging exchanges in response well beyond what has already occurred elsewhere. I, as editor, reaffirm that the purpose of this volume is to disclose to the reading public some cardinal aspects of the character and dimensions of this ongoing and sometimes impassioned debate. Each contributor is a recognized expert in his or her chosen area of scholarship and is understood to stand behind his or her claims as expressed herein.

Alan S. Rosenbaum

Acknowledgments

I wish to thank the following individuals, whose expertise and assistance in a variety of areas helped to guide me in the preparation of the manuscript: Mr. Spencer Carr (Editor, Westview Press); Dr. Michael Berenbaum (Project Director of the United States Holocaust Memorial Museum, Washington, D.C.); Dr. Joseph P. DeMarco (Chairman, Department of Philosophy, Cleveland State University, Cleveland, Ohio); Barry Epstein (President, Eppco Enterprises, Cleveland, Ohio); and Ricardo Teamor, Esq. (Teamor, Thomson, and Associates).

A. S. R.

"The things I saw beggar description. . . . The visual evidence and the verbal testimony of starvation, cruelty and bestiality were . . . overpowering. . . . I made the visit deliberately in order to be in a position to give first-hand evidence of these things if ever, in the future, there develops a tendency to charge these allegations merely to 'propaganda.'"

General Dwight D. Eisenhower, April 15, 1945

"There Were No Nazi 'Gas Chambers'; the Holocaust was 'propaganda.'"

Marco Polo, *a Japanese magazine,* February 1995

"The best medicine for the vulgar exercise of comparative victimization is not the copious assertion of Jewish uniqueness, but an end to the fruitless debate between the uniqueness and universality of suffering in the first place."

David Biale, TIKKUN, January/February 1995

"The uniqueness of the Jewish experience can best be documented by comparing it with the Nazi treatment of other persecuted populations. The study of the Holocaust can provide insights that have universal import for the destiny of all humanity."

Michael Berenbaum, A Mosaic of Victims, 1990

"Events happen because they are possible. If they were possible once, they are possible again. In that sense the Holocaust is not unique, but a warning for the future."

Yehuda Bauer, The Holocaust in Historical Perspective, 1978

Introduction

ALAN S. ROSENBAUM

The time has come to fix the place of the Nazi-engineered Holocaust against the Jews, Gypsies, and millions of others so that it may be accurately integrated into the mainstream of recorded history. For it remains disturbingly obvious, even to those with merely a passing exposure to this area of scholarship, that the variety of radically different opinions on this matter may contribute unwittingly to the nihilistic impression that any one view is as valid or invalid as any other view. This outcome would be most unfortunate and would be rejected unequivocally by this editor and the contributors to this book.

Normalizing the Holocaust in this manner recognizes both its continuities and discontinuities with the past. It is not an attempt to marginalize or dilute its horror but rather to point out that a social phenomenon that is treated as external to history and literally beyond the reach of human understanding (which it may be to those who endured and survived its ravages) will undoubtedly be seen quite differently from the perspectives of future generations. Indeed, some theorists in the scholarly world are in the throes of a struggle to articulate the abiding significance of the Holocaust. The purpose of the process of normalization is to influence responsible opinion about this matter in the future, now that the fiftieth anniversary of the liberation of Auschwitz—the "largest Jewish cemetery in the world" and the worst of the Nazi's death camps—and the defeat of the Third Reich have passed. Unfortunately, this historiographic process has become burdened with serious impediments. The most critical problem concerns how best to characterize the Holocaust: Should it be regarded as a unique historical phenomenon?

If indeed it is true that the Holocaust is genuinely and significantly unique and unprecedented, as a number of prominent scholars argue, then questions arise as to whether that perspective assures that future generations will better understand this historical phenomenon than would otherwise be so. Accordingly, we may ask: Is this claim about uniqueness historically inconsequential because it is an understandable expression, perhaps based in a mixture of motives and circumstances, of a generation of people who were in some way personally touched by the effects of World War II? Is it inevitable, as many people today fear, that the attenuating hold it has on our generation will gradually yield to a more generalized notion that the Holocaust was merely only one of many significant horrors that occurred in this century's most horrific conflict? Are the authentic victims of the Holocaust and the proponents of the claim of its uniqueness ultimately asserting in this unusual mode of expression a fearful plea for remembrance? Will the current exercise in the "politics" of uniqueness be displaced by the sheer quantity and magnitude of atrocities that have occurred as they become better known (as in Mao's China) and, unfortunately, happen in the future? And will the received concept of the Jewish-centeredness of the Holocaust be overwhelmed by the persistent cries of other aggrieved groups and by new evidence attesting to their own serious losses in the Holocaust? Of course, none of these questions can definitely be answered now. Nevertheless, some considered reflections about these matters can be offered based on the idea that the chapters in this volume are written by scholars who regard the overall issue of uniqueness very worthy of response.

Granted, history is replete with instances of mass death in a "widening circle of genocide." In order to avoid the unseemly appearance of a competitive martyrdom in attributing a certain specialness sui generis to the Holocaust, a sound defense of this ascription must be marshaled by its proponents at the very least in the context of the relevant empirical demographics of this history. The chapters in this volume are intended to promote clarity and understanding of the various claims about the comparability of other egregious instances of mass killing and death to the Holocaust. In this context, the term *Holocaust* usually refers to what the Nazis called the "Final Solution to the Jewish question," namely, the deliberate, systematic extermination of all Jewish people (nota bene: They succeeded in murdering at least 6 million people, including over 1.5 million children; this means that Jewish losses amounted to two-thirds of European Jewry). It also encompasses the relentless persecution, enslavement, and murder of many millions more: Gypsies (or Roma, or Romani), Poles, Slavs, gays, the mentally ill, the handicapped, and political dissidents. Of these non-Jewish victims of the Holocaust, numbering some 5.5 million people, it is clear that the fate of the Gypsies is generally accepted as being nearest to that of the Jews in the Nazi vision of a future "world without Jews" and Judaism.[1] As a more complete record becomes known, it may well be that the Gypsies can no longer be assumed to share a relatively separate experience from the Jews under the Nazi regime. Therefore, some scholars assert that "uniqueness" must also be held to encompass the Gypsy genocide. This is the cardinal point of Chapter 3, by Ian Hancock. In any case, the arguments marshaled in defense of the uniqueness of the Holocaust are almost never drawn on the basis of numbers of people killed alone, because Russia under Stalin and China under Mao had considerably larger numbers of people slain than did Germany under Hitler. Thus, the focus is usually placed on the Nazis' ideologically motivated intent to exterminate wholly the seed of the Jewish people—all men, women, and children everywhere.

In general, this book is premised upon the life-affirming proposition that no determinate group's suffering ought to be consigned to perpetual misconception, insignificance, invisibility, or silence. For, if it could, the collective voice of every group would seek to have its anguished cries of suffering and pain both heard and accurately enshrined in history's Book of Life as a legacy of instruction about warning signs of a possible recurrence for future generations to heed. Inasmuch as this is the only way to rescue a historical reality such as the Holocaust from oblivion—in that history does not speak for itself because it is dead and silent and, in and of itself, teaches us nothing—great care and attention must be dedicated to documentable specifics. Also, our focus must include contextual and interpretive considerations in the scholarly enterprise of framing and conveying information and establishing perspective from which future generations may learn, particularly so that those who are able to recall the genocidal past will move to thwart its recurrence (as the sanguine philosopher George Santayana once implicitly counseled).

Therefore, as I note at the outset and reaffirm here, any presumption about the uniqueness of the Holocaust may be entirely warranted provided that, upon proper scrutiny, it does not in any manner diminish or still the certain moral authority that must be accorded to other groups whose members have also been forced to endure unspeakable atrocities during their history. And yet any acknowledgment of the persecutions and mass deaths endured by members of other groups should not be construed as vitiating or denying, in the absence of honest and rational debate, claims as to the uniqueness of the Holocaust.

Too often, however, philosophical reflections and theoretical discussions about historically significant realities such as the Holocaust are sterile because they trade in some unnecessarily vacuous abstractions. These abstractions only serve to confuse, undermine, and prevent a full and accurate grasp of the realities in question. Typical of such dialogues, which are pointless because they arrest further constructive thought, is the tendency to attribute the occurrence of the Holocaust, or, for that matter, *any* act of violence, to "Man's inhumanity to Man" or to a presumed "evil or bestial human instinct."[2] Two other well-known approaches that yield a similar sterile outcome concern: first, a mystification that ensues from treating the Holocaust as essentially unthinkable owing to its extrahistorical and profoundly idiosyncratic, evil nature; and, second, a trivialization of its unprecedented character that accrues to the notion that the Holocaust, like *all* other sociohistorical events, is unique. Recourse to such abstract universalisms fails to account for real event-specifics like context, scope, and dimension; intention; methods; opportunity; blame; and responsibility. These chapters seek to avoid such usage because it obscures the genocidal realities that the contributors propose to compare and evaluate. In any case, there is a rational and honest disagreement among them about a precise, adequate definition of uniqueness itself.

It is in this spirit that the distinguished contributors to this book intend to assess the claims about whether the Holocaust is unique as viewed from the standpoint of other well-known and apparently analogous instances of genocide or mass deaths. Each chapter has been written specifically for this book, prompted by the firestorm of controversy surrounding, among other things, how best to remember the Holocaust and integrate our understanding into the historical mainstream of the scholarly literature. Hence, it is to be expected that prominent scholars in the interrelated areas of history, political science, religion, and philosophy have important contributions to make toward advancing a fair and reasonable resolution to this dispute.

One particularly insidious and nasty undercurrent of all this is a newfound cottage industry dedicated to voicing distortions and contrived falsifications of history in the form of "Holocaust denials."[3] It is reasonable to conjecture that this industry will be transitory, despite the fear, indignation, and outrage it currently provokes, because the testamentary evidence to the contrary is so overwhelming that it has become institutionalized (e.g., the United States Holocaust Memorial Museum) and readily accessible to the general public. In addition, responsible scholars[4] have made timely and persuasive refutations of specific fraudulent claims, laying bare the Holocaust deniers' incredulity and antisemitic motivation.

Nevertheless, when Holocaust denials are considered in tandem with another set of recent tendencies to "normalize," historicize, relativize, marginalize, and trivialize the reality of the Holocaust, the debate seriously intensifies. In this sense, efforts to deny its uniqueness converge with attempts to deny its existence altogether. Again, the core issue in this debate is whether the Holocaust has a special or unique place on history's continuum of persecution, genocide, and mass death. It appears that it does on its face, if we consider such factors as the magnitude of murders, ideology, and prior government planning and executions, the wholesale involvement of the legal and medical professions, the major business and industrial enterprises, academic institutions, the military forces, and the civil service, as well as the widespread bureaucratization and technoindustrialization of genocide.

However, if such normative inferences about "uniqueness"—much like its paradigmatic character of genocide and of evil—are to be warranted and enduring given the factors noted above, the Holocaust requires a rigorous, empirical comparison to other historical instances of mass death with sufficiently relevant similarities. For this reason, I have chosen to include such tragedies as the Atlantic slave trade, which is examined by Seymour Drescher in Chapter 4; the Soviet-engineered Ukrainian famine and mass kulak killings and population transfers, as discussed by Barbara B. Green in Chapter 7; the decimation and population transfers of Native American peoples, addressed by both Steven T. Katz (Chapter 2) and David E. Stannard (Chapter 8); and the Gypsy holocaust and the Armenian genocide at the hands of the Turks, analyzed by Vahakn N. Dadrian (Chapter 6) and also by Katz. References to the recent civil strife in the Balkans, Rwanda, and Cambodia will also be presented for the reader's analysis, particularly in Chapter 5, by Robert F. Melson. Again, the idea is not to invite a cynical politics of competitive suffering but rather to offer an assessment of the uniqueness claim regarding the Holocaust in light of other commonly cited and seemingly comparable instances of mass death.

There exists some question as to why some people think it important to attribute a "uniqueness" to the Holocaust[5] or to mount a rebuttal to the attribution,[6] given that there are a number of other historical events that are patently "unique" in a nontrivial sense. For instance, no such necessity seems to prompt those scholars who readily acknowledge a definite uniqueness to the nuclear devastation of the Japanese cities of Hiroshima and Nagasaki at the end of World War II to engage in a debate about its specialness, to challenge the ascription or uniqueness, or, for that matter, to deny its existence. Of course, some dispute has surrounded the matter of the rationale behind the putative military necessity to drop the bombs (for example, in a revanchist spirit some Japanese politicians, not unlike some disingenuous Germans who point to the Allied saturation bombing of Dresden as a moral equalizer, seek to cast Japan either as a co-sufferer or victim with equal moral standing alongside the true victims of Japanese militarism such as the people of Nanking in the 1930s or as would-be liberators of Asia from Western colonial domination as justification for its attack on Pearl Harbor on December 7, 1941). But no thinking person would seriously contest the uniqueness of the use of atomic weaponry on Japan. So why are Holocaust studies burdened with this curious challenge? I think the answer is conveyed in the words of Oxford professor Isaiah Berlin: "There must be a good deal more to the question of uniqueness—the 'placing in context' of this event than a mere historical assessment of an objective kind. It has a conspicuously political motive."[7] Nowhere else is this impression better confirmed than in the German historians' debate (the *Historikerstreit*) about reshaping a positive German national identity post-Auschwitz[8] and in the recent cultural politics of Jewish history and identity.

The debate among (mostly) German historians involves the question of interpreting Germany's Nazi past and the evil criminality of the Holocaust in view of certain current political purposes. One such purpose is to provide a special conceptual historicist framework for understanding and evaluating the Holocaust by reference to Hitler's antibolshevism (equally if not more important than his antisemitism) and a general violent and unavoidable response to rapid industrialization. Ernst Nolte, the German theorist, articulated this stratagem for minimizing Nazi genocide by attempting to rationalize and justify it.[9] The problem with this approach concerns, among other things, an attempted justification for Nazi wrongdoing by casting aside moral and legal principles to serve preferred political ends, for example, burying the past without really confronting it or downplaying the responsibility of the German nation today in view of its antisemitic and Nazi past. It is a transparent form of rationalizing evil by relativizing (or worse) its occurrence.

Another approach that politicizes history is found in claims that the Third Reich's actions as regards the Holocaust basically were no different than what others have done in furthering national interests in war or peace: destroy enemies by whatever means are at their disposal. This view also seeks to normalize the Holocaust. Still others argue that the future cannot be faced squarely unless and until former adversaries reconcile and agree to leave behind past wartime antagonisms. In this vein, we have a 1985 event that triggered a bitter worldwide dispute—the wreath-laying ceremony by U.S. President Ronald Reagan and German Chancellor Helmut Kohl at Germany's Bitburg cemetery, the burial ground for some German soldiers and Nazi SS criminals. A wave of indignation swept over those who felt this ill-conceived political effort at reconciliation came at the expense of a fair and honest appraisal of Germany's responsibility for its Nazi past. At the same time, however, many others were able to embrace the notion that the demands of future international relations and affairs required leaving the past behind by unfettering Germany from the stultifying grip of its shameful and blameworthy past, that is, from its moral and historical responsibility for the Holocaust. The political nature of continuing attempts to rehabilitate Germany by short-circuiting well-founded charges of culpability and responsibility, in a strategy designed to blunt criticism against Germany, is mentioned earlier (i.e., the deliberate recasting of the Dresden firestorm as a victimization of Germany that assigns it—or so the expositors of this notion hold—a standing worthy of equal moral consideration with the victims of German aggression).

Among some scholars, both Jewish and non-Jewish, there continues to be a certain current of thought that strives to retrieve the pain and suffering of the Jewish people in the Holocaust, arguably the worst fate to have befallen the Jews from time immemorial, and to give it a permanent and uniquely significant place in the annals both of Jewish and world history.[10] As may be expected, variations on this theme range from a plea for universal and perpetual recognition of the Holocaust as the worst case of genocide ever (as Katz proposes), certainly as the ineradicable nadir in all Jewish history as crucial to Jewish identity[11] and to the right to have its identity publicly validated; to the quasireligious concept of evil as best exemplified and embodied in the Holocaust;[12] to the theological query concerning God's whereabouts during the exterminative process of His Chosen People at the hands of the Nazis and their co-persecutors.[13]

As the chapters in this book demonstrate, the Holocaust is in many crucial respects an unparalleled or singular event. The historical singularity of the Holocaust does not imply by that fact alone that it is "unique" in some significant sense. And though an assertion of its uniqueness appears unavoidably to invite invidious comparisons with others' pain and suffering, this consequence alone should not render the inquiry fruitless.

In my opinion, research, argument, and clarity of comprehension belie any charge of fruitlessness because accurate empirical differentiation between instances of mass death and killing demonstrate how the Holocaust will probably be remembered, not only as "the epitome of evil, of cruelty," in the words of Elie Wiesel, but also as an event unlike any other and thus with special significance for all humanity.[14]

In this editor's opinion, one of the universal lessons that Holocaust study aspires to teach involves, above all else, the honest consideration about how we ought to respond in the future when confronted with unqualified evil. If "evil" means the use of a maleficent power to deliberately destroy the physical, cultural, or spiritual being of an individual human being or a people,[15] then, in the wake of the Holocaust, we must forthrightly acknowledge its presence and resist a modern cultural bias to blur the distinction between good and evil. Second, our deepest sense of moral redemption demands unequivocal resistance to the workings of evil in any feasible manner; or at the very least to make the doers of evil accountable for their actions. Finally, the enduring significance implicit in sustained teaching or preaching of contempt and hatred for others who differ from ourselves or, in a word, to satanize others simply because they are and not for what they may have done, will lead, we now know, under a conducive mix of circumstances, to a policy of relentless persecution and even extermination.[16] For there is certainly an abiding wisdom in the recognition that the Holocaust has seared into the collective historical consciousness of humanity a new, indefeasible standard of evil. In other words, it may be that George Santayana's trite admonition about remembering the past as a way of not condemning ourselves to repeating it might also occasion among future genocidists a recollection of barbaric Nazi methods for more efficiently destroying their enemies. So we must be ever vigilant about the warning signs of a possible turn toward genocide. In light of these many lessons, only thus may we salvage our humanity and reaffirm the fundamental values at the heart of our civilization: respect for individual human life, dignity, and freedom; for human rights; and for a just rule of law.[17]

NOTES

1. In support of this view, we may cite the following authoritative works: Michael Berenbaum, "The Uniqueness and Universality of the Holocaust," in *A Mosaic of Victims*, ed. M. Berenbaum (New York: New York University Press, 1990), p. 33 (where Berenbaum argues that the Roma "shared much but not all the horrors assigned to the Jews"); Steven T. Katz, *The Holocaust in Historical Context*, vol. 1 (New York: Oxford University Press, 1994), pp. 27–63; and George L. Mosse, *Toward the Final Solution: A History of European Racism* (Madison: University of Wisconsin Press, 1978), pp. 220–221 (Mosse cited the Nazi expert, Eva Justin, on the Gypsy question). For contrary views, see Angus Fraser, *Gypsies* (Oxford: Blackwell Publishers, 1992); and Gerhard L. Weinberg, *Germany, Hitler, and World War Two* (New York: Cambridge University Press, 1995), pp. 218–219.

2. For instance, see "Freeing the Survivors," *U.S. News and World Report*, April 3, 1995, p. 65; also, for a variation on the same theme, see Alan S. Rosenbaum, *Prosecuting Nazi War Criminals* (Boulder: Westview Press, 1993), pp. 5, 9 at n. 4.

3. Deborah L. Lipstadt, *Denying the Holocaust: The Growing Assault on Truth and Memory* (New York: Free Press and Plume, 1994).

4. In this regard, such prominent scholars as Deborah Lipstadt and Harold Brackman have exposed the distortions and falsifications of some pseudohistorical but dangerous

14. See Cargas's interview with Emil Fackenheim, in Harry James Cargas, *Voices from the Holocaust* (Lexington: University Press of Kentucky, 1993), p. 134.

15. A similar definition of evil is found in Fred E. Katz, *Ordinary People and Extraordinary Evil* (Albany: State University of New York Press, 1993), p. 5.

16. Lawrence L. Langer, *Admitting the Holocaust* (New York: Oxford University Press, 1995), pp. 179 and 184.

17. In philosopher Richard Rorty's words, which generally express a similar sentiment: "It does not diminish the memory of the Holocaust to say that our response to it should not be a claim to have gained a new understanding of human nature or of human history, but rather a willingness to pick ourselves up and try again." Richard Rorty, "Human Rights, Rationality, and Sentimentality," in *On Human Rights: The Oxford Amnesty Lectures 1993*, ed. Stephen Shute and Susan Hurley (New York: Basic Books, 1993), p. 246 at n. 7.

❀ 1 ❀

Religion and the Uniqueness of the Holocaust

RICHARD L. RUBENSTEIN

*F*ew events of the twentieth century have been the object of as much persistent popular interest as the Holocaust. When the United States Holocaust Memorial Museum opened its doors in April 1993, museum officials estimated that 1 million people would visit the museum during its first year. They vastly underestimated the actual number that first year, hosting approximately 2 million visitors, two-thirds of whom were non-Jews. It is difficult to account for this interest simply in terms of the number of Holocaust victims or the fact that the Shoah was perpetrated by the government of one of the best-educated and technically competent nations in the world, although that fact cannot be discounted. There have been many other large-scale, demographic catastrophes perpetrated by human beings in the twentieth century. Nevertheless, it is unlikely that a museum devoted to Stalin's murders or the Armenian genocide of 1915 would consistently draw so large a number of visitors as has the Holocaust Museum.

What, then, accounts for the persistence of interest in the Holocaust half a century after the end of World War II? It is, I believe, the fact that the Holocaust, more than any other twentieth-century disaster, resonates with the religio-mythic traditions of biblical religion, the dominant religious tradition of Western civilization. Put differently, the response to the Holocaust reflects the pervasiveness in Western civilization of what Stephen R. Haynes has called the "witness-people myth"—the belief that whatever happens to the Jews, for good or ill, is an expression of God's providential justice and, as such, is a sign "for God's church."[1] According to Haynes, the witness-people myth is "a deep structure in the Christian imagination . . . a complex of ideas and symbols that, often precritically and unconsciously, informs ideas about Jews among persons who share a cultural heritage." The myth has its roots in the biblical doctrine that God has chosen Israelis as His people by bestowing upon them a covenant stipulating that Israel's fidelity would be rewarded by divine protection, as surely as infidelity would be harshly punished. As we know, the rabbis interpreted the Fall of Jerusalem as God's punishment of a sinful Israel for failing to keep the commandments. Christian thinkers agreed that the Fall of Jerusalem was divine punishment, but they argued that the rejection of Jesus as Lord and Messiah was God's motive for laying waste to Jerusalem and the Holy Temple. According to the Christian interpretation, the Jews could only regain God's favor by truly accepting baptism. As long as they refused, God would condemn them to the suffering, humiliation, and indignity of exile. The suffering of the witness people was thus understood as a confirmation of Christian faith, and Jews were seen as justly paying a bitter price for their refusal to accept the truth as taught by Christianity.

Given the enormous weight Judaism and Christianity place on the interpretation of Jewish disaster as an expression of God's justice and providence, it was inevitable that both Jews and Christians would respond to the Holocaust in accordance with their respective traditions. It is, for example, possible for believing Christians to view the Armenian genocide or the Pol Pot massacres in Kampuchea as purely secular events without raising the question of whether transcendent religious meaning is involved in such events. Not so the Holocaust. The Holocaust almost inevitably elicits some form of religious interpretation at every level of intellectual sophistication, as is evident in the popular response to the Holocaust museum. The same phenomenon can be seen in the rise of Holocaust theology as a distinctive discipline among a large number of post–World War II Jewish theologians and a smaller but influential group of Christian thinkers. The latter include John Pawlikowski, Paul van Buren, Franklin Littell, Alice and Roy Eckhardt, and John K. Roth. Never before in Jewish history had there been a catastrophe of such magnitude, and if one believes, as do most Jews and Christians, in a God who is the ultimate author of the drama of history, then the question of divine involvement in the Holocaust is bound to arise.

No matter how the question of God's involvement is resolved, neither academically trained theologians nor ordinary laypersons can entirely ignore it. For some, the Holocaust is ipso facto proof that a sinful Israel had been justly punished by a righteous God. Many others—both Jewish and Christian—are unable either to abandon some semblance of faith in the biblical God-who-acts-in-history or to assert that the Holocaust was in any sense God's righteous judgment. Unable to abandon either position, they are impaled on the horns of a dilemma, made more painful by their respective liturgical traditions that stress the righteous and saving acts of the Lord.

Most academically trained historians argue that events like the Holocaust can be adequately explained in terms of the conflicting material interests of the perpetrators and their victims. Undoubtedly, much can be learned from a socioeconomic reading of history. Nevertheless, such a reading underestimates the power of religion and myth to define reality. The overwhelming majority of human beings understand the world in terms of the way their religions and cultures define reality for them. A given society's religio-mythic inheritance is normally opaque to critical scrutiny by its members, because that same inheritance is a crucially important part of the interpretive matrix by which individuals comprehend reality.

Even in a relatively secular age, the power of religion to define reality largely determines the experiences available to Jews and Christians alike, at least in relation to each other. In the case of the witness-people myth, most Christians can be said to *dwell within the myth* and to comprehend Jewish history and experience in and through it.[2] That is why the deicide accusation has been so potent a force throughout the ages. That is also why the image of Judas has played so important a role in determining the way Jews have been perceived by Christians, especially in times of stress.[3]

The fate of the Jews as a distinctive people is too closely connected with the religio-mythic inheritance of both Judaism and Christianity for the Holocaust to have lacked profound religious significance for either believing Jews or Christians, especially at the level of unreflective, pretheoretical consciousness. The Holocaust is linked to the Fall of Jerusalem in 586 B.C.E. (to the Babylonians) and in 70 C.E. (to the Romans). It is also linked to the responses to those events of the prophets, the rabbis, the authors of the New Testament, and the Church Fathers as is no other event in modern history.

No other instance of genocide or attempted genocide in modern times elicits associations so directly to the Bible and its worldview as does the Holocaust. Other peoples have depicted themselves as "Christ among the nations" and have interpreted their suffering as an assault on God's people, but in no other instance did the event occur to those who were directly linked to the biblical drama of God's involvement in history as the Jews. More people died under Stalin than in the Holocaust, albeit a lesser proportion of the peoples of the Soviet Union perished than was the case with Europe's Jewish population. Ethnic cleansing in former Yugoslavia and the recent massacres in Rwanda are horrendous examples of mass slaughter and inhumanity. Nevertheless, these events do not have the same religio-mythic overtones for Jews and Christians as does the Holocaust.

My conviction that the religious dimension is responsible for the uniqueness of the Holocaust has been strengthened by frequent visits to Asia. Starting in the late 1970s, I have made more than fifteen trips to Japan and Korea. As I came to know Japanese, Chinese, and Korean scholars, it became apparent that, except for the Christians among them, the Holocaust had very little meaning for them. It did not happen on their continent, and, terrible as it was, it was perceived as simply one of the many bloody chapters in human history, of no distinctive importance in and of itself. The scholars were by no means indifferent to human suffering. Nevertheless, except for Asian Christians, the Holocaust was seen as a purely Western secular event.

Most Asians do not respond to Jews, either positively or negatively, in as emotionally complex a manner as do Westerners. During World War II, for example, even Japanese antisemites were largely incapable of the kind of visceral anti-

Jewish hatred that pervaded much of Europe.[4] Japanese antisemitism first became a significant force in the aftermath of the Bolshevik Revolution when the 75,000-man Japanese Expeditionary Force and its White Russian allies were defeated by the Bolsheviks and forced to retreat from eastern Siberia. According to the defeated White Russian officers who fought alongside the Japanese, the Bolshevik Revolution was the result of a secret Jewish conspiracy for world domination. The Japanese found this explanation credible. As "proof," White Russians had offered an infamous forgery, *The Protocols of the Elders of Zion*, which was speedily translated into Japanese. In addition to finding the Bolshevik system repugnant given their profound reverence of the emperor, the Japanese were horrified at the murder of Tsar Nicholas II and his family. Convinced that the Jews were deeply implicated in the revolution, a group of Japanese officers and ultranationalists began to study Jews and Judaism in the 1920s. They concluded that many of the disorders brought about by modernity were deliberate elements in a grandiose Jewish plot. Although they saw the Jews as a potential danger to Japan, in the 1930s they decided on a radically different strategy than that of the National Socialists in dealing with them. If the Jews were as powerful and as potentially dangerous as the *Protocols* alleged, they were to be handled with great care in order to turn their alleged abilities and influence into an advantage for Japan.

In the 1920s and 1930s, Captain Norihigo Yasue and naval Lieutenant Koteshige Inuzuka were regarded as leading "experts" on Jews and Judaism. Both had been attached to the White Russian military command during the unsuccessful campaign against the Bolsheviks. Captain Yasue translated the *Protocols* into Japanese. He was also the author of several tracts warning of a Jewish conspiracy to take over the world. In 1927, the Foreign Ministry borrowed Yasue from the army and sent him to Europe and the Middle East, where he met with Zionist leaders such as David Ben Gurion, Chaim Weizman, and Menahem Ussishkins, as well as rabbis and ordinary Jews. He was impressed by the *kibbutzim,* which he believed the Jews would use to colonize the countries they would eventually conquer. Nevertheless, he reported honestly to his superiors that he heard no hint of any conspiracy for world domination while among the Jews of Palestine.[5]

Like Yasue, Lieutenant Inuzuka was as convinced of a Jewish world conspiracy as any hard-core Nazi, but he and his fellow "experts" reacted very differently than did the Nazis. In a January 18, 1939, report to the navy's general staff, Inuzuka spelled out the difference: "[The Jews are] just like a *fugu* [blowfish] dish. It is very delicious but unless one knows well how to cook it, it may prove fatal to his life."[6] The *fugu* fish is regarded by the Japanese as a great delicacy *when properly prepared*. There is, however, no margin for error. An improperly prepared *fugu* can result in almost instantaneous death. However, the "experts" were convinced that they knew how to prepare this particular *fugu*.

Yasue was also a key figure in protecting the 17,000 Jews residing in Shanghai during the war. In July 1942, Colonel Joseph Meisinger—the Gestapo chief for Japan, China, and Manchukuo—and two other German officials met with local authorities in Shanghai to demand that the Japanese exterminate their Jewish charges "like garbage" on Rosh Hashanah.[7] Meisinger had previously served in Warsaw in 1939. Shanghai's Japanese authorities were initially inclined to accede to Meisinger's demands, but Vice Consul Mitsugi Shibata found both Meisinger and his proposals revolting. He took the highly unusual step of warning the leaders of Shanghai's Jewish community. He urged them to use their contacts in the Japanese government to thwart Meisinger. Shibata was imprisoned and dismissed from the Consular Service when his activities became known to local Japanese authorities.[8] Nevertheless, the Shanghai Jews got word to Dr. Abraham Kaufman, a leading Jew in Harbin, Manchuria, who enjoyed the favor of some of Japan's most important leaders, including members of the ultranationalist Black Dragon Society. When Kaufman used his contacts to apprise Foreign Minister Y[amo]suke Matsuoka and Colonel Norihigo Yasue of the impending danger, the Japanese government rejected Meisinger's proposals.[9] To appease its German ally, the government decreed on February 18, 1943, that "stateless refugees" would be confined to a ghetto in the Hongkew section of Shanghai, one of the poorest sections of the metropolis. Nevertheless, within Hongkew, the Jews were not harmed.

In spite of persistent German efforts to bring Japan's policy into line with national socialism on the "Jewish question," more than 20,000 Jews found a safe haven during the war in Japanese-occupied Shanghai, several other Chinese cities controlled by Japan, and the puppet-state of Manchukuo (Manchuria). Moreover, with a few exceptions, some of Japan's leading antisemites were among the most effective protectors of the Jewish refugees. Protecting Jews under their own names, they followed a consistent pattern of writing and translating antisemitic tracts under pseudonyms.

There have been periods, such as the present, when Japan has been flooded with antisemitic literature.[10] World War II was such a period, but Japanese anti-Jewish feeling has never had the emotionally overladen content that has characterized European antisemitism. The reason is fairly obvious: The vast majority of Japanese are not Christians influenced by the witness-people myth. The emotions engendered by the Judeo-Christian rivalry are largely absent among the Japanese.

As noted, many Japanese have seen Jews as responsible for the Bolshevik Revolution. Today, some Japanese blame the Jews for the strengthening of the yen and the newly activist U.S. trade policies toward Japan. Nevertheless, the Jews have not been perceived as deicides, and Jewish history is not seen as a continuing record of divine chastisement for failure to accept Christ as Lord, something the overwhelming majority of Japanese have yet to do.

Thus, the Holocaust is not a unique event for the Japanese or for most other Asians. The same cannot be said of the Western world, where it is difficult to extricate the Holocaust from the matrix of meanings concerning Jews and Judaism to be found in the biblical religions. To repeat, as a catastrophic event in Jewish history, the Holocaust can only be compared to the Fall of Jerusalem in ancient times. Inevitably, it elicits a religious response as did the earlier catastrophe. This is especially true in the United States, with its pervasive biblical tradition. For a very large number of Americans, by no means all of them Fundamentalists or Dispensationalists, the Bible is a living document, and contemporary events tend to be comprehended in its terms. Moreover, far more Christians than care to say so in public regard the Holocaust, as did the early Christians at the time of the Fall of Jerusalem to the Romans, as God's punishment for Israel's continuing refusal to accept faith in Christ.

Elsewhere, I have written that the Holocaust was a holy war in which post-Enlightenment European Christendom's goal of eliminating Jews and Judaism from its midst was fulfilled by Hitler, albeit by means other than most religious authorities would have preferred. Put differently, far more Europeans objected to the methods Hitler employed to eliminate the Jews than to his objectives.

In spite of national socialism's unremittingly racist antisemitism, Europe's motives for seeking the elimination of the Jews were largely religious. To understand the Holocaust as a modern holy war, we must keep in mind the fact that in Europe's formative centuries all those who rejected baptism, apart from the Jews, were either expelled or exterminated.[11] For example, in 1995, Norway celebrated a millennium of adherence to Christian religion. It is instructive, however, to remember how Christianity won the day in that country: According to the Norse sagas, in 995 King Olaf I Tryggvason returned from Dublin to give Norwegians a stark choice—death or baptism.[12]

Put differently, the king was offering his subjects the choice of death or becoming Europeans. For the king, as well as for Europe's princes and prelates in the centuries that followed, the price of admission to full participation in European civilization was membership in the Christian church. Moreover, today, no less than yesterday, few aspects of European civilization—art, literature, music, philosophy, religion, politics, universities, status hierarchies—can be entirely divorced from their Christian roots. Even European secularism is an unintended consequence of Europe's Christian culture, as Max Weber and others have recognized.[13]

My characterization of the Holocaust as a modern version of a Christian holy war carried out by a neopagan National Socialist state hostile to Christianity is based in part on the answer to the following question: *Which groups and institutions in the 1930s regarded the total elimination of the Jews and Judaism from Europe as a long-term benefit?* The answer is clear: *All those for whom the integrity of the Christian symbolic universe was indispensable to a genuinely civilized existence.* In 1939, the overwhelming majority of European Christian leaders were convinced that the greatest threats to the integrity of their symbolic universe came from two sources: bolshevism and unconverted Jews, whether religious, socialist, Zionist, secular, or assimilationist. Moreover, these same leaders thought of bolshevism as largely Jewish in origin and spirit. In their minds, the two often merged into one.

Europe has never valued genuine religious diversity. Whenever a group or a movement arose to challenge the primacy of Christianity anywhere in Europe—

whether it was the external challenge of Islam or the internal challenge of the Cathari in thirteenth-century southern France—the response of European Christendom was to eliminate the nonbeliever. Before the Enlightenment, Jews were tolerated in parts of Europe as long as they were perceived as useful. When that perception no longer held, they were expelled.

As a result of the Enlightenment, the Jews came to participate in European life under conditions of more or less civic equality. This resulted in the rise of a class of Jewish writers, thinkers, intellectuals, and academics who for a time were able to influence European Christendom from within. Neither the Catholic Church nor the Protestant churches found that development acceptable. After the Bolshevik Revolution, perceived by both the churches and the European right as a Jewish assault on Christendom, the Jewish presence within European Christendom became intolerable to important political and religious elites throughout the continent. All that remained was for someone to find a feasible method of population elimination. As was the case with the Cathari in the thirteenth century, it was only a question of time before the highly popular objective of eliminating the Jews from the European continent was achieved. Although never proclaimed as such, the Holocaust bore much resemblance to a holy war in which the Nazis did the dirty work for institutions that were destined to outlast them.

It is the religious element that makes the Holocaust unique. The Holocaust can be likened to a one-sided holy war or a latter-day crusade, most closely resembling the Albigensian Crusade. Never before in history was one religion eliminated so brutally or so efficiently by adherents of another religion with almost no protest. Like the Fall of Jerusalem, the Holocaust arouses speculation concerning God's absence or presence in history for Jews and Christians alike. Although the motives for initiating the Holocaust were by no means solely religious, the event did achieve an extraordinarily important goal for most Europeans—the elimination for all practical purposes of the Jewish demographic presence and Jewish religio-cultural influence within European Christendom. In vast areas of central and eastern Europe, today's surviving Jews constitute little more than a living museum to be exhibited or suppressed as suits the momentary political objectives of the governing elite.

NOTES

1. See the introduction to Stephen R. Haynes, *Jews and the Christian Imagination: Reluctant Witness* (Louisville, Ky.: Westminster/John Knox Press, 1995), pp. 8ff.

2. Ibid., p. 9.

3. On the influence of Judas on Christian perceptions of Jews, see Richard L. Rubenstein, *After Auschwitz: History, Theology, and Contemporary Judaism*, 2d ed. (Baltimore: Johns Hopkins University Press, 1992), pp. 21–22, 45, 50–51.

4. For an examination of Japanese attitudes toward Jews during World War II, see David Kranzler, *Japanese, Nazis, and Jews: The Jewish Refugee Community of Shanghai, 1935–1945* (Hoboken, N.J.: KTAV, 1988).

5. Marvin Tokayer and Mary Swartz, *The Fugu Plan: The Untold Story of the Japanese and the Jews During World War II* (New York: Paddington Press, 1979), p. 49.

6. Cited by Kranzler, *Japanese, Nazis, and Jews*, p. 169.

7. Tokayer and Swartz, *The Fugu Plan*, pp. 222–226.

8. Kranzler, *Japanese, Nazis, and Jews*, pp. 478–479.

9. The sources disagree concerning Colonel Yasue's first name. Kranzler, *in Japanese, Nazis, and Jews*, lists the name as "Senko." Tetsu Kohno lists the name as "Norihigo." I have accepted the latter. See Tetsu Kohno, "The Jewish Question in Japan," in *Jewish Journal of Sociology* 29(1) (June 1987).

10. See David G. Goodman, "Japanese Anti-Semitism," *World and I* (November 1987).

11. On this point, see Robert Bartlett, *The Making of Europe: Conquest, Colonization, and Cultural Change, 950–1350* (Princeton: Princeton University Press, 1993).

12. "Norway Celebrates a Millennium of Christianity Despite Fires," *New York Times*, June 4, 1995.

13. For a brief discussion of the Christian roots of secularization, see Peter Berger, *The Sacred Canopy: Elements of a Sociological Theory of Religion* (Garden City, N.Y.: Anchor Books, 1969), pp. 105–126.

✤ 2 ✤

The Uniqueness of the Holocaust: The Historical Dimension

STEVEN T. KATZ

I

Introduction

Given the focus of this book on the issue of the uniqueness of the Holocaust, I wish to state clearly at the outset my position on this matter: The Holocaust, that is, the intentional murder of European Jewry during World War II, is historically and phenomenologically unique. No other case discussed in this book parallels it. My burden in the remainder of this chapter is to document and defend this statement.

In arguing for the uniqueness of the Holocaust, I am *not* making a *moral* claim, in other words, that the Holocaust was more evil than the other events discussed in this collection, for example, the murder of Armenians in World War I, the devastation of the Native American communities over the centuries, the decimation of Ukraine by Stalin, the treatment of the Gypsies during World War II, and the enslavement and mass death of black Africans during the enterprise of New World slavery. I know of no method or technique that would allow one to weigh up, to quantify and compare, such massive evil and suffering, and I therefore avoid altogether this sort of counterproductive argument about what one might describe as comparative suffering.

In addition, I am not suggesting that the Holocaust involved the greatest number of victims of any mass crime. It did not. Numbers of victims will not establish the uniqueness of the Holocaust—quite the contrary.

When I argue for the uniqueness of the Holocaust I intend only to claim that the Holocaust is phenomenologically unique by virtue of the fact that never before has a state set out, as a matter of intentional principle and actualized policy, to annihilate physically every man, woman, and child belonging to a specific people. A close study of the relevant comparative historical data will show that only in the case of Jewry under the Third Reich was such all-inclusive, noncompromising, unmitigated murder intended.

Given the limits of this short chapter, my presentation must be selective and schematic. I will, therefore, consider only three of the cases discussed by others in this volume in order to show how they differ from the Holocaust. If space allowed, a similar decipherment in support of *difference* could be made in every case said to be comparable to the Holocaust in this collection.[1]

II
The Case of the Native Americans:
Colonial America and the United States

The Native American people(s) have been the subject of exploitation, despoliation, rape, violence, and murder since the arrival of Columbus. This centuries-long record of subjugation and abuse is incontrovertible and tragic. However, I would argue that the structure, the character, of the assault against the Native American peoples differs radically from that represented by the Holocaust for several fundamental reasons, the most basic of which is the role that disease has played in this history. That is to say: All serious contemporary students of the demographic collapse of the Indian peoples of America (that is, populations north of Mexico) are now agreed that its primary cause, whatever other factors contributed to this phenomenon, was newly imported pathogens against which the native community, estimated at anywhere between 1 million (plus or minus 10 percent) and 18 million, had no immunity. Henry Dobyns lists ninety-three pandemics and epidemics, most of which occurred in the territory that now comprises the United States, caused by European pathogens that struck the Native American peoples between 1500 and 1900. And for the sixteenth century alone—the period of the greatest decimation—Alfred W. Crosby Jr. cites fourteen major epidemics between 1524 and 1600.

As occurred also in the unparalleled demographic collapse of the South American Indian population in the sixteenth century, not only did the American aborigines lack the biological ability, the immunological prerequisites, to resist the unfamiliar and unfriendly microbes that now assaulted them, the European invaders and settlers who were directly responsible for their (often unknowing) importation lacked the scientific knowledge required to halt their deadly work once it had begun. Thus, infectious killers were unintentionally let loose within the Americas, and literally nothing was able to intervene to limit the massive damage they would do.

This phenomenon defined the history of the Native American peoples right through the nineteenth century. In the most complete analysis of nineteenth-century Indian demography undertaken to date, Henry Dobyns enumerates no less than twenty-seven epidemic outbreaks during that century, the most deadly of which were thirteen smallpox epidemics, the two worst occurring in 1801–1802 and 1836–1840. During the first of these, James Mooney estimates that, for example, "the prairie tribes . . . lost more than half of their population at this time, while the Wichita, Caddo, and others in the South suffered almost as severely."[2] Nearly everywhere in the United States, Indians continued to die, and disease was the primary cause of their death.

For example, Sherburne Cook attributes only 8.64 percent of the decline in California's Indian population to military casualties, most of the remainder, that is, the rate of loss, being due to disease. This ratio of loss due to disease versus other factors evidenced in California also obtained more generally, with modification from location to location, throughout the country in Indian-white relations. Thus, Cook concluded that only approximately 6,750 Indians had been killed by white settlers in New England between 1634 and 1676, even though this half-century included the Pequot War of 1637 (and saw the native population of New England decline by many times that number). Even Russell Thornton, who has vigorously attempted to highlight the roles of warfare and genocide in the decline of the Indian population, is forced by the unassailable demographic evidence to conclude that, at most, "45,000 American Indians [were] killed in wars with Europeans and Americans between 1775–1890. To this might be added . . . 8,500 American Indians killed in individual conflicts during the period, to arrive at a total of 53,000 killed."[3]

That is to say, in a period of 115 years, during which the indigenous population declined by over 1.5 million, only 53,000 casualties, or 3.7 percent of the total lost, can be counted as having been intentionally murdered. For the pre-1775 period, the percentage of loss due to warfare (and individual murder) is even lower. Thornton, for example, in attempting to configure losses in the prerevolutionary era, suggests doubling the post-1775 figure of 53,000 to arrive at the pre-1775 aggregate. Accordingly, if we follow this suggestion, if only for purposes of argument, we have a projection, however crudely arrived at, of 106,000 casualties due to war and conflict situations in this earlier epoch. However, given the much higher total native population in this initial contact period—anywhere up to 10 or more times as great as what it was after 1775—the percentage of loss represented by this hypothesized 106,000 casualties shrinks to some fraction of 1 percent.

When mass death occurred among the Indians of America, and it did occur, it was almost without exception caused by microbes, not militia—although militias were much in evidence and did their damage—that is, this depopulation happened unwittingly rather than by design, even transpiring in direct opposition to the expressed and self-interested will of the white empire-builder or settler. This is true for the colonial era as well as for the period of American domination. It should be specifically remarked, contra the genocidal reading of these historical events, that after the discovery of the smallpox vaccination in 1797, all Indians were encouraged to be vaccinated, and following the epidemic of 1831–1832, U.S. government policy required the vaccination of Indians. The resistance of the western tribes to this statute contributed directly to their decimation by epidemics in the late 1830s and early 1840s.

Certainly the fatigue, the unaccustomed and punishing hunger, and a host of related psychological dilemmas that attended white conquest, in conjunction with direct military conflicts and acts of violence, reduced the inherent ability of the native population to withstand the heretofore unencountered pathogens. Yet these important factors do not alter the *unintentional* character of the spread of these infectious visitations—the primary killer—nor our appreciation of the notorious inability to control these pandemics once they began. Moreover, in contradistinction to those who would overemphasize the nonpathogenic causes of Indian decline, it needs to be understood that the most widespread and demographically significant epidemics—claiming an estimated one-third or more of the still very large native population—were the very earliest ones, in other words, those connected with the initial contact, that occurred *prior* to any full-scale program of enforced labor or removals north of Mexico.

Disease unaided, disease per se, along with the internal social and communal dislocations it created, was the primary, unavoidable, and ubiquitous agency of death among North American Indians between 1492 and 1900.

In addition, further mediating factors are to be considered in drawing the disjunction between the Native American case and the Holocaust. Foremost among these is the vast enterprise of mission that was first established and supported by all the colonial powers and then continued under American auspices.

After American independence, between 1787 and 1820, eleven denominational and interchurch groups created missionary agencies, the most active being the American Board of Commissioners for Foreign Missions, an interdenominational group with a predominance of Presbyterian and Congregational missionaries founded in 1810. By 1824, twenty-one missionary schools were being supported by federal and private funds—six by the American Board of Commissioners, five by the Baptists, four by the United Foreign Missionary Society, four by the Methodists, and one each by the Moravians, Presbyterians, Cumberland Missionary Society, and the Catholics. The Indian Department reported in 1824–1825 that in 1824 a total of $192,064.48 had been spent on Indian education from all sources (government, Indian annuities, and private donations) and that this amount had increased to $202,070.85 by 1825. By 1826, the total of Indian missionary schools had grown to thirty-eight, and a number of new missionary societies had come into being. These thirty-eight schools had 281 teachers and 1,159 students and received $13,550 from the federal government. The most notable conversionary successes were in the South among those nations later known as the Five Civilized Tribes, the Cherokee, Choctaw, Chickasaw, Creek, and Seminole, with the Cherokee providing the single most remarkable case in point.

By the 1830s, despite significant setbacks connected with the Jacksonian removals, which had seriously divided the diverse missionary groups (and differing denominations), both Protestant and Catholic missionaries were working intensively among the Native Americans from Florida to California and from New York to the Great Northwest. In the 1840s, Jesuits were active in Idaho, Washington, and the Dakota Territory, and Presbyterians, Methodists, and Congregationalists were to be found in the Dakota Territory and in the Northwest. The 1850s witnessed the spread of missions to the Santee and the Ojibway in Minnesota. Now, too, the Mormons established missions to the Shoshoni and Delaware in Utah, Wyoming, Kansas, and Idaho. All this at the cost of many millions of dollars. For example, between 1818 and 1830 the Choctaw Mission in Mississippi, which converted a total of 360 individuals and established four small churches, spent $140,000 on its relatively limited activities, and the Baptists spent on its missionary work in the West $131,888 ($72,184 provided by the federal government) between 1826 and 1842 and an additional $139,750 ($69,475 from the federal government) between 1843 and 1864. By 1865, the American Board of Commissioners of Foreign Missions had spent no less than $1.25 million on its Indian missionary activity.

After the Civil War, President Ulysses Grant's "peace policy," begun in 1869, encouraged still more intensive missionary activity under the leadership of the Quakers. At Grant's request, the Board of Indian Commissioners, composed of wealthy and influential Protestant laymen (no Catholics were nominated), was established by an act of Congress on April 10, 1869. Along with the creation of this new board, the selection of Indian agents, with obvious disregard for the First Amendment, was, at least in part, given over to church groups in the hope that they would be able to reform and improve the Indian service. In all, thirteen denominations came to control seventy-three agencies dealing with approximately 235,000 Indians. However, their inexperience and lack of a coherent design in such matters proved fatal, and, in the end, this reformist system, for all its considerable ambition and undoubted goodwill, did not work. By 1882, this Christian reform program was abandoned—even the Quakers having lost faith in it; in its place the country moved to adopt a radically alternative strategy for solving the "Indian problem"—the allotment of Indian lands.

What is of particular and compelling interest vis-à-vis the post-1880 reformist effort to resolve the fate of the Indian peoples is the naive, quasi-Utopian, exceedingly insensitive, ultimately destructive, though kindly meant, ideology that governed this short-lived experiment. At the core of this initiative, undertaken by well-intended, thoroughly ethnocentric men, was the orthodox white opinion that Indian culture was inferior and that in order to "advance," the Indians had to shed their traditions as they "progressed" up the ladder of "civilization." The Indian modes of existence (personal and corporate), in all their distinctive particulars, were, by definition, doomed. Like the liberals of Europe who a priori demanded the complete eradication of Jewish identity as the fair, obligatory price for Jewish emancipation and civic equality before and after the French Revolution, the "friends" of the Indian, with clear consciences, demanded a comparable extinguishing of Native American identity. The liberals in both Europe and America—and this is what made them liberals—were for the rapid acculturation and (eventual) equality of the Jew and the Indian respectively, but only after all vestiges of their traditional *tribal* consciousness and classical forms of life had been eliminated. As such, the most revolutionary constructions of ethnocide were seen not only as thoroughly compatible with authentic friendship for the Native American (and the European Jew) but, actually, as an entailment of that friendship. "Poor Indian, Poor Jew, savages and primitive obscurantists respectively, we know better." Native American*ism* (like Juda*ism*) would be, had to be, exterminated—but through an ethnocidally generous process that preserved the fundamental Native American stock now to be refashioned and recycled in a more acceptable majoritarian image.

Put simply, the reality of mission, the implication of all the conversionary activity here described, is contragenocidal in its intent.

The creation of Indian reservations also bears directly on this issue of putative Indian genocide. In fact, after 1850, the policy of reservations became the primary national response to the "Indian question," because, unless the indigenous peoples could be protected against the tidal flow of white settlement that was in the process of creating a vast settler nation stretching from the Atlantic to the Pacific, all hope of preventing the extinction of the Indian would prove a cruel illusion. That is, *as an alternative to extinction*, and as a new, if in many ways equivocal, manifestation of America's historic paternalistic and imperialistic colonial attitudes toward the nation's aboriginal peoples, a second round of Indian removals, now to newly established reservations, began. This policy, first articulated in a programmatic way by William Medill, commissioner of Indian affairs in the James Polk administration, allowed the majority of western Indian territory to be opened up to white settlement while establishing a "controlled" and protected environment—all too often actually uncontrolled and unprotected—wherein intercourse, laws, white-directed educational reform (there were forty-two Indian schools by 1842 with some 2,000 pupils of both sexes), and missionary activity could, working together, begin to transform the indigene into a peasant-style Christian farmer. Indian culture would give way to "civilization," but the Indians themselves, that is, as a biological entity, would survive, if in a starkly different sociocultural guise.

Beginning in the early 1850s, under the administration of President Millard Fillmore, the implementation of this policy on a broad scale was accelerated. For example, the Fort Berthold Indian Reservation was created in 1851 for the Hedatsa, Mandan, and Arikara; the Otoe were moved to the Blue River Reservation in Nebraska and Kansas in 1854; and the Cheyenne and Arapaho were "settled," temporarily as it turned out—for they had another decade of overt resistance left in their system—in areas south of the Arkansas. Various California Indian nations were enclosed on the Fresno Farm Reservation in 1852, the El Tejon Reservation in 1853, and the Nome Lackee Reservation in 1854, with six additional loci created between 1856 and 1870 (though only three of these reservations remained open by 1871). The Chippewa of Michigan and Wisconsin began their entry onto reservations in 1854. In fact, in 1854 alone, the various

Indian nations ceded, in twelve treaties, 18 million acres in return for reservations of 1.5 million acres. In 1865, the Kiowa, Comanche, and Kiowa-Apache were established in northern Texas and western Oklahoma. In 1866, the Santee Reservation was created in Nebraska, and, in 1867, the White Earth Reservation was created for the Chippewa. In 1868, the Navajo were moved to a reservation in northern New Mexico and Arizona; the Utes were relocated to western Colorado and parts of Utah; and a number of other Utah tribes were installed in the Uintah Valley. The Sioux, under the Treaty of Fort Laramie, settled in Montana and the Dakotas after 1868, and the Oglala Sioux settled at the Red Cloud Reservation in 1870. In 1873, the Mescaleros were lodged on a reservation in their traditional lands in south-central New Mexico; in 1869, a final settlement with the Southern Cheyenne and Southern Arapaho was reached that created a nearly 4.3-million-acre reservation in western Oklahoma; in 1874, the Kickapoo, who had previously been moved west of the Mississippi, were moved once more to a newly created reservation; the Pawnee were installed on a reservation in Indian Territory in 1875; and then in 1876–1877, following further wars and General George Custer's massacre, the Northern Cheyenne were likewise moved to this territory. In the Northwest beginning in 1855, the Nez Percé were given a 3-million-acre territory in the Grande Ronde, Clearwater, and Snake and Salmon Valleys of Idaho; the Cayuse, Umatilla, and Wallawalla were provided with a grant of 800 square miles in the Blue Mountains beginning in 1855; and the Klikitat, Yakima, and Paloo (Palouse) were settled on the Yakima River in the Washington Territory. The Flathead, Upper Pend d'Oreille, and Kutenai were ceded a 1.25-million-acre reserve in northern Montana. In Oregon, the indigenous peoples were contained in the Warm Springs Reservation, and the Numa (Northern Paiute) who spread across parts of Oregon, California, Idaho, and Nevada were removed to the Walker Lake and Pyramid Lake (and other) reservations after the Pyramid Lake War of 1860. By 1876, even some Apache had accepted their fate and joined reservations. Indeed, by the mid-1870s Secretary of the Interior Columbus Delano estimated that Indian reservations outside of the Indian Territory occupied 96,155,785 acres (containing 172,000 people). Accordingly, as late as 1887, Indian lands totaled 156 million acres.

This enterprise of protected resettlement was, ultimately but not surprisingly, unable to transcend the broader crosscurrents and deeply partisan politics of the period. Pressure to reduce Indian landholdings continued, justified by various reformist ideologies as well as outright avarice, often offering only a "fig leaf." However, even a cursory study of the inventory of the reservations already listed indicates that the U.S. government, despite the inhumanity and injustice incarnate in this grossly unfair resolution of the territorial question, never came, relative to the American Indian, to the Hitlerian conclusion: "You cannot live at all." During this era physical abuse and moral indifference were present in abundance in Indian affairs, but the substantial criminality and severe neglect that reigned supreme were not the consequence of, and were not accompanied by, a consciously enacted program of extermination.

In the years following the Civil War, especially during President Grant's terms in office, the U.S. government carried through its decision that the Indian people qua a people could not live *among* the white population but could continue their separate communal life in their degraded and reduced circumstances, with official America's consent in the special Indian territories created for this purpose. It did so because, as the commissioner of Indian affairs wrote in 1867, the policy of "preservation by gradual concentration on territorial reserves [was the only alternative to] swift extermination by the sword and famine."[4] This was not a noble choice. White society, even as it "saved" the aboriginal inhabitants of the land, was guilty of colossal wrongdoing. Yet, despite the monumentality and endurance of the crime, this was not a crime without limits and self-imposed constraints. The maintenance of 141 reservations (by 1880), controlling well over 100 million acres (including the Indian territory), inhabited by hundreds of thousands of Indians—housing 11,328 students in school, 177 church buildings, and 27,215 Indian church members—is indisputable evidence of this. The reservation, for all the ethical and existential transgressions that it represents, is a concession to survival, a commitment to continued individual and tribal existence. (As proof of its success in at least providing for native survival, I note that in the mid-1980s, the Native American population of the United States was put at 1.532 million by the U.S. Census Bureau, with 631,574 persons still living on 278 reservations; the 1990 census put the native Indian population at over 1.8 million.)

In this often misrepresented historical context, it is important to recognize explicitly that the Indian Wars, begun in the 1850s and 1860s against the great western tribes (Navajo, Comanche, Sioux, and Apache), were fought not to exterminate the Indians outright but rather to break their serious and continued resistance to removal to reservations. The federal government and the U.S. Army sought to crush Indian autonomy, eradicate Indian territorial attachments, put an end to the extremely expensive Indian Wars, and reduce the Indians to a subservient and acquiescent mode of behavior that would allow the national authorities to dictate the sociopolitical, economic, and existential conditions of Indian life. This description applies even to such humanly costly encounters as occurred, for example, in the Washington Territory in the mid-1850s during the Rogue River War and the Yakima War. For these military conflicts, too, were fought so that the federal authorities could successfully relocate Indian tribes drawn from Oregon and Washington onto eight reservations established for them. This nonexterminatory reading of the great Indian Wars is reinforced, moreover, by the treatment of (to take just one example) the Nez Percé, who chose not to join their Northwest Indian neighbors in the military conflicts of the 1850s and were, at least for a time, spared their depredations as a consequence. That is to say, reflective of a larger, conscious American design, there was no national homicidal scheme directed at the Washington and Oregon Indians. Likewise, the great climactic Indian Wars on the plains in the 1870s and 1880s against the Kiowa, Cheyenne, Arapaho, Comanche, and Sioux, among others, were, for all their lethal ferocity, a continuation of the dominant-submissive pattern that the federal authorities now sought to impose on white-Indian relations. Contra the misconceived genocidal school of historical interpreters, it is here relevant to recognize the salient fact—not forgetting particular massacres perpetrated by American military forces, indeed, precisely in light of them—that once the U.S. Army had subdued the great western tribes on the field of battle, it could have slaughtered all the remaining tribal members had genocide been its determinate purpose. It was not and it did not.

III
The Famine in Ukraine

The widespread and consequential famine in Ukraine between 1930 and 1933 also has to be accounted for in light of the current argument contra genocide. There are two main lines of scholarly interpretation as to what happened in Ukraine and why. The first of these emphasizes the nationalist dimensions of the event. Under this interpretation, both the indigenous Ukrainian population and the alien Soviet ruling class knew that Ukraine, as recently as 1918, had been independent—with its own separate historical and cultural traditions—and that it wished to be politically independent again. Accordingly, the confrontation of the late 1910s and of the 1920s and 1930s in this region is seen as having been defined by the collision of two competing claims to sovereignty: one nationalist and the other putatively internationalist, though, increasingly, the latter was merely a cover for an ever more visible Russian national chauvinism. For Stalin, the ultimate objective is seen to have been the full integration without national remainder of Ukraine into the larger, ideally homogenized, Soviet state. Anything less was dangerous, both practically—because it would interfere with Bolshevik control of the agricultural market and the essential issue of grain collection and distribution, a circumstance that often divided the local leadership—and potentially—because of the geopolitically divisive character of nationalist aspirations. In consequence, Stalin, under this nationalist reading, consciously decided on a deadly campaign—most accurately described through the political category of internal colonialism—to eradicate this recurring threat to Soviet hegemony. Beginning with the purge of Ukrainian academics and political and cultural leaders that began in April 1929 and continued into 1930, Stalin is believed to have set in motion a movement that would eventually consume literally millions of Ukrainians.

The object of the entire terror campaign was, under this exegesis, the complete annihilation of Ukrainian nationalism (a goal that was also consistent with the larger Stalinist policy of the socialization of agriculture). Much like Hitler's later strategy in, for example, Poland (and elsewhere in eastern Europe), Stalin sought to expunge local autonomy and all manifestations of cultural and political independence in order to facilitate continued domination from Moscow. Here, as in many other cases that easily come to mind (Cambodia, Nigeria, Sudan, and, most recently, Rwanda), the purpose of state-organized violence is the maintenance of political control.

Given the importance of the independent, economically autonomous peasantry in Ukraine's socioeconomic structures, Stalin's plan for the extermination of national identity required—in addition to the removal of the national intelligentsia—a crusade against this "protocapitalist" strata. As Semen O. Pidhainy has described it, Stalin had to move against Ukrainian nationalism's "social base"—the individual landholdings.[5] "Only a mass terror throughout the body of the nation—that is, the peasantry—could reduce the nation to submission."[6] As long as the *selianym* (a euphemism now for all free Ukrainian peasants) existed, nationalist (and capitalist) sentiment would remain: Both needed to be crushed.

The dominant method used to achieve this collective submission to socialism, this elimination of the base of Ukrainian national sentiment, was the forced collectivization of the agricultural sector. At the same time, and not unimportant, such a centralized agrarian policy gave the Communist Party—in the form of the All-Union Commissariat of Agriculture—control over the region's grain supply. It was the task and responsibility of this commissariat, in conjunction with the Soviet planners, to calculate, coordinate, and organize the yearly grain harvest, in other words, to set and oversee the state exactions to be levied and collected. In the event, when this direct control was expressed in an overly demanding target for grain exports from the region—ostensibly justified by the increased program of industrialization that was to be financed by the agricultural surplus—it effectively translated into a man-made famine in Ukraine in 1931 that grew worse in 1932 and 1933. For example, in 1931, the procurement quota for the region was set at 7 million tons out of a total of 18.3 million tons (much of which had been lost to inefficient collective harvesting). Such a level of national procurement almost certainly spelled trouble for the local community. Matters of food supply only got worse in 1932 when the procurement total was again set at 7 million tons while that year's harvest, due to drought, inefficiency, and a decline in the number of acres sown—the last partly in protest to Stalinist policy—came in at the very reduced level of 14.7 million tons. Although the local leadership, in the face of the total decline in tonnage, managed to persuade Moscow, at great cost to itself in the suspicions of disloyalty (and suspect nationalism) that such appeals raised, to reduce the quota to 6.6 million tons—itself a target never fulfilled—even this reduced sum was still far too high to make it possible to avoid massive starvation. Stalin, despite the mounting death toll, did not believe, or did not *want* to believe, the claim that the harvest was too small both to feed the Ukrainian people and to provide sufficient grain for export. Instead, already intensely suspicious of Ukrainian separatism and fearful of local disloyalty, he chose to interpret the failure to meet the inordinate quotas sent down from the center as deliberate acts of "sabotage," the peasants as no better than "wreckers" of the socialist dream. Therefore, in a deliberate act intended to punish the population of Ukraine—though justified as an act of socialist self-defense—he continued to export grain from the region, if at a lower rate: 1.73 million tons in 1932 and 1.68

million tons in 1933, compared to 5.2 million tons in 1931. This export of grain, given the greatly reduced supplies, turned an already grave situation into an occasion of mass death.

Increased pressure was now also applied against the *selianym*-class enemy, local party officials (37.3 percent of the new Ukrainian Communist Party members and candidate members were purged and 75 percent of local Soviets and members of local committees were replaced, with many of those who were replaced being arrested for failing to produce the required quota), those involved in local agricultural middle management (many of these officials were arrested in the second half of 1932 for sabotaging Bolshevik policy), and all channels of Ukrainian economic, cultural, and nutritional self-sufficiency. On December 14, 1932, the Central Committee of the All-Union Communist Party accused the leadership of the Ukrainian Communist Party "of tolerating a Ukrainian nationalist deviation in its ranks"[7] and then proceeded, on January 24, 1933, to replace it with a new ruling clique headed by Pavel Postyshev. At the same time, all available food aid to the stricken population, it is argued, was consciously denied, existing grain reserves in the region and elsewhere were not made available, and the importation of food was stopped at the border of Ukraine—all while Stalin, in an act of depravity, continued, as already noted, to export more than 3 million tons of grain in 1932 and 1933. As a result, there was massive—under this decoding, *intentional*—starvation throughout Ukraine climaxing in 1933 and 1934. Of a peasant population of upwards of 25 million, I estimate that up to 5 million persons, or 20 percent of the rural population, plus from 500,000 to 750,000 persons in the urban areas of Ukraine, died from lack of food and related medical problems in this period. In some areas, the death rate was as low as 10 percent, in others nearly 100 percent, depending largely upon local agricultural and ecological conditions, for example, and most importantly, the ability to find other sources of nutrition, such as fish or wildlife—in many places this also led to cannibalism and infanticide—to replace the lost grain harvests.

So goes the nationalist account of the Ukrainian famine interpreted as an intentional, man-made "genocide." Stalin purposely killed 5 million or more Ukrainians, plus hundreds of thousands of additional individuals belonging to other ethnic groups, such as the Volga Germans and Kuban Cossacks, in order both to decapitate opposition to agricultural collectivization and to eradicate Ukrainian, and other, nationalist aspirations.

Now, accepting this nationalist interpretation of Ukrainian history, at least for the sake of argument, what are we to conclude about these events constituting an instance of genocide? This is neither an irrelevant nor a trivial question given the size of the human losses involved and the evil will that is asserted to have directly caused, to have been knowingly responsible for, these losses. Moreover, I do not want to support any diminution or denial of this vast collective tragedy, the existence of which is not in doubt. However—and here I recognize that given the loss of millions of persons this conclusion will seem at first counterintuitive—even if the nationalist intentionalist thesis is correct, the results—at least 5 million deaths—do *not* constitute the technical crime of genocide, and the event, in its phenomenological specificity and totality, is not, for all of its murderous ferocity and demographic enormity, comparable to the Shoah. I would argue—assuming the correctness of this account—that the ruthless campaign against Ukrainian nationalism that destroyed a majority of the indigenous Ukrainian cultural and political elite, in addition to a significant segment of the peasant population of the region, is most correctly categorized as an instance of nationalist conflict and internal colonialism rather than as an example of genocide. Stalin did not intend to exterminate the entire population of Ukraine.

This conclusion finds immediate support from the apposite statistical indicators: Though the human carnage was enormous—approaching the number of Jewish victims during the Second World War—the portion of the Ukrainian peasant population lost was somewhere near 20 percent (plus or minus 5 percent), and the losses for the Ukrainian population as a whole were in the area of 15 percent. These demographic results resemble (if being slightly higher than) the figures for population decline in those eastern European countries overrun by the Nazis, and in both cases the numbers do not indicate that a policy of total population eradication was pursued. Had Stalin in Ukraine—and Hitler in eastern Europe—sought to pursue a genocidal war, given the destructive possibilities that lay open to him, more than 15 percent of the population would have been done away with. More people were not killed because, amid the murder that did occur, there was, odd as this may seem, restraint. There was restraint because Stalin did not want to eradicate the people of Ukraine; he wanted to exploit them. Eliminating the whole of a vanquished helot population makes no more sense than slaughtering one's slaves. However, in contrast, eliminating a conquered people's controlling elite, leaving it leaderless, anxious, and vertiginous, is a rational and functional strategy, long pursued by conquerors and adopted by Stalin, in order to achieve both enduring subordination of the subjugated and political stability in one's empire. This is not a humane imperial strategy—a regular course of action to be recommended as a form of empire maintenance—but neither is it genocide.

Ironically, this judgment is confirmed by the heartrending condition of the children, especially infants and the newborn. Throughout Ukraine, youthful cadavers lay strewn across the landscape; the entire territory had become a crude necropolis for children under the age of twelve who were unable to obtain enough nourishment to stay alive. Yet even here, in the midst of the most intense human suffering, the relevant population statistics require careful decipherment. The latest demographic data indicate that fewer than 760,000 children died,[8] largely from starvation, between 1932 and 1934. This represents, depending on one's estimation of other relevant demographic variables, between 6 percent and 33.5 percent of the age cohort and a significant percentage of the total population decline. However, recognizing the great tragedy that occurred here, even the maximum loss rate of 33.5 percent does not support a genocidal reading of this event. For, on these numbers, that is, a loss rate of between 6 and 33.5 percent, 66.5 percent of Ukrainian children, at a minimum, survived. Once the famine was past its peak in May 1933, the surviving two out of three children were not singled out for further harassment or worse. Most of those who survived the crisis of 1932–1933 survived.

This historical outcome regarding the children is not trivial. What makes the Ukrainian case non-genocidal, and what makes it different from the Holocaust, is the fact that the majority of Ukrainian children survived and, still more, that they were *permitted* to survive. Even the mountain of evidence pertaining to Stalin's evil actions produced by the proponents of the nationalist-genocide thesis—for example, James Mace and Robert Conquest—does not indicate an intent to eliminate, or any motive that would plausibly justify the extermination of, the Ukrainian biological stock. Though the number of Ukrainian children who died and, under the intentionalist reading, were murdered, was almost as high as (or higher than) the number of Jewish children who were exterminated, their deaths were the consequence of, represented, and intended something wholly different from what the murder of Jewish children at Auschwitz and Treblinka represented and intended. In the Ukrainian case, the focused object of the violence and death was national enfeeblement and political dismemberment. In the Shoah, the focused object, given its racial determinants, was physical genocide. Stalin intended that after the famine there should still be Ukrainians, though not Ukrainianism; Hitler intended that after Auschwitz there would be neither Jews nor Judaism. The loss of every child in both contexts, employing the calculus of the talmudic sages, was the loss of a world. The death of each child was an act of equal immorality. Nonetheless, there is an important, nonreductive, phenomenological difference to be drawn between mass murder (including children) and complete group extinction (including children), between a war for political and territorial domination (including children) and a war of unlimited biological annihilation (including children).

The issue, the interpretive inquiry, the dialectic of evidence and meaning regarding the Ukrainian tragedy, is still more complex. For, as noted (nonpolemically) at the outset of this analysis, there are two possible explanations of the Ukrainian tragedy. The second possible, plausible, non-nationalist deconstruction of the Ukrainian tragedy argues that the famine was neither intended nor man-made—though, ultimately, it was the result of human errors connected with the program of forced collectivization. That is to say, under this alternative reading, the famine, the reality and extent of which no one denies, was not the consequence of a premeditated plan to murder large numbers of Ukrainians in support of an antinationalist political outcome in the region. Therefore, by definition, what transpired, though baleful and full of bile, was not genocide.

The case for this very different interpretation has been made by a number of scholars including, most recently, J. Arch Getty, Walter Laqueur, Mark B. Tauger, and R. W. Davies, and is supported by both Robert C. Tucker's narrative in his *Stalin in Power* and Adam Ulam's conclusion in his *Stalin: The Man and His Era:* "Stalin and his closest collaborators had not willed the famine."[9]

Now, under either interpretation of the Ukrainian tragedy, the fact is that, though something very terrible occurred in Ukraine, what happened was a very different sort of thing—structurally and as regards intention—than what transpired in the Holocaust.

IV
The Armenian Tragedy

The Armenian tragedy was an enormous historical outrage. As I understand this event, the controlling ambition, the collective civic agenda, behind Turkish inhumanity was primarily nationalist in character and, in practice, limited in scope and purpose. The Armenian massacres were an indecent, radicalized manifestation of a most primitive jingoism activated by the exigencies of war from without and the revolutionary collapse of the Ottoman empire from within. Turkish nationalism—the extreme nationalist elites in control of the Turkish state—now under the violent cover of war, envisioned and pursued the elimination of (*not* the murder of) *all* non-Turkish elements—and most especially and specifically the eradication of the Armenian community—from the national context. The anti-Armenian crusade was, therefore, for all its lethal extravagance, a delimited political crusade. Of course, mixed into the noxious brew that represented itself as national destiny were other obsessions: a loathing of Christians if not all non-Muslims, xenophobia, greed, jealousy, fear, desire, and the like. But, above all else, the "war against the Armenians" was a vulgar and desperate manifestation of raw nationalist politics.

As a direct and immediate consequence, anti-Armenianism is not expressed in the baroque language of metaphysical evil, nor does it require (paraphrasing Heinrich Himmler's assertion that "all Jews without exception must die") the complete annihilation of *every* Armenian man, woman, and child. It does not represent a racial collision as that term came to be understood in the ornate ontological schema of Nazism. There is no assertion of primordial reciprocity between power and being, between intrahuman aggression and metahistoric causations, between biological contingencies and noumenological principles. Rather, the elemental rationale almost universally cited by the Turks in defense of their actions is political: The Armenians were secessionists, Russian spies, fifth-columnists, and divisive nationalists who would subvert the Turkish people's revolution and destroy Turkish national and political integrity. This explanatory tack, this nationalist warrant, is already determinative in the prewar Turkish interpretation of, for example, the Armenian massacres at Adana in April 1909, and it reappears in full force in the explication of the events of 1915–1916. Repeated Turkish reference to the Armenian revolution at Van in 1915 is perhaps the outstanding example of this "legitimating" mode of moral-political reasoning.

This is to argue that contrary to, for example, Helen Fein's contention that the Armenians were "enemies by definition,"[10] that is, on a priori ideological or racial grounds—thereby allowing her erroneously to equate the action against Jews and Gypsies in World War II with that against the Armenians in World War I—the Armenians were "enemies" to the degree that they were enemies in this context, on practical and political grounds centering around long-standing policies of internal colonialism, the implications—and machinations—of national self-determination, and the provocative issue of loyalty in time of war. Accordingly, the objective of Turkish action, when it came in 1915–1916, was the destruction, once and for all, of Armenian national identity. The criminality of the Armenians did not require (as I shall show in detail in a moment) the biological extinction of every Armenian man, woman, and child—especially if such individual and collective survival took place outside Turkish national boundaries and, therefore, made no claims upon Turkish sovereignty or national territory.

This is not to ignore the magnitude of the crime perpetrated against the Armenian people, the misery and death entailed by the mass deportations, the continual abuse of Armenian women, the mix of ideology, sadism, and self-interest in the massacre of Armenian men, and the theft and murder of infants and children. It is, however, to insist that these deliberate acts of despoliation and near-unlimited cruelty be deciphered aright. To decipher them aright means recognizing their particular strategic causation that (odd as this may sound, given the vast inhuman carnage that occurred) entailed limits. Being a political-national assault against a political enemy, the Young Turks could achieve their preeminent goal—the protection of the nation as they defined it—without requiring the complete physical extirpation of every person of Armenian heritage. To this degree (and here I make only this limited and very precise claim), the intentionality behind, as well as the actualized structure of, the Turkish program for the eradication of Armenian national existence was *unlike* the biocentric war that Nazism carried on against the Jews—because the "Armenian question" differed in its quintessential character from the "Jewish question." The former had been a conflicted political issue for nearly a century, had created manifold pressures and functional compromises for the Ottoman state, and now could be, once and for all, resolved by the annihilation of the organized Armenian *community* within Turkey. In contrast, the Jewish question, which had likewise been a central, exceedingly controversial, political concern in Europe since the beginning of Jewish emancipation in the eighteenth century, was categorically transformed by Hitler into an inescapable metaphysical challenge ("blood" in the Nazi universe of discourse being understood as the elementary vehicle by which ontological values become incarnate in history) that could *only* be resolved by an uncompromisingly genocidal assault. The Third Reich, therefore, insisted not only on the elimination of Jewish collective identity and communal existence, but also on the murder of *every* Jewish person of whatever age and gender.

At this juncture of our argument, three seminal factors that strengthen the morphological *dis*analogy between the Armenian tragedy and the Holocaust need to be introduced. They are: (1) the possibility of Armenian Christian conversion to Islam as a way of avoiding deportation and worse; (2) the specific character of the forced deportations; and (3) the *nontotalistic* nature of the anti-Armenian crusade.

As regards the mediating role of conversion to Islam, the eyewitness accounts of the tragedy repeatedly mention this lifesaving, though communally destructive, possibility. Both "willingly" and unwillingly, large numbers of Armenians became Muslims. In particular, there appears to have been extensive, forced proselytization of Armenian women and children. It is difficult to ascertain just what role official Ittihadist ideology played in these coerced prophylactic rituals, though it is clear that the Committee of Union and Progress (CUP), devoid as it was of a racist ideology, did not oppose such re-creative, death-deflecting actions. Indeed, to the degree that Islamicization constructively reinforced the Young Turks' normative political agenda—Islam being a fundamental buttress of Turkification (whereas Christianity was the key element in Armenian self-identity)—this survivalist (flagrantly inhumane) program was consistent with CUP ambitions; and it found wide instantiation. So wide, in fact, that Johannes Lepsius again and again excoriates the Turkish government for allowing, even encouraging, this tyrannical policy, and Arnold Toynbee accusingly refers to "survival being purchased by apostatizing to Islam."[11] Likewise, the German, U.S., British, and other governments are on record as protesting this unwelcome practice.

In that neither Islam nor Turkism is predicated on inelastic, biologistic concepts, both possess absorptive capacities that create existential as well as sociopolitical possibilities unavailable in Nazism. Accordingly, the "other" is not only defined differently by the Ittihad elites than in Hitler's Reich—not genetically and without reference to metaphysical canons of ontic pollution and decadence—but the required response to the "other" allows for the remaking of the "other," primarily through the mysterious rite of conversion, so as to obviate still more complete—that is, exterminatory—forms of overcoming. We have evidence that the children in Christian orphanages were converted en masse. It was not only women and children who were forcibly converted. Lepsius, for example, records that the entire male medical staff of the German Mission Hospital in Urfa were coerced into becoming Muslim, as were Armenian army physicians at Sivas.[12] In Aleppo, the entire Armenian labor battalion was converted in February 1916, and further large-scale conversions of Armenian males occurred in March and April 1916. Lepsius also reports that "all Armenian villages in the Samsun area and in Unich has been Islamicized. No favors were granted to anyone, apart from renegades."[13] In fact, Lepsius conservatively estimates that 200,000 men, women, and children, approximately 12 to 13.5 percent of the entire Armenian community, were forcibly converted and thereby saved,[14] however objectionable the instrument of their salvation. In this respect, Turkish policy reproduces medieval pro-

cedures of cultural homogenization, not modern procedures of physical genocide. As such, it kept Armenians, if not Armenianism, alive.

Secondly, the Armenian deportations were not uniform events of total annihilation. Though these Armenian removals, carried out under the most brutal conditions, were regularly occasions of mass death that sealed the fate of hundreds
of thousands, several hundred thousand Armenians did survive these horrific
journeys. Lepsius, for example, (under)estimates the remnant at 200,000 individuals. Toynbee cites a total of 600,000 Armenian survivors up to 1916—the combined total of those who lived through the deportations and those who fled into
Russian territory. He summarizes:

> In general wastage [death during the deportations] seems to fluctuate, with a wide
> oscillation, on either side of 50 percent; 600 out of 2,500 (24 percent) reached Aleppo
> from a village in the Harpout district; 60 percent arrived there out of the first con-
> voy from the village of E. (near H.), and 46 percent out of the second; 25 percent ar-
> rived out of a convoy from the village of D. in the same neighborhood. We shall cer-
> tainly be well within the mark if we estimate that at least half those condemned to
> massacre or deportation have actually perished.[15]

Supporting these large estimates of the number of those who were *not* killed
during these forced evacuations are the figures for Armenians who found refuge
in Arab countries and then, later, in western Europe and the United States.
Richard Hovannisian, writing of their acceptance in the Arab world, indicates
that "many of the deportees suffered a cruel fate at the hands of certain Bedouin
tribes in the Syrian desert, but most were accorded sympathetic asylum by the
Arab peoples, who had themselves endured four centuries of Ottoman domination. In all, the number of Armenian deportees who found refuge in Arab lands,
by 1925, is estimated at well over 200,000."[16] This figure excludes the 50,000 persons who found refuge in Iran. More specifically, Hovannisian breaks these
refugee figures down as follows: Syria accepted 100,000 Armenian refugees;
Lebanon, 50,000; Palestine and Jordan, 10,000; Egypt, 40,000; Iraq, 25,000; and
Iran, 50,000, making a total of 275,000 survivors. These numbers are supported
by later governmental statistics issued by the respective Arab countries. Census
data released between 1931 and 1945 by the individual Middle East states indicate that Syria had an Armenian population of 125,550 (1945); Lebanon, 72,797
(1944); Palestine, 3,802 (1931); and Egypt, 19,596 (1937). Moreover, in addition
to these aggregates, we also have evidence in various national census counts of
the inter-war period of sizable new Armenian communities, in France, Greece,
Cyprus, Bulgaria, and the United States, with additional small populations in
Czechoslovakia, Switzerland, Greece, Hungary, Austria, Yugoslavia, Italy, and
Canada. (The population figures for these communities overlap with Hovan-
nesian's figures for the Arab World—though to what exact degree is uncertain.)
Therefore, if we put the number of survivors of these inhumane transfers at be-

tween 300,000 and 400,000, we shall be on secure grounds—or at least grounds that are as secure as possible given all the statistical uncertainties—remembering that Hovannisian's total of 275,000 does not include any survivors in Russia, Europe, or the United States. This translates into a survival rate somewhere between 17.7 percent (300,000 out of 1.7 million, the maximum Armenian population) and 26.6 percent (400,000 out of 1.5 million, the minimum Armenian population). Then, too, beyond the mathematics alone, these substantial statistics indicate that the Turkish oppressor did not require nor demand the death of all Armenians. The Turks had all of these individuals, this entire defenseless population, within their control and could have murdered them all, despite the practical difficulties involved in murdering an entire people in a country as large as Turkey, had they so desired. Evidently, this was not necessary.

Thirdly, the enacted policy of deporting Armenians was not universally applied even within the borders of Turkey. The Armenians of Constantinople, numbering up to 200,000, and the Armenians of other large cities—for example, Smyrna, where between 6,000 and 20,000 Armenians lived, Kutahia, and, to some degree, Aleppo—were not uprooted en masse during the entire war period. Lepsius estimated (and, in his own words, perhaps "overestimated") that the number of Armenians so protected represented one-seventh to one-ninth of the total Armenian population, or some 204,700 persons (out of what he projected as an original Armenian population of 1,845,450).[18] Although recent studies[19] require that we temper Lepsius's figures and indicate that up to 30,000 Armenians were, in fact, deported from Constantinople, the need to modify all generalizations as to Turkish intentions, given the very real limitations placed upon evictions from Constantinople and elsewhere, stands.

To gain a full picture of all the relevant statistics bearing upon the question of Armenian survival, we must also add in the 300,000 or so Armenians who retreated with the Russian army back into Russian territory after the final defeat at Van in the summer of 1915 and the 4,200 who survived the famous battle at Musa Dagh and were rescued by the French in mid-September 1915. Accordingly, the comprehensive demographic picture regarding casualties and survival looks like this:

1914 Armenian Population	1,500,000–1,700,000
Converts to Islam	200,000–300,000
Survive Deportations (outside Turkey)	300,000–400,000
Survive in large Turkish Cities	170,000–220,000
Survive in Russia	250,000–300,000
Survivors of Musa Dagh	4,200–4,200
TOTAL SURVIVORS	924,200–1,224,200
TOTAL DEATHS (1915–1918, based on 1,700,000 total)	475,800–775,800

This is not the Holocaust.

V
Conclusion

The spatial limits imposed on this chapter prevent further comparative review and analysis. However, I believe that in all the other cases that are said to parallel the Holocaust, close study would show that they also are dissimilar insofar as they, too, would not be examples of an unlimited war that required complete annihilation—the death of every man, woman, and child—of the victim population. The Holocaust is a unique historical reality.

NOTES

1. I discuss all of these historical events at great length in volume 2 of my study entitled *The Holocaust in Historical Context* (New York: Oxford University Press), forthcoming. Volume 1, published in 1994, deals with premodern cases, for example, medieval anti-semitism, the witch craze, the medieval crusades against heretics, and the French wars of religion, that bear on this subject.

2. James Mooney, "Calendar History of the Kiowa Indians," in the *Seventeenth Annual Report of the Bureau of American Ethnology, 1895–1896* (Washington, D.C.: Bureau of Ethnology, 1898), part 1.

3. Russell Thornton, *American Indian Holocaust and Survival* (Norman: University of Oklahoma Press, 1987), p. 49.

4. Cited from Brian Dippie, *The Vanishing American: White Attitudes and U.S. Indian Policy* (Middletown, Conn.: Wesleyan University Press, 1982), p. 151.

5. Semen O. Pidhainy et al., eds., *The Black Deeds of the Kremlin: A White Book*, vol. 1 (Detroit, 1955), p. 205.

6. Robert Conquest, *The Harvest of Sorrow: Soviet Collectivization and the Terror-Famine* (New York: Oxford University Press, 1986), p. 219. Repeated in the *U.S. Commission on the Ukraine Famine* (Washington, D.C., 1990), p. xiii: "Crushing the Ukrainian peasantry made it possible for Stalin to curtail Ukrainian national self-assertion."

7. Cited from George O. Liber, *Soviet Nationality Policy* (Cambridge: Cambridge University Press, 1992), p. 166. On these political activities, interpreted from a radical Ukrainian perspective, see Hryhory Kostiuk, *Stalinist Rule in the Ukraine* (New York: Praeger, 1960), pp. 18–37; and from a less ideological perspective, see Robert S. Sullivant, *Soviet Politics in the Ukraine* (New York: Columbia University Press, 1962), pp. 195–208.

8. Robert Conquest's maximum total of child deaths of 4 million—3 million as a result of the famine and 1 million due to the program of dekulakization—appears, based on currently available evidence, too high. See *Harvest of Sorrow*, p. 297. Moreover, this total includes non-Ukrainian children, for example, those of Kazakhstan, thus reducing the number and percentage of child losses in Ukraine (even on Conquest's numbers) significantly.

9. Adam Ulam, *Stalin: The Man and His Era* (New York: Viking, 1973), p. 349.

10. Helen Fein, *Accounting for Genocide* (New York: Free Press, 1979), p. 30.

11. Arnold Toynbee, "The Murderous Tyranny of the Turks" (pamphlet: New York, 1917).

12. Johannes Lepsius, *Deutschland und Armenien, 1914–1918* (Potsdam: Tempelverlag, 1919), p. 283.

13. Ibid., p. 160.

14. Ibid., p. lxv.

15. Arnold Toynbee in Viscount Bryce, *The Treatment of the Armenians in the Ottoman Empire, 1915–1916* (London: The Knickerbocker Press [for His Majesty's Stationery Office], 1916), p. 650.

16. Richard Hovannisian, "Ebb and Flow of the Armenian Minority in the Arab Middle East," *Middle East Journal* 1(28) (Winter 1974):20.

17. I will provide a fuller accounting of these statistics in my analysis of the Armenian Tragedy in Vol. 2 of my *Holocaust in Historical Context.*

19. See Vahakn N. Dadrian's important qualification regarding the Armenians of Constantinople, "Genocide as a Problem of National and International Law: The World War I Armenian Case and Its Contemporary Legal Ramifications," *Yale Journal of International Law* 14(2) (Summer 1989):262, n. 131; and again, "The Documentation of the World War I Armenian Massacres in the Proceedings of the Turkish Military Tribunal," *International Journal of Middle East Studies* 23(4) (November 1991):570, n. 26. According to Dadrian's reconstruction, based on the testimony of German Ambassador Wolff-Metternich on December 7, 1915, who gave as his source the Turkish chief of policy, 30,000 Armenians were deported from Constantinople and more deportations were feared.

❀ 3 ❀

Responses to the Porrajmos: The Romani Holocaust[1]

IAN HANCOCK

Ignorance and arrogance are in full flower ... [including] the notion that not only Jews ... but Gypsies were chosen by the Nazis for annihilation.
Edward Alexander, "Review of Lopate," 1990[2]

"Holocaust" has been used to encompass more than the murder of the Jews. From the casualties in our Civil War to the wholesale murder of gypsies in World War II.
William Safire, "On Language: Long Time No See," 1983[3]

Just four years after the fall of the Third Reich, Dora Yates, the Jewish secretary of the Gypsy Lore Society, noted in the pages of *Commentary* that:

> It is more than time that civilized men and women were aware of the Nazi crime against the Gypsies as well as the Jews. Both bear witness to the fantastic dynamic of the 20th century racial fanaticism, for these two people shared the horror of martyrdom at the hands of the Nazis for no other reason than that they were—they existed. The Gypsies, like the Jews, stand alone.4

And, the following year, the *Wiener Library Bulletin*, organ of what is now the Jewish Institute of Contemporary History in London, published the statement that "Germany had in 1938 a gipsy population of 16,275. Of these, 85 per cent. were thrown into concentration camps, and no more than 12 per cent. survived."5

Despite these very early observations[6] and the overwhelming amount of documentation relating to the fate of the Gypsies in Nazi Germany, which has been examined during the fourteen years the U.S. Holocaust Memorial Council has been in existence, that body, more than any other, rigorously persists in underestimating and underrepresenting that truth, made plain forty-five years ago, a position reflected in the permanent exhibit in the United States Holocaust Memorial Museum—whose staff, it should be said, has generally been much more favorably disposed to the Gypsy case. In their 1989 book *Holocaust: Religious and Philosophical Implications*, editors John Roth and Michael Berenbaum ask, "Why should the fate of the Jews be treated differently than the fate of the Gypsies or the Poles. . . . The answer will be found in these essays."[7] But the answer to that question, at least for the Gypsy case, appears nowhere in any of the twenty-three essays that appear in the book. More recently still, Martin Gilbert, in his foreword to Carrie Supple's *From Prejudice to Genocide: Learning About the Holocaust*, published for use in British schools, refers to the Holocaust as "the attempt by the Nazis to destroy all the Jews of Europe between 1941 and 1945," then mentions the fate of the Romani victims as being among "other attempts at genocide, such as the slaughter of the Armenians,"[8] thereby placing Gypsies with a group outside of the Holocaust altogether and echoing the statement in his *The Holocaust* that "it was the Jews alone who were marked out to be destroyed in their entirety."[9] And though Michael Burleigh and Wolfgang Wippermann discuss in detail a "final solution" of the "Gypsy problem" in their book *The Racial State*, Antony Polonsky is still moved in his introduction to that book to maintain that "as emerges clearly from the arguments of Burleigh and Wippermann, the mass murder of the Jews *was* unique in that every Jew, man, woman and child, assimilated or deeply orthodox, was singled out for destruction."[10] It is abundantly clear that some historians see only what they want to see, that a very blind eye is being turned in the direction of Gypsy history, and that where the Romani genocide in Nazi Germany is acknowledged, it is kept, with the fewest of exceptions,[11] carefully separated from the Jewish experience. Some authors, such as Emil Fackenheim and Charles S. Maier, seem not yet to have made up their minds about whether to include Gypsies or not: "With the possible exception of the Gypsies, Jews were the only people killed for the 'crime'" of existing."[12] And in Maier's words:

> Why . . . does it seem important to insist on the uniqueness of the Nazi crimes? Because nowhere else but in Nazi-occupied Europe from 1941 to 1945 was there an apparatus so single-mindedly established to carry out mass murder as a process in its own right. And not just mass murder, but ethnic extermination—killing, without even a pretext of individual wrongdoing, an entire people (if gypsies are counted, two peoples).13

Similarly, Richard Breitman admits that Gypsies might eventually also get higher billing once more details become available: "The Nazis did try to wipe out virtually all Jews, whereas their murderous policies for other groups were more selective. In some cases, for example with the gypsies, further research is needed to show what distinctions were made, why some were killed and others spared."[14]

This is a profoundly emotionally charged issue, one fraught with subjective interpretation and response. Assumptions are made, and repeated with confidence, by individuals who have no special expertise in (Romani) holocaust history, and unqualified statements are reiterated that automatically assume a lesser status for Gypsies in the ranking of human abuse. These take the form of entire articles, such as that by Steven Katz.[15] He systematically compares the fate of Jews in the Holocaust with the medieval witch craze, North American Indians, black slavery, Gypsies under the Nazis, homosexuals during World War II, and Polish and Ukrainian losses during World War II, concluding that "all . . . are to be fundamentally distinguished from the Holocaust, even when they reveal horrifyingly large casualty figures."[16] The same is found in the writings of Yehuda Bauer, who states with assurance in his entry on "Gypsies" in *Encyclopedia of the Holocaust* that "the fate of the Gypsies was in line with Nazi thought as a whole: Gypsies were not Jews, and therefore there was no need to kill all of them."[17] Then, like Katz, he substantiates this claim by selectively citing sources (none more recent than 1979) and makes no comparisons with Jewish populations that were also exempted from death and for whom there was likewise "no need to kill all." The three-and-a-half-page "Gypsies" entry in the two-volume, 2,000-page *Encyclopedia of the Holocaust*, incidentally, amounts to less than one-quarter of 1 percent of the whole book, despite the enormity of Gypsy losses by 1945, which proportionately at least matched, and possibly exceeded, losses of Jewish victims. In his more recent book, Katz elaborates upon these comparisons and expands upon the criterion of "intentionality," which, he says, characterized the fate of Jews in the Holocaust but not that of any other victims of mass-scale murder. Indeed, he claims that "the Nazi attack on the Jews was the only true genocide in history."[18]

Typically accompanying these statements and assumptions is the acknowledgment that yes, there were other victims of Nazism, but they belong under a separate heading of non-Jews, and their fate was different. Berenbaum places the Gypsy victims in a category we might easily call "unnamed afterthought" in his own definition of the Holocaust—"the systematic state-sponsored murder of six million Jews by the Nazis and their collaborators during World War II; as night descended, millions of others were killed in their wake."[19] Berenbaum presumed what the effect of the United States Holocaust Memorial Museum upon the public consciousness would be fully five years before its opening, in *Newsday*, when he said, "People had to grow. Jews had to learn to be sensitive to non-Jewish victims, and they, in turn, had to learn to be sensitive to the uniqueness of the Jewish experience."[20] The central issue rests squarely upon this notion of "uniqueness"; it was the basis of my presentation at the first "Remembering for the Future" conference in Oxford, which was published in an expanded version in my *Without Prejudice*.[21] Phillip Lopate seems to be the only writer to have listed the criteria for "uniqueness" in an unequivocal way:

The position that the Jewish Holocaust was unique tends to rest on the following arguments: (1) scale—the largest number of deaths extracted from one single group; (2) technology—the mechanization of death factories; (3) bureaucracy—the involvement of the state apparatus at previously unheard-of levels; (4) intent—the express purpose being to annihilate every last member of the Jewish people.[22]

I will enumerate these and other principal challenges to the Romani case that have emerged since the Oxford conference and that argue for categorization separately from the Jewish case and thereby support the perceived "uniqueness" of the latter, commenting upon each in turn:

1) Jews were targeted to the last man, woman, and child for complete extermination, a policy that held true for no other population.

There were in fact numbers of categories of Jews who were exempt and who escaped death. Raul Hilberg discusses these in detail in the first chapters of his *The Destruction of the European Jews*.[23] As early as 1938, the Third Reich asked various foreign governments to extend invitations to German Jews as a means of getting them out of the country, but this policy was not extended to include Gypsies. Mention can also be made of the September 1, 1941, law confining Jews and Gypsies to their place of residence, which exempted Jews married to non-Jews but did not similarly spare Gypsies. Ronald Smelser discusses the Brand Mission of 1944 (named for Hungarian Jew Joel Brand, who led this effort to free Jewish countrymen), when Adolf Eichmann himself was prepared to spare the lives of 1 million Jews in return for 10,000 trucks, and the effort of the American Jewish Joint Distribution Committee, which successfully secured the release of 318 Jews from Bergen-Belsen the same year.[24] As the Holocaust intensified, most of these exemptions, for both groups, were progressively rescinded. When making statements of this kind, the year should be specified to incorporate policy changes. Ultimately, *only* Jews and Gypsies were singled out for complete extermination (with the exception of certain exempted groups within each population) on the basis of race and/or ethnicity. No other targeted populations were thus identified, and for this reason Gypsies must not be placed in the residual category of "Others."

2) Gypsies "come closest" to the Jewish situation but, as Messrs. Mais, Bauer, Wiesel, and Berenbaum and others have said, close is still a miss.

In this connection and most recently, Michael Berenbaum has said, in the introduction to *The World Must Know*, "At the center of the tragedy of the Holocaust is the murder of European Jews—men, women and children—killed not for the identity they affirmed or the religion they practiced, but because of the blood of their grandparents. Near that center is the murder of the Gypsies. Historians are still uncertain if there was a single decision for their complete annihilation, an enunciated policy of transcendent meaning to the perpetrators."[25] He further says "Gypsies (Roma and Sinti) had been subject to official discrimination in Germany long before 1933, but even the Nazi regime never promulgated a comprehensive law against them,"[26] a statement that seems to have been paraphrased from David M. Luebke, who wrote that "no comprehensive 'Gypsy Law' was ever promulgated."[27] To this might also be added Richard Breitman's statement that "whatever its weaknesses, 'Final Solution' at least applies to a single, specific group defined by descent. The Nazi are not known to have spoken of the Final Solution of the Polish problem or of the gypsy problem."[28] What makes a decree calling for racial obliteration "comprehensive" or not isn't discussed, but the statement is neither correct nor serves in any way to relegate the fate of the Gypsies to some less stringent category. But, as Penelope Keable asserts in her refutation of those who claim that no so-called Gypsy Law ever existed, "while denial threatens . . . oblivion, facts require repetition if they are to remain facts."[29] There are numerous Nazi policy statements available to us calling for the total elimination of the Romani population, several of which I have included in my chronology, together with references.[30] Thus in the Auschwitz *Memorial Book* we find "the final resolution, as formulated by Himmler, in his 'Decree for Basic Regulations to Resolve the Gypsy Question as Required by the Nature of Race,' of December 8th, 1938, meant that preparations were to begin for the *complete extermination* of the Sinti and Roma."[31] In 1939 Johannes Behrendt of the Office of Racial Hygiene issued a brief stating that "all Gypsies should be treated as hereditarily sick; the only solution is elimination. The aim should therefore be the elimination without hesitation of this defective element in the population." Benno Müller-Hill writes:

> Heydrich, who had been entrusted with the "final solution of the Jewish question" on 31st July 1941, shortly after the German invasion of the USSR, also included the Gypsies in his "final solution." . . . The senior SS officer and Chief of Police for the East, Dr. Landgraf, in Riga, informed Rosenberg's Reich Commissioner for the East, Lohse, of the inclusion of the Gypsies in the "final solution." Thereupon, Lohse gave the order, on 24th December 1941, that the Gypsies "should be given the same treatment as the Jews."[32]

Reinhard Heydrich, who was head of the Reich Main Security Office and the leading organizational architect of the Final Solution, ordered the *Einsatzkommandos* "to kill all Jews, Gypsies and mental patients."[33] Although there is no dispute about the Heydrich directive, in their 1991 work Burleigh and Wippermann draw attention to the fact that not all of the documentation regarding its complete details, relating to both Jews and Gypsies, has been found:

> A conference on racial policy organized by Heydrich took place in Berlin on 21 September 1939, which may have decided upon a "Final Solution" of the "Gypsy

Question." According to the scant minutes which have survived, four issues were decided: the concentration of Jews in towns; their relocation to Poland; the removal of 30,000 Gypsies to Poland, and the systematic deportation of Jews to German incorporated territories using goods trains. An express letter sent by the Reich Main Security Office on 17th October 1939 to its local agents mentioned that the "Gypsy Question will shortly be regulated throughout the territory of the Reich." . . . At about this time, Adolf Eichmann made the recommendation that the "Gypsy Question" be solved *simultaneously* with the "Jewish Question," . . . Himmler signed the order despatching Germany's Sinti and Roma to Auschwitz on 16th December 1942. The "Final Solution" of the "Gypsy Question" had begun.[34]

The *Memorial Book* for the Roma and Sinti who died at Auschwitz-Birkenau interprets this somewhat differently:

The Himmler decree of December 16th, 1942 (*Auschwitz-Erlaß*), according to which the Gypsies should be deported to Auschwitz-Birkenau, had the same meaning for the Gypsies that the conference at Wannsee on January 20th, 1942, had for the Jews. This decree, and the bulletin that followed on January 29th, 1943, can thus be regarded as a logical consequence of the decision taken at Wannsee. After it had been decided that the fate of the Jews was to end in mass extermination, it was natural for the other group of racially-persecuted people, the Gypsies, to become victims of the same policy, which finally even included soldiers in the *Wehrmacht*.[35]

In a paper delivered at the March 1987 conference on the non-Jewish victims of the Holocaust sponsored by the U.S. Holocaust Memorial Council, Dr. Erika Thurner of the Institut für Neuere Geschichte und Zeitgeschichte at the University of Linz stated:

Heinrich Himmler's infamous Auschwitz decree of December 16th, 1942, can be seen as the final stage of the final solution of the Gypsy Question. The decree served as the basis for complete extermination. According to the implementation instructions of 1943, all Gypsies, irrespective of their racial mix, were to be assigned to concentration camps. The concentration camp for Gypsy families at Auschwitz-Birkenau was foreseen as their final destination . . . opposed to the fact that the decision to seek a final solution for the Gypsy Question came at a later date than that of the Jewish Question, the first steps taken to exterminate the Gypsies were initiated prior to this policy decision; the first gassing operations against Gypsies did indeed take place in Chelmno as early as late 1941/early 1942.[36]

On September 14, 1942, following a meeting in Berlin with Minister of Propaganda Josef Goebbels, *Reichminister* of Justice Otto Thierack wrote that "with respect to the extermination of antisocial forms of life, Dr. Goebbels is of the opinion that the Jews and the Gypsies should simply be exterminated."

Six years earlier, on March 4, 1936, a memorandum was sent to State Secretary of the Interior Hans Pfundtner that addressed the creation of a "Gypsy Law" (the *Reichzigeunergesetz*), the purpose of which was to deal with the complete registration of the Romani population, their sterilization, the restriction of their movement and means of livelihood, and the expulsion of all foreign-born, stateless Gypsies.

3) Another argument, discussed by Emil Fackenheim[37] and most recently given voice by Israeli Rabbi Eliezer Schach, is that "God used the Holocaust to punish Jews for their sins."

This would certainly exclude other groups and is perhaps the most difficult defense of "uniqueness" to address, from a non-Jewish perspective. But no doubt speaking for most of the Jewish religious community, Rabbi Yitzak Kagan of the Lubavitch Foundation of Michigan responded that Schach's statement "borders on heresy";[38] we must wonder how the murder of innocent Jewish babies can possibly be rationalized by this argument. It is of some significance that some Roma and Sinti today have succumbed to survivor's guilt and have also wondered, rhetorically, whether the Holocaust was "punishment" for imagined transgressions.

There is also the argument that the Jewish experience cannot be compared to that of any other people because Jews alone "dwell inside divine history"[39] (or "outside of history," as it has also been stated, for example, by Elie Wiesel). Such an argument is likewise a difficult one to reconcile with prosaic historical detail.

4) Certain Romani groups sedentary for two or more years were to be exempted from death.[40]

This two-year exemption was only a recommendation and was never actually implemented, as it was overridden by Himmler's own directive that all migratory Gypsies be killed and sedentary Gypsies worked to death in labor camps. In any case, this potential situation would only have applied to the Soviet Union and the Baltic lands and nowhere else. A similar situation did, however, operate for Jews in these countries; thus Hilberg writes of the *Gebietskommissar* for northern Lithuania in September 1941 complaining about the killings, explaining that "the Jews were needed as skilled laborers."[41] Hilberg continues, "In October 1941, the Reichskommissar forbade the shooting of Jews . . . [and] during the quiet months of the winter and spring of 1942, they began to adjust themselves to their hazardous existence." By the end of 1943, "some tens of thousands of Jews were being kept alive at Lida and Minsk in Byelorussia, and looked forward to evacuation, or death." Nazi extermination of the Baltic Roma was particularly effective, almost the entire population having been destroyed by 1945.

5) Some Gypsies were even allowed to fight in the German army.[42]

Donald Kenrick and Grattan Puxon discuss Gypsies who served in the armed forces, saying that "Gypsies had officially been excluded from the army by law as early as November, 1937 . . . on the grounds of racial policy no more Gypsies should be called up. . . . The release of servicemen took some time and Gypsies could still be found in the army as late as 1943."[43] The sentence following this, however, reads, *"Certain classes of Jews with mixed parentage were retained in the armed forces throughout the war"* (emphasis added).

6) Kenrick and Puxon discuss certain categories of exemptions that applied to Gypsies.[44]

Kenrick and Puxon do deal with these and also include the statement that "these exemptions compare with similar arrangements for Jews."[45] If such an argument is to be used to characterize the treatment of Roma and Sinti, then it must likewise be used to characterize the treatment of Jews. And since it does apply to both populations, it cannot be used to support the "unique" treatment of the latter.

7) It has been claimed, including by the German government itself as a means of avoiding the payment of war crimes reparations, that Roma and Sinti were targeted not for racial reasons but rather for social reasons.

Yehuda Bauer has supported this argument also, stating that "the Gypsies were not murdered for racial reasons, but as so-called asocials . . . nor was their destruction complete."[46] But this argument originates in the deliberate and despicable move on the part of the German government to take advantage of the shattered condition of the surviving Romani population, which was in no condition to contest it and for which the Romani population is still suffering today. The racial identity of the Gypsy people and the genetically based rationale for their extermination are abundantly documented and referenced.[47] "In his report on the matter, the Bonn Correspondent of the *Manchester Guardian* . . . points out that the Supreme Court's decision 'is at direct variance with the known facts of Nazi policies for concentrating and later exterminating the gypsies.'"[48]

It is still the case that Gypsies are widely believed to be a population defined by behavior and social criteria rather than by genetic heritage or ethnicity. Professor Seymour Siegel, former chairman of the U.S. Holocaust Memorial Council, questioned, in the pages of the *Washington Post* and in the context of their right to full inclusion, whether Gypsies did in fact constitute a distinct ethnic people,[49] a particularly insensitive remark since Roma have a far more demonstrable claim to a "racial" identity than do Jews; this latter has been the subject of many studies.[50] A report on the health of the U.S. Romani population by a team of Harvard geneticists, which appeared in the prestigious medical journal *Lancet*, concludes,

"Analysis of blood groups, haptoglobin phenotypes, and HLA types establish the Gypsies as a distinct racial group with origins in the Punjab region of India. Also supporting this is the worldwide Gypsy language Romani, which is quite similar to Hindi."[51]

The fact remains, however, that whether Gypsies and Jews are "races" or not does not matter; Hitler believed both populations to constitute a racial threat, and race was his justification for their attempted extermination. Bauer's further observation, that "nor was their destruction complete," is a baseless and peculiar argument, since the same statement applies, mercifully, to Jews, nearly 300 times as many of whom survived the Holocaust than did Gypsies (see Key Point 10, below).

8) Some families of "pure" Gypsies were to be preserved in special camps for future anthropologists to study.[52]

This has also been noted by Bauer, where he includes "pure" Gypsies with yet another category (apparently of his own devising: "racially safe" Gypsies—in direct contradiction of his reference in Key Point 7, above, to Gypsies as a *non*racially targeted population) in his statement that "Gypsies who were of pure blood, or who were not considered dangerous on a racial level, could continue to exist, under strict supervision."[53] In the United States Holocaust Memorial Museum's published Holocaust history we find the same argument made by Mais and Bauer repeated in slightly modified form, that "pure Gypsies were not targeted for extermination until 1942."[54] The wording here gives the impression that there was an existing policy that was then revoked in 1942, rather than its having been (like Key Point 4, above) nothing more than a suggestion, by Himmler, which was mocked by his peers as "one more of Himmler's hare-brained schemes"[55] and rejected outright by Martin Bormann, head of the Nazi Party Chancellery. Thus on December 16 of that same year, in compliance with this rejection of his idea, Himmler issued the order that "all Gypsies are to be deported to the Zigeunerlager at Auschwitz concentration camp, with no regard to their degree of racial impurity." This order may even have been the result of a direct decision from Hitler himself.[56] Nazi SS Officer Percy ("Perry") Broad, who worked in the political division at Auschwitz and participated directly in the murders of several thousand prisoners there, wrote that "it was the will of the all-powerful Reichsführer to have the Gypsies disappear from the face of the earth."[57] Richard Breitman reproduces the statement made by Streckenbach following a policy meeting with Hitler and Heydrich held in Pretsch in June 1940: "The Führer has ordered the liquidation of all Jews, gypsies and communist political functionaries in the entire area of the Soviet Union."[58] Even if Himmler's "Gypsy Zoo" had been a reality, it would only have involved the lives of several dozen individuals, fewer by several hundred percent than the six thousand Karait Jews who were able to argue successfully for their own lives to be spared.

9) Gypsies received kinder treatment because parents and children were allowed to stay together in special family camps, unlike other prisoners.

Lucette M. Lagnado and Sheila Cohn Dekel are among those who have referred to this: "The Gypsies were allowed to stay together, perhaps because they were faithful Christians. Despite their inferior racial stock, it was their one privilege . . . the Gypsies alone among the inmates had the comfort of being with their loved ones."[59] Their unqualified reference to Roma as constituting "inferior racial stock," their guess at their faithful Christianity, and their stunningly unfeeling description of the Gypsy camp in Auschwitz as resembling a "vast playground, an ongoing carnival" can only reflect the authors' stereotypes about Roma and Sinti, and it is abundantly obvious that neither one of them ever spoke to a Romani survivor or was there at the camp at Birkenau. Ulrich König makes it very clear that the "family camps" were not created out of any humanitarian motive or desire to bestow any "privilege" but rather because the Gypsies became completely unmanageable when separated from family members.[60] Michael Zimmermann also discusses this:

> The Nazi institutions involved with the persecution of the Gypsies knew about the particularly close family ties in this ethnic group. If these family ties were not taken into account, as happened in part with the deportation of 2,500 Sinti to Poland in 1940, there were certainly difficulties for the police, which were recorded negatively. To this extent, the RSHA [the *Reichssicherheitshauptamt*, or State Security Office] order of 29 January 1943 to deport the Sinti and Roma to Auschwitz "in families" reflected efforts to keep the friction and resultant bureaucratic problems associated with the deportation and internment as small as possible.[61]

First Lieutenant Walther of Infantry Regiment 734 and head of the execution squad wrote in his *Report on the Executions of the Jews and the Gypsies* that "the execution of the Jews is simpler than that of the Gypsies. One must admit that the Jews go to their deaths very composedly; they remain very calm. The Gypsies, however, wail and scream and move about incessantly as soon as they get to the place of execution." It was simply more expedient and caused the guards less problems to keep families together for processing. König writes of their sometimes having to smash the hands and feet of the Gypsies, who even used loaves of stale bread as weapons, in order to render them docile as they were being herded to the ovens. His book is a monument to Romani heroism and resistance in the camps and should be required reading for any student of the Porrajmos. Romani families were not kept together in every camp, incidentally (compare those shipped to Poland in 1940 referred to above by Zimmermann); this seems to have been a policy enacted at Auschwitz-Birkenau in particular. Jews transported to Auschwitz from Theresienstadt in September 1943, for example, were also allowed to remain together with their families.

10) "The denial of the right to live is what singles out the fate of the Jews from all other victims—Gypsies, Poles, Russian prisoners of war, Jehovah's Witnesses . . . their fate was different from the fate of the Jews."[62]

Michael Berenbaum, in a better position than most to know the details of the Romani experience during the Holocaust, repeats these arguments in his book, where he says "Gypsies shared much, but not all of the horrors assigned to Jews. Romani were killed in some countries but not others. . . . Even though the Romani were subject to gassing and other forms of extermination, the number of Gypsies was not as vast. . . . In contrast, all Jews lived under an imminent . . . sentence of death."[63] Jews were killed in some countries but not others, too, and the number of Gypsies was "not as vast" because (according to the Nazis' own census conducted by Behrendt in 1939) there were nine times as many Jews as Gypsies to start with at the outbreak of World War II, so obviously the numbers were greater. Selma Steinmetz's argument that "numbers decide" would only be valid if the number of Jews and the number of Gypsies had been equal to begin with.[64] But when we discuss genocide we must do so in the context of the *destruction of entire peoples*, and, in terms of overall percentage, the losses of the Roma and Sinti almost certainly exceeded those of any other group; their *percentage* was "vaster." If there had been 17.4 million Gypsies in 1939 (the government's estimate of the number of Jews in that year), the Nazis would surely have murdered 6 million, too.

The question of the numbers of Roma and Sinti who were killed is a vexed one. Given the nature of their mode of life, no reliable estimate of the prewar European Romani population exists. Similarly, the circumstances of their dispatch at the hands of the Nazis make this a question that can never be fully answered. I dealt with this in some detail but rely on König's statement:

The count of half a million Sinti and Roma murdered between 1939 and 1945 is too low to be tenable; for example in the Soviet Union many of the Romani dead were listed under non-specific labels such as Liquidierungsübrigen [remainder to be liquidated], "hangers-on" and "partisans." . . . The final number of the dead Sinti and Roma may never be determined. We do not know precisely how many were brought into the concentration camps; not every concentration camp produced statistical material; moreover, Sinti and Roma are often listed under the heading of "remainder to be liquidated," and do not appear in the statistics for Gypsies.[65]

In the eastern territories, Russia especially, Gypsy deaths were sometimes counted into the records under the heading of Jewish deaths. The *Memorial Book* for the Gypsies who perished in Auschwitz-Birkenau also discusses the means of killing Roma:

Unlike the Jews, the overwhelming majority of whom were murdered in the gas chambers at Birkenau, Belzec, Treblinka and all the other mass extermination camps, the Gypsies outside the Reich were massacred at many places, sometimes only a few at a time, and sometimes by the hundreds. In the *Generalgouvernement* [the eastern territories] alone, 150 sites of Gypsy massacres are known. Research on the Jewish Holocaust can rely on comparison of pre- and post-war census data to help determine the numbers of victims in the countries concerned. However, this is not possible for the Gypsies, as it was only rarely that they were included in national census data. Therefore it is an impossible task to find the actual number of Gypsy victims in Poland, Yugoslavia, White Ruthenia and the Ukraine, *the lands that probably had the greatest numbers of victims.*[66]

This means that statements such as "somewhere between 20 and 50 percent of the entire population of European Gypsies was killed by the Nazis"[67] and the low figure of 250,000 Romani deaths displayed at the United States Holocaust Memorial Museum must be considered underestimations. Several published estimates[68] put the figure in excess of 1 million, and even thirty years ago Louis Pauwels and Jacques Bergier listed it at 750,000.[69] That perhaps an even higher number of Gypsies were murdered in the fields and forests where they lived than were murdered in the camps has been recognized for some time. The most recent reference to this appeared in the *Financial Times* (London) in an article by C. Tyler, who noted that "between 500,000 and 750,000 were killed in the German death camps during the war, and another million may have been shot outside."[70] New information is reaching us all the time that is pushing the death toll upwards. Dr. Paul Polansky of the Iowa-based Czech Historical Research Center recently published a report on his discovery of a hitherto unrecorded concentration camp at Lety in the Czech Republic, which was used for the disposal of Gypsies. Now used as a pig farm, Lety, as well as a chain of other camps, processed mainly Roma, killing them on the spot or sending them on to Auschwitz. Numbers from here, like those from the Gypsy camps in northern Italy, have not yet been figured into the estimate.[71] We should nevertheless rejoice in the numbers of those who lived and not glorify those of the dead in some horrible body count; but if we *are* obliged to argue with numbers and quantity in this peculiarly American way, then let us look at the situation from the other side and count the Romani *survivors* of the Holocaust, only 5,000 of whom are listed in the official register of the Zentralrat Deutscher Sinti und Roma in Heidelberg, only four of whom have been located in the United States, where over 80,000 Jewish survivors live today out of 350,000 still living worldwide. My respected colleague Donald Kenrick, coauthor of *The Destiny of Europe's Gypsies*, the first full-length treatment of the Porrajmos, has claimed with some gladness that his own research points to the *lowest* figures for Romani deaths by 1945; in his new book he estimates that they did not exceed 200,000.[72] Surely this is the kind of dialogue we should be striving for, not a competition over whose losses were greater.

11) The "uniqueness" of the Jewish case should be defended at all costs because it justifies the existence of the Jewish homeland, Israel.

On the main mall of the campus at the University of Texas at Austin, where I teach, there stands a structure some nine feet high, erected by the Jewish Students' Association as a monument to Israel. It is covered with photographs and newspaper articles, and in the very middle of it is a yellow placard bearing the words, "Israel: The Six Million: Never Forget." This is not a new argument; indeed it has been suggested to me by more than one well-disposed U.S. Holocaust Memorial Council member, and Zygmunt Bauman explicitly refers to the way in which "the Jewish state tries to employ the tragic memories as the certificate of its political legitimacy, a safe-conduct pass for its past and future policies, and above all, as the advance payment for the injustices it might itself commit."[73] But it is a specious argument. Israel, a Jewish state, should exist under any circumstances; speaking as a member of a people without a country, I can feel very deeply the emotion associated with the (non)possession of a homeland. To acknowledge that Gypsies received the same treatment as Jews, as Miriam Novitch says, "for the same reasons using the same methods" cannot take anything away from the enormity of the Jewish tragedy or diminish the strength of the right to Israel. I am reminded of Dermot Mulroney's words in *Where the Day Takes You*: "What's mine is mine, and if I share it with you, it becomes less mine!"[74] I cannot imagine that the rest of the world would interpret the Romani claim in this way or see it as a threat to the right to the existence of a Jewish state.

12) No other group was viewed with such disgust and contempt, so relentlessly and methodically persecuted, or selected for total eradication from the face of the earth.

Gypsies don't match this, I have been told, because Gypsies weren't mentioned in *Mein Kampf* or at the Wannsee Conference, because some Gypsies were exempt from the death machine, and because a much higher number of Jews had died by 1945.

Gypsies were not mentioned specifically in the documentation of the Wannsee Conference, because by that time (January 20, 1942) policies against Jews, subsequent to the December 24 directive issued four weeks earlier, automatically applied to the Gypsies. The Wannsee Conference in any case was not a policy or decision-making meeting, although it has acquired that interpretation; its purpose was rather to coordinate existing policies. And no argument was necessary in *Mein Kampf* because it was totally unnecessary on Hitler's part to make any case for anti-Gypsyism. There was simply no need to convince anybody of the subhuman status of Gypsies, against whom laws were already firmly entrenched in Germany, despite the guarantees of the constitution of the Weimar Republic. No public conscience ever provoked a defense of the Romani case, a fact Angus Fraser comments upon in his book *The Gypsies*: "From about 1937 onwards, [Nazi] pressures . . . on Gypsies built up swiftly and remorselessly, with no hostile public reaction, abroad or at home, of the kind which had made the Nazis a little more circumspect in their dealings with the Jews, at least in the early days, because of respect for world opinion."[75]

When the question of this indifference was raised following the war, one French physician commented, rhetorically, that "everyone despises Gypsies, so why exercise restraint? Who will avenge them? Who will bear witness?"[76] Nor can the excuse that the rest of the world was ignorant of what was happening be maintained in the Romani case:

> Whatever the real state of knowledge or ignorance among the German civilian population during the Second World War about the transport and the murder of millions of German and non-German Jews in Europe, the initial internment of the Roma was kept secret from no one. Concentration camps were built on the outskirts of the capital city, and the internment of the Sinti and Roma was not only covered by a number of Berlin newspapers, but was even joked about in their columns. Psychologists engaged in racial research paid official visits to Marzahn to study and take extensive film footage of the Romani children at play there. A major trainline ran right past that camp, and its few survivors recall that train passengers who pitied their situation, and who knew or suspected that the interned Roma were surviving on only minimal rations, occasionally threw packages of food down into the camp enclosure as their train passed by.[77]

German antisemitism, like anti-Gypsyism over the centuries, has bordered upon the pathological,[78] yet there was no one to argue in support of the Gypsies, unlike those who defended the Jewish position. As Burleigh and Wippermann make clear,[79] antisemitism was *not* an undisputed part of the early German racial hygiene movement. Alfred Ploetz and a number of other racial hygienists, such as Wilhelm Schallmayer, fiercely denounced antisemitism; indeed, in his 1895 treatise, Ploetz classified Jews as a part of the superior "white race."[80] On the contrary, in the early 1890s the Swabian Parliament organized a conference on the "Gypsy scum" (*Das Zigeunergeschmeiß*), and in 1899 Alfred Dillmann established the Gypsy Information Agency (*Nachrichtendienst in Bezug auf die Zigeuner*), which began to collect data in the form of genealogical information, fingerprints, and photographs of Gypsies throughout the territory. This led to the publication in 1905 of Dillmann's *Zigeuner-Buch*,[81] which laid the groundwork for what was to come a quarter-century later. It consisted of a lengthy argument for controlling Gypsies, stressing their inherent criminality and calling them "a plague against which society must unflaggingly defend itself." The bulk of the volume consisted of a register of over 5,000 individuals that gave date and place of birth, genealogy, criminal record if any, and so on. The third part of the book consisted of photographs of Gypsies taken from police files throughout the German states. On February 17, 1906, the Prussian minister of the interior issued a directive to "Combat the Gypsy Nuisance" (*Die Bekämpfung des Zigeunerunwesens*) and established bilateral, anti-Gypsy agreements with all neighboring countries. Licenses were required by all Romani people wanting to live and work in Prussia.

In 1909 the Swiss Department of Justice began a national register of Gypsies, and in Hungary it was recommended at a "Gypsy Policy Conference" that all Romani people be branded on their bodies for easy identification. In 1912, France introduced the *Carnet Anthropométrique*, a document containing personal data (including photograph and fingerprints) that all Gypsies were henceforth required to carry.

"The first anti-Jewish law was promulgated in 1933,"[82] at a time when scores of anti-Gypsy laws had already been in effect in Germany for centuries. In 1920, the minister of public welfare in Düsseldorf forbade Gypsies from entering any public washing or recreational facilities, such as swimming pools, public baths, spas, or parks; this restriction also came to be applied to Jews after 1933.[83] More ominously, in that same year, Karl Binding and Alfred Hoche published their treatise[84] on "lives undeserving of life" (*Lebensunwertes Leben*), which argued for the killing of those who were seen to be "dead weight" (*Ballastexistenz*) within humanity, including Gypsies. This notion of "unworthy life" was incorporated into Nazi law on July 14, 1933, less than six months after Hitler came to power, in his "Law for the Prevention of Hereditarily Diseased Offspring." In 1934, Roma and Sinti were expelled from the trade unions. In June 1935, the main Nazi institution to deal with Gypsies, the Racial Hygiene and Criminal Biology and Research Unit, was first established, its express purpose being to determine whether Gypsies and blacks were human or subhuman, the groundwork on genetic evaluation that provided the model for the subsequent classification of Jews. Five months later, on November 26, the Ministry of the Interior, which partially funded the Research Unit, circulated an order forbidding marriages between Germans and "Gypsies, Negroes, and their bastard offspring." On September 15, 1935, the *Nürnberger Gesetze* (the "Nuremberg Law for the Protection of Blood and Honor") was passed, making marriage between "Aryan" and "non-Aryan" people illegal. It stated that "of the foreign blood common in Europe, there are only Jews and Gypsies." In 1936, in preparation for the Summer Olympic Games and for fear of negative world opinion, "anti-Semitic posters and placards were temporarily removed" from the streets of Berlin by the Nazis;[85] at the same time, Gypsies were being cleared from those streets as an eyesore, because visitors had to be "spared the sight of the 'Gypsy disgrace,'"[86] just as they were at the 1992 Summer Olympic Games in Barcelona. Just before the Berlin games, 600 Gypsies were forcibly detained in a cemetery and next to a sewage dump at Marzahn, which was "particularly offensive to a people hyper-sensitive about cleanliness";[87] in Spain fifty-six years later, they were placed in the Campo de la Bota outside of the city. More significantly, we have now learned that Nazi propaganda encouraging public support for the incarceration of Gypsies was widely distributed together with the program for those games in 1936. In 1938, more stringent criteria came to be applied to the definition of "Gypsy": If two of an individual's eight great-grandparents were even part Gypsy, that individual later was deemed to have too much "Gypsy blood" to be allowed to live—a criterion twice as strict as that defining who was Jewish. Indeed, if criteria for the latter had applied equally to Gypsies, some 18,000 (nine-tenths of the total Romani population of Germany at that time) would have escaped death.[88] One could argue, therefore, that Gypsies in fact were seen as posing twice the genetic threat to the *Herrenvolk* that Jews did.

According to eyewitness accounts, in January or February 1940, 250 Gypsy children from Brno in the concentration camp at Buchenwald were used as guinea pigs for testing the Zyklon B cyanide gas crystals, a lethal insecticide that from 1941 onward was used for the mass murders at Auschwitz-Birkenau. "At Buchenwald then, for the first time, this gas was used for mass murder, and it was for the murder of innocent Gypsy children."[89]

The night of November 9, 1938, is remembered in the annals of the Jewish Holocaust as *Kristallnacht*, or "The Night of Broken Glass," for it was on this night, in response to the murder of a German embassy official in Paris by a Jewish teenager, that over 1,000 synagogues were desecrated and nearly a hundred Jews were killed, with thousands more arrested. This blatant public display of hatred marked the beginning of the open and official sanctioning of the persecution of an "inferior race." In effect, it sent a message to the general public that such violence had full state approval. From this date onward, anti-Jewish hostility escalated steadily toward the Holocaust. But this was not the first massive anti-Jewish outbreak in twentieth-century Germany; in November 1923, a violent attack took place in Berlin against numbers of eastern European Jews who had come there to live.[90] For the Romani victims, there were also mass roundups and displays of military and police brutality, designed to show them—and the German public— exactly where they stood in the German hierarchy and how they could be treated by ordinary citizens with the approval and encouragement of the government. As early as 1927, between November 23 and November 26, armed raids were carried out in Gypsy communities throughout Prussia to enforce a decree issued on November 3 of that year, which required that all Gypsies be registered through documentation "in the same manner as individuals being sought by means of wanted posters, witnesses, photographs and fingerprints."[91] Even infants were fingerprinted, and those over six years of age were required to carry identity cards bearing fingerprints and photographs. Eight thousand Gypsies were processed as a result of that raid, more than a third of the entire Romani population in Germany. The second such action took place between September 18 and September 25, 1933, when the *Reichsministers* for the interior and for propaganda ordered the apprehension and arrest of Gypsies throughout Germany in accordance with "The Law Against Habitual Criminals." Many were sent to concentration camps as a result, where they were forced to do penal labor and where some underwent sterilization. The most significant military action, however, occurred during the summer of 1938, between June 12 and June 18, when *Zigeuneraufräumungswoche*, or "Gypsy Clean-Up Week," was ordered. Hundreds of Gypsies throughout Germany and Austria were rounded up, beaten, and imprisoned. In Mannswörth, Austria, 300 were arrested in this way in a single night.

Following the collapse of the Third Reich, nothing was done to assist the Romani survivors, no effort made by the liberators to reorient them; instead, the terms of a 1926 pre-Nazi anti-Gypsy law still in effect ensured that those lacking a trade remained out of sight, hiding in the abandoned camps, for fear of arrest and incarceration. Since that time, all of the programs used by the Nazis to deal with Gypsies have been either suggested or implemented by various European nations—sterilizations in Slovakia, recommendations for incineration in a furnace from an Irish government official, forced incarceration and deportation in Germany.[92] Today, the Romani population faces its severest crisis since the Holocaust; neo-Nazi race crimes against Gypsies have seen rapes, beatings, and murders in Germany, Hungary, and Slovakia; anti-Gypsy pogroms in Romania and Bulgaria, including lynchings and home burnings, are increasing. For my people, the Holocaust is not yet over.

The United States Holocaust Memorial Museum has not yet done enough to educate the world about the Romani experience; there, the "Gypsy" artifacts on display in the "other victims" corner of the museum's third floor consist of a violin, a wagon, and a woman's dress—more Hollywood than Holocaust—and very, very few of the Romani victims and inmates depicted in the photo exhibits (especially those involving Josef Mengele's experiments with twins) are identified as such. Most galling of all was the total absence of the key words "Gypsy," "Rom," "Sinti," "Romani," "Zigeuner," and so on in the computerized question-and-answer bank provided for the public to consult. This led, in June 1993, to an organized protest at the museum by a group represented by Mary Thomas of Adoptive Parents and Friends of Romani Children demanding that more details of the fate of Roma and Sinti be included in the museum. They argued that when their newly acquired children grow older and begin to ask about their background and the history of their people, and about the Holocaust in particular, the United States Holocaust Memorial Museum would not be the place to go for their answers, that the Gypsy story had been downplayed to the extent of differently representing historical fact, of revision by omission. That protest led to the circulation of a petition asking, among other things, that more Romani scholars (rather than non-Gypsy specialists) be directly involved and that more documentation on the Romani holocaust be displayed and made available to visitors to the museum; this has resulted in the inclusion of one or two Gypsy entries in the computerized data bank.

I have been both praised and criticized for bringing attention to these issues. The director of one Holocaust center referred to me as a troublemaker; another writer on the Holocaust called my discussion of the Romani case in the Jewish context "loathsome." A representative of the U.S. Holocaust Memorial Council, whom I have never met, told a researcher who called to find out how to reach me that I was a "wild man." People have walked out when it was my turn to speak at conferences about the Porrajmos, and one former professor at the university where I teach adamantly refused even to *mention* Roma and Sinti in his regular course on the Holocaust. Others have intimated that I should not be pursuing this because I am not a historian and therefore not qualified to engage in this kind of research. If you think these things don't hurt me, they do, deeply. There are those reading this chapter who I'm sure are angered by what is being said in these pages, who are ready to challenge me. Why should this be? I have tried to remain objective and let the facts argue my case. If I can be proven wrong, I am happy to acknowledge that. I am well aware that for some people insistence upon getting all the facts of the Romani experience properly acknowledged has been regarded as confrontational and even threatening; Yehuda Bauer[93] felt that "anti-Gypsy sentiment" in Europe was, in his words, "in competition" with "radical anti-Semitism" there, the "sentiment" in question having led to the murders and pogroms against Gypsies mentioned above, during the same period for which the *1990 Country Report on Human Rights* reported "no incidents of anti-Semitic violence." At the same time, however, an August 1993 report issued by the Nemzetközi Cigány Szöveség quoted a physician from the Romanian town of Teleorman who said "our war against the Gypsies will start in the fall. Until then, preparations will be made to obtain arms; first we are going to acquire chemical sprays. We will not spare minors, either."[94] Events indicating that this persecution began to happen shortly thereafter were described in the December 19, 1993, issue of the *San Francisco Chronicle*, where the following appeared:

> An orgy of mob lynching and house-burning with police collaboration, has turned into something even more sinister for Romania's hated Gypsies: the beginnings of a nationwide campaign of terror launched by groups modeling themselves on the Ku Klux Klan. . . . "We are many, and very determined. We will skin the Gypsies soon. We will take their eyeballs out, smash their teeth, and cut off their noses. The first will be hanged."[95]

Anti-Gypsyism is at an all-time high, and it can only begin to be combated by sensitizing the general public to the details of Romani history and suffering. My purpose in this chapter, a follow-up to a paper given at the 1994 "Remembering for the Future" conference in Oxford, is to get these issues into the open, to air them publicly, in hopes that a more accurate, and more compassionate, attitude will prevail.

Resistance to the Gypsy case must be due at least in part to the lateness of its arrival on the academic scene; scholarship on the Porrajmos is comparatively new, so much so that it has brought charges of "bandwagoning" from some quarters. Our people are traditionally not disposed to keeping alive the terrible memories from our history—nostalgia is a luxury for others, and the Porrajmos was not the first but the second historical attempt to destroy the Roma as a people, following Charles VI's extermination order in 1721. Roma in the United States, for example, have obliterated entirely from their collective memories all recollection of the five and a half centuries of slavery in Romania, which their great-great-grandparents came to America to escape during the last century.[96] Survivors of the Holocaust are today likewise reluctant to speak about their experiences, and so it is that the story is only now beginning to unfold. The task of those collecting testimonies is made all the more difficult because, for some groups, the Sinti in particular, there are cultural restrictions upon speaking about the dead.

It has to be said too that there is an element of racism evident in the Jewish response; after all, Gypsies are a "Third World people of color," as Lopate coins the term in his discussion of the relative value of victimhood; Anton Fojn ("Bubili") wrote of the SS guards' whipping him and his father off the transport and through the gates of Dachau and calling them "Congo niggers" on account of their dark skin.[97] I have been told—off the record—that some U.S. Holocaust Memorial Council members do not want to be judged by the company they fear they might have to keep. In every single public opinion poll, including one conducted in the United States (and reported in the January 8, 1992, issue of the *New York Times*), Gypsies are listed as the most discriminated-against minority, the most despised ethnic population, and some of the stereotypes have evidently rubbed off on some councilmembers. At one presentation I gave at a Hillel center, I was interrupted by a woman who leapt to her feet and angrily demanded why I was even comparing the Gypsy case to the Jewish case when Jews had given so much to the world and Gypsies were merely parasites and thieves. On another occasion a gentleman in the audience stood up and declared that he would never buy a book on the Holocaust written by a Gypsy. I learned recently from James Michael Holmes of Phoenix Productions International that two Hollywood studios have already declined to consider an updated script of the 1947 film *Golden Earrings*, because it is a screenplay about the Holocaust that does not deal with Jewish victims.

Working to alter attitudes of this kind is a mighty task indeed and was one reason behind my cofounding the Romani-Jewish Alliance some years ago, which works to dispel anti-Jewish and anti-Romani stereotypes and to educate both populations about the other's experience. I should say here, incidentally, in answer to an often-asked question, that there are many Roma and Sinti who are Jewish and many more Romani-Jewish marriages. During the war, such "marriages" characterized one concentration camp in eastern Serbia in particular, where Gypsies and Jews were held before transportation. Even popular attempts to document our story can do more harm than good; an example is the film version of Alexander Ramati's *And the Violins Stopped Playing* (1988), which is so full of misrepresentation and distortions of the truth that it would have been better left undone (among other things it suggests that Gypsies were murdered in Auschwitz, for example, lest they survive as witnesses to the fate of the Jewish prisoners).

It might also be acknowledged that some resistance is grounded simply in disbelief, in the assumption that "if this is true, why haven't we heard about it before?" I must admit that for a very long time, as I searched the "shelves tightly packed," through the innumerable books on the Holocaust looking for references to Gypsies, I would skim right over sections dealing with the non-Romani victims; I am ashamed to say that they just were not as important to me, so consumed was I with my search. It was only later that I began to take the time to learn about what happened to other groups and to be appalled and aggrieved by what I read. When the existence of one's entire people is threatened so barbarously, anything else simply gets in the way. But others have come to do as I did and are examining the cases of those besides their own without prejudgment, and I am encouraged by the responses forthcoming from those who have made the effort, with an open mind, to examine the details of what Roma and Sinti suffered at the hands of the Nazis. I have said many times that only Jews can really come close to understanding the impact the Porrajmos has had on the Romani population, and I venture to think that only Gypsies can come close, on an emotional level, to understanding the Jewish tragedy. The Holocaust, sadly, just doesn't seem to mean as much for anyone else. But neither Jew nor Roma can *fully* understand the other's experience, then or now, nor should either begin to presume to interpret for the other. For this reason I would like to see the individual "uniquenesses," if you like, emphasized by a greater use of the ethnic terminology: *Shoah* or *Khurbn* for the Jewish Holocaust, *Porrajmos* for the Romani. The word "Holocaust," I feel, is used too casually to have the meaning intended for it.

I have been deliberately critical of the U.S. Holocaust Memorial Council and the museum in this chapter and make no apology for that, for our relationship over the past decade has been stormy and has caused me considerable personal frustration. It is, after all, the national memorial to the victims of Nazism and an international educational resource. Many factors, many personalities, have been involved in the misunderstandings and anger generated by the dialogue between Roma and the council. Speaking at the council's conference on non-Jewish victims in Washington, D.C., in 1987, Erika Thurner drew attention to the evident lack of concern for the Holocaust's Romani victims:

> Gypsies have generally been forgotten or been reserved for the footnotes of historical investigation. . . . This very position, as a fringe social group with negligible social status, is responsible for the fact that, after 1945, the Gypsy Holocaust was not acknowledged for so many years, and continues to be neglected to a certain degree to this very day. Ignorance as to the fate of the Sinti and Roma in the Third Reich has made historical reconstruction especially difficult. It has led to further discrimination against Gypsies, and to the *refusal* to recognize their right to restitution of both a material and ideal nature.[98]

In the years since Erika Thurner made those observations, there has been a steadily growing acknowledgment of the Romani tragedy and an acceptance of the fact that the Jews and the Gypsies were equally victim to the techniques and policies of the Nazi death machine. But along with this recognition at the academic and historical levels, so efforts to singularize the Jewish experience have gained, at least for some of its champions, an almost desperate impetus.[99] Perhaps we should be examining not what the challenges are to the procedural and historical details with which scholars attempt to make their case, but rather *why* it is so vitally important to some of them to privatize the Holocaust—why they strive so passionately to do so.

I am confident that open recognition of the Romani position will continue to grow. From having no representation at all on the council we now have one member; from having no Gypsy-related entries in the data bank we now have some. The council has gone so far as to protest formally against anti-Gypsyism at the administrative level.[100] My greatest hope is that we will eventually be moved out of the category of "other victims" and fully recognized as the only population, together with Jews, that was slated for eradication from the face of the earth. I want to be able to thumb through any of the many published treatments of the Holocaust at my local bookstore and find comprehensive information in them about what happened to my people—at present, we're usually not listed in indexes at all. My most recent purchase was Louis Snyder's *Encyclopedia of the Third Reich;* not only does it not contain one single reference to Gypsies, but neither does Robert Ritter nor Eva Justin nor Gerhard Stein nor Sophie Erhardt find a place in its list of entries. This is true also for the *Encyclopedia of the Second World War,*[101] *Who's Who in Nazi Germany,*[102] and *Who Was Who in World War II,*[103] as well as for most other books on the Holocaust. It is an eerie and disheartening feeling to pick up such books and find the attempted genocide of one's people written completely out of the historical record. Perhaps worse, in the English-language translation of at least one book, that by Lucjan Dobroszycki of *The Chronicle of the Lodz Ghetto*, the entire reference to the liquidation of the Gypsy camp there (entry number 22 for April 29 and 30, 1942, in the original work) has been deleted deliberately. I have been told, but have not yet verified, that translations of other works on the Holocaust have also had entries on Roma and Sinti removed. Furthermore, I do not want to read references to the United States Holocaust Memorial Museum in the national press and learn only that it is a monument to "the plight of European Jews," as the *New York Times* told its readers on December 23, 1993. I want to be able to watch epics such as *Schindler's List* and learn that Gypsies were a central part of the Holocaust, too; or other films, such as *Escape from Sobibór*, a Polish camp where, according to Kommandant Franz Stangl in his memoirs, thousands of Roma and Sinti were murdered, and not to hear the word "Gypsy" except once, and then only as the name of somebody's dog. This latter example is not merely offensive, it is cruel and callous. Camp survivor B. Stawska is one who has described the transportation of Sinti and Roma to Sobibor:

In November, 1942, the pogrom against the Jews and Gypsies began, and they were shot on a mass scale in street executions. The Gypsies were driven into the square at the fore of the crowd, and after them the Jews. It was cold, and the Gypsy women were weeping loudly. They had all their possessions on their backs, including eiderdowns; everything that they had, but all of that was taken away from them later. The

Jews behaved very calmly, but the Gypsies cried a lot—you could hear one loud sobbing. They were taken to the station and loaded into goods wagons, which were sealed and taken to stations beyond Chełm, to Sobibór, where they were burnt in the ovens.[104]

National Public Radio (NPR) in Washington, D.C., covered extensively the fiftieth anniversary of the liberation of Auschwitz-Birkenau on January 26, 1995, but Gypsies were never once mentioned, despite being well represented at the commemoration. In his closing report on NPR's "Weekend Edition" on January 28, Michael Goldfarb described how "candles were placed along the tracks that delivered Jews and Poles to their death." But it is little wonder that Gypsies weren't mentioned; they were not allowed to participate in the candle ceremony. An article on the Auschwitz commemoration that appeared in the British press (though not in the U.S. press) dated January 28 included a photograph of a group of Roma staring mournfully through a wire fence, with a caption reading "Cold-shouldered: Gypsies, whose ancestors were among Auschwitz victims, are forced to watch the ceremony from outside the compound."[105] In a speech given at that ceremony, Elie Wiesel said that the Jewish people "were singled out for destruction during the Holocaust." The British Broadcasting Corporation's "World at War" segment entitled "Genocide" mentions the 1935 law forbidding Aryans from marrying Jews but fails to say that the very same law also referred to Gypsies; it mentions the Polish victims repeatedly but remains completely silent about Roma, against whom—unlike Poles—the Final Solution *did* operate. The first concentration camp inmates pictured in that documentary are Sinti prisoners at Buchenwald, but the viewer isn't told this. And in Germany, where it all began, Roma and Sinti have even yet to be included in the national Holocaust memorial, an omission that attracted the international media,[106] even though the chairman of the Jewish community in Berlin, Heinz Galinski, speaking at a ceremony commemorating the Romani victims of the Porrajmos fifteen years ago, acknowledged publicly that "Jews and Gypsies were both singled out as 'lives unworthy of life.'"[107] Surely genocide of the magnitude suffered by the Romani people deserves acknowledgment far beyond that which it now receives.

NOTES

1. This chapter is an expanded version of a paper first presented at "Remembering for the Future International Conference on the Holocaust," held at Berlin, Germany, March, 13–17, 1994.

2. *Congress Monthly*, May/June (1990), p. 13.

3. *New York Times Magazine*, September 20, 1983, p. 12.

4. Dora Yates, "Hitler and the Gypsies," *Commentary* 8 (1949):455, reprinted in *On Prejudice: A Global Perspective*, ed. Daniela Gioseffi (New York: Anchor Books 1993), pp. 103–110.

5. *Anon.*, "How the Gipsies Were Persecuted," *Wiener Library Bulletin* 4(3/4) (1950):18.

6. Earlier references to the situation of Roma and Sinti in Nazi Germany are Sultzberger (1939), Max (1946), Kochanowski (1946), and Maximoff (1946).

7. John Roth and Michael Berenbaum, eds., *Holocaust: Religious and Philosophical Implications* (New York: Paragon House, 1989), pp. 6–7.

8. Carrie Supple, *From Prejudice to Genocide: Learning About the Holocaust* (Stoke-on-Trent: Trentham Books, 1993).

9. Martin Gilbert, *The Holocaust: A History of the Jews of Europe During the Second World War* (New York: Henry Holt), 1985.

10. Michael Burleigh and Wolfgang Wippermann, *The Racial State: Germany, 1933–1945* (Cambridge: The University Press, 1991).

11. For example, see Annegret Ehmann, "A Short History of the Discrimination and Persecution of the European Gypsies and Their Fate Under Nazi Rule," Lecture, Institute of Contemporary Jewry, The Hebrew University, January 27, 1981; Sybil Milton, "The Context of the Holocaust," *German Studies Review* 13(2) (1990):269–283, "Gypsies and the Holocaust," *History Teacher* 24(4) (1991):375–417, "The Racial Context of the Holocaust," *Social Education* (February 1991):106–110, "Nazi Policies Towards Roma and Sinti, 1933–1945," *Journal of the Gypsy Lore Society* 2(1), 5th series (1992):1–18; "Antechamber to Birkenau: The *Zigeunerlager* after 1933," in *Die Normalität des Verbrechens,* ed. Helge Grabitz et al. (Berlin: Hentrich, 1994), pp. 241–259, and "Sinti und Roma als 'vergessene Opfergruppe' in der Gedenkstättenarbeit," in *Der Völkermord an den Sinti und Roma in der Gedenkstättenarbeit,* ed. Edgar Bamberger (Heidelberg: Dokumentations-und Kultur-zentrum Deutscher Sinti und Roma, 1994), pp. 53–62; Erika Thurner, "Nazi Policy Against the Gypsies," Paper delivered at the U.S. Holocaust Memorial Council Conference on Other Victims, Washington, D.C., March 1987; and David Young, *A Mulano Place: Paradox and Ambivalence in the Romani Holocaust,* B.A. (Hons.) Thesis, Macquarie University, Sydney, Australia, 1994.

12. Emil Fackenheim, *To Mend the World* (New York: Schocken Books, 1982), p. 12.

13. Charles S. Maier, *The Unmasterable Past: History, Holocaust, and German National Identity* (Cambridge: Harvard University Press, 1988), p. 82.

14. Richard Breitman, *The Architect of Genocide: Himmler and the Final Solution* (Hanover, N.H.: University Press of New England, 1991), p. 19.

15. See Steven Katz, "Quantity and Interpretation: Issues in the Comparative Analysis of the Holocaust," *Remembering for the Future: Jews and Christians During and After the Holocaust,* vol. 3 (Oxford: Pergamon, 1988), pp. 200–216.

16. Ibid., p. 216.

17. Israel Gutman, ed., *Encyclopedia of the Holocaust* (New York: Macmillan, 1990).

18. Steven Katz, *The Holocaust in Historical Context, Volume 1: The Holocaust and Mass Death Before the Modern Age* (Oxford: University Press, 1994); see also David Nemeth, "Contrasting Realities and the Gypsy Holocaust," *Newsletter of the Gypsy Lore Society* 17(3) (August 1994):3–4.

19. Michael Berenbaum, *The World Must Know: The History of the Holocaust as Told in the United States Holocaust Memorial Museum* (Boston: Little, Brown, 1993), p. 1; see also Michael Shermer, "Proving the Holocaust," *Skeptic* 2(4) (1994):32–57.

20. As quoted in Susan Brenna, "Housing the Memories of Genocide," *Newsday,* September 2, 1988, pp. 2–5.

21. Ian Hancock, "'Uniqueness' of the Victims: Gypsies, Jews, and the Holocaust," *Without Prejudice: International Review of Racial Discrimination* 1(2), 1988, pp. 45–67.

22. Phillip Lopate, "Resistance to the Holocaust," in *Testimony: Contemporary Writers Make the Holocaust Personal,* ed. David Rosenberg (New York: Random House, 1989), pp. 285–308.

23. Raul Hilberg, *The Destruction of the European Jews* (Chicago: Quadrangle Books, 1961).

24. Ronald Smelser, "The 'Final Solution' and the War in 1944," unpublished manuscript, University of Utah, Salt Lake City, 1991.

25. Berenbaum, *The World Must Know,* p. 2.

26. Ibid., at p. 51.

27. David M. Luebke, *The Nazi Persecution of Sinti and Ròma,* U.S. Holocaust Memorial Museum Research Brief, April 18, 1990, p. 3.

28. Breitman, *The Architect of Genocide,* p. 20.

29. Penelope Keable, *Creators, Creatures and Victim-Survivors,* doctoral diss., University of Sydney, Australia, 1995, p. 24.

30. See David Crowe and John Kolsti, eds., *The Gypsies of Eastern Europe* (Armonk, N.Y.: E. C. Sharpe, 1991), pp. 11–30.

31. State Museum of Auschwitz-Birkenau (for Documentary and Cultural Centre of German Sintis and Roma), *Memorial Book: The Gypsies at Auschwitz-Birkenau* (Munich: K. G. Saur, 1993), p. xiv (emphasis added).

32. Benno Müller-Hill, *Murderous Science: Elimination by Scientific Selection of Jews, Gypsies, and Others, 1933–1945* (Oxford: University Press, 1988), pp. 58–59.

33. Ibid.

34. Burleigh and Wippermann, *The Racial State,* pp. 121–125.

35. State Museum of Auschwitz-Birkenau, *Memorial Book,* p. 3.

36. Thurner, "Nazi Policy Against the Gypsies."

37. See Emil Fackenheim, *The Jewish Return into History* (Syracuse, N.Y.: University Press, 1978).

38. Kate DeSmet, "Comments Outrage Area Jews," *Detroit News,* December 31, 1990, p. B-3.

39. See, e.g., Vico and Keable.

40. Based on the author's personal correspondence with Yitzchak Mais, dated May 11, 1988.

41. Hilberg, *The Destruction of the European Jews,* pp. 142–144.

42. Based on the author's personal correspondence with Yitzchak Mais, dated May 11, 1988.

43. Donald Kenrick and Grattan Puxon, *The Destiny of Europe's Gypsies* (London: Sussex University Press, Chatto and Heinemann, 1972, new edition in preparation), p. 82.

44. Based on the author's personal correspondence with Yitzchak Mais, dated May 11, 1988.

45. Kenrick and Puxon, *The Destiny of Europe's Gypsies,* p. 78.

46. Yehuda Bauer, "Whose Holocaust?" *Midstream* (November 1980):42–46.

47. See, e.g., Hancock, *Chronology,* in Crowe and Kolsti, *The Gypsies of Eastern Europe.*

48. *Manchester Guardian,* January 9, 1956.

49. Lloyd Grove, "Lament of the Gypsies: 40 Years After Auschwitz, Petitioning for a Place," *Washington Post,* July 21, 1984, p. C4.

50. For example, see C. S. Coon, "Have the Jews a Racial Identity?" in *Jews in a Gentile World,* ed. I. Graeber and S. H. Britt (New York: Greenwood, 1942), pp. 20–37; R. Patai and

J. Patai-Wing, *The Myth of the Jewish Race* (Detroit: Wayne State University Press, 1989); and William Petersen, "Jews as a Race," *Midstream* (February-March 1988):35–37.

51. J. D. Thomas et al., "Disease, Lifestyle, and Consanguinity in 58 American Gypsies," *Lancet* 8555 (August 15, 1977):377–379.

52. Based on the author's personal correspondence with Yitzchak Mais, dated May 11, 1988.

53. Bauer, "Whose Holocaust?"

54. Berenbaum, *The World Must Know,* p. 51.

55. Gabrielle Tyrnauer, *The Fate of Gypsies During the Holocaust,* Special Report prepared for the U.S. Holocaust Memorial Council, Washington, D.C., 1985, restricted access document, p. 24.

56. Sybil Milton, "Nazi Policies Towards Roma and Sinti."

57. Percy Broad, "KZ Auschwitz: Erinnerungen eines SS-Mannes," *Hefte von Auschwitz* 9 (1966):7–48.

58. Breitman, *The Architect of Genocide,* p. 164.

59. Lucette M. Lagnado and Sheila Cohn Dekel, *Children of the Flames: The Untold Story of the Twins of Auschwitz* (New York: William Morrow, 1991), p. 82.

60. Ulrich König, *Sinti und Roma unter dem Nationalsozialismus* (Bochum: Brockmeyer Verlag, 1989), pp. 129–133.

61. Michael Zimmermann, "From Discrimination to the 'Family Camp' at Auschwitz: National Socialist Persecution of the Gypsies," *Dachau Review* 2 (1990):87–113, quote at 107–108.

62. Yitzhak Mais, in the brochure published by the Museums at Yad Vashem.

63. Roth and Berenbaum, *Holocaust: Religious and Philosophical Implications,* p. 33.

64. See Selma Steinmetz, *Oesterreichs Zigeuner im NS-Staat,* Monographien zur Zeitgeschichte (Frankfurt: Europa Verlag, 1966).

65. König, *Sinti und Roma unter dem Nationalsozialismus,* pp. 87–89.

66. State Museum of Auschwitz-Birkenau, *Memorial Book,* p. 2 (emphasis added).

67. Berenbaum, *The World Must Know,* p. 129.

68. See references in Hancock, "'Uniqueness' of the Victims."

69. Louis Pauwels and Jacques Bergier, *Le Matin des Magiciens* (Paris: Gallimard, 1960), p. 430.

70. C. Tyler, "Gypsy President," *Financial Times,* March 26, 1994, pp. 3–4.

71. Susan Strandberg, "Researcher Claims Thousands of Gypsies Exterminated by Czechs," *Decorah Journal* (May 5, 1994):1–2.

72. Donald Kenrick, *Gypsies Under the Swastika* (Hatfield: Hertfordshire University Press, 1995).

73. Zygmunt Bauman, *Modernity and the Holocaust* (Cambridge: Polity Press, 1989).

74. Kurt Voss and Mark Rocco, *Where the Day Takes You.* Cinetel Films, Inc., 1992.

75. Angus Fraser, *The Gypsies* (Oxford: Blackwell, 1993), pp. 261–262.

76. Christian Bernadec, *L'Holocaust Oublié* (Paris: Editions France-Empire, 1979), p. 34.

77. Katie Trumpener, "The Time of the Gypsies: A 'People Without History' in the Narratives of the West," *Critical Enquiry* 18(4) (1992):843–884, quote at 844.

78. See especially Stephen Wilson, *Ideology and Experience: Anti-Semitism in France at the Time of the Dreyfuss Affair* (London: Fairleigh Dickinson University Press, 1982), ch. 13, "Racial Anti-Semitism: A Race Apart," pp. 456–495.

79. Burleigh and Wippermann, *The Racial State,* p. 36.

80. Robert Proctor, "From *Anthropologie* to *Rassenkunde* in German Anthropological Tradition." In George W. Stocking, ed., *Romantic Motives: Essays on Anthropological Sensibility* (Madison: University of Wisconsin Press, 1988): 138–179.

81. Alfred Dillmann, *Zigeuner-Buch* (Munich: Wilsche Verlag, 1905).

82. Burleigh and Wippermann, *The Racial State,* p. 4.

83. Ibid., p. 77.

84. Karl Binding and Alfred Hoche, *Die Freigabe der Vernichtung Lebensunwerten Lebens* (Leipzig: Felix Meiner, 1920).

85. Burleigh and Wippermann, *The Racial State,* p. 84.

86. Zimmermann, "From Discrimination to the 'Family Camp' at Auschwitz," p. 91.

87. Burleigh and Wippermann, *The Racial State,* p. 117.

88. Kenrick and Puxon, *The Destiny of Europe's Gypsies,* p. 68; see also Ehmann, "A Short History of the European Gypsies," p. 10.

89. F. Proester, *Nacistická okupace: Vraždeni čs. Cikánů v Buchenwaldu*. Report prepared for Miriam Novitch, Document No. ÚV ČSPB K-135 on deposit in the Archives of the Museum of the Fighters Against Nazism, Prague, 1968.

90. Detlev Peukert, *The Weimar Republic* (New York: Hill and Wang, 1987), p. 160.

91. Eva von Hase-Mihalik and Doris Kreuzkamp, *Du Kriegst Auch einen Schönen Wohnwagen: Zwangslager für Sinti und Roma Während des National-sozialismus in Frankfurt am Main* (Frankfurt: Brandes and Apsel, 1990), p. 140.

92. Stephen Kinzer, "Germany Cracks Down: Gypsies Come First," *New York Times,* September 27, 1992, p. 1.

93. See his "Continuing Ferment in Eastern Europe," *SICSA Report* 4(1/2) (1990):1, 4.

94. Sandor Balogh, "Following in the Footsteps of the Ku Klux Klan: Anti-Gypsy Organization in Romania," Nemzetközi Cigány Szövetség *Bulletin,* No. 5, New York, 1993.

95. Louise Branson, "Romanian Gypsies Being Terrorized," *San Francisco Chronicle,* December 19, 1993, pp. A1, A15.

96. See Ian H. Hancock, *The Pariah Syndrome: An Account of Gypsy Slavery and Persecution,* 2d ed. (Ann Arbor, Mich.: Karoma, 1988).

97. Lopate, "Resistance to the Holocaust," p. 292; Ina R. Friedman, *The Other Victims: First-person Stories of Non-Jews Persecuted by the Nazis* (Boston: Houghton Mifflin Co., 1990): 7–24.

98. Thurner, "Nazi Policy Against the Gypsies," p. 7.

99. For example, see Steven Katz, *The Holocaust in Historical Context, Volume 1.*

100. Harvey Meyerhoff, "Council Decries Germany's Treatment of Gypsies," *U.S. Holocaust Memorial Council Newsletter,* Winter Issue (1992–1993):8.

101. Elizabeth-Anne Wheal, Stephen Pope, and James Taylor, *Encyclopedia of the Second World War* (Secaucus, N.J.: Castle Books, 1989).

102. Robert Wistrich, *Who's Who in Nazi Germany* (New York: Bonanza, 1982).

103. John Keegan, ed., *Who Was Who in World War II* (New York: Thomas Crowell, 1978).

104. In Jerzy Fickowski, *The Gypsies in Poland* (Warsaw: Interpress, 1989), p. 43.

105. Margaret Stapinska, "Faceless, Stateless, Endless Victims," *Yorkshire Post,* January 28, 1995, p. 5.

106. Anon., "Holocaust Memorial Omits Gypsies," *Atlanta Constitution,* July 15, 1992, p. A-5.

107. Heinz Galinski, "Dieses Gedenken sei uns Mahnung zum Handeln," *Sinti und Roma in Ehemaligen KZ Bergen-Belsen am 27 Oktober 1979* (Göttingen: Gesellschaft für Bedröhte Völker, 1980), pp. 76–81, 77.

❀ 4 ❀

The Atlantic Slave Trade and the Holocaust: A Comparative Analysis

SEYMOUR DRESCHER

The Comparative Impulse

The vastness of some historical events and processes attracts scholars into postulates marked by singularity. Like the Holocaust, modern slavery intuitively appeals to the historical imagination as a candidate for uniqueness: "There was nothing quite like black slavery, in scale, importance or consequence," writes one of slavery's recent chroniclers.[1] Beyond slavery's challenge to scholarly understanding, recently, considerable popular pressure has generated a demand that greater attention be paid to the story of slaves and their descendants in the world at large. The enormous increase in scholarly discussion and in the public visibility of the Holocaust in the United States has contributed to corresponding reflections on the place of slavery in American and world history. In April 1995, a *New York Times* front-page story on the commemoration of slavery reported that "some scholars compare this widespread reflection to that of Jews who have vigilantly preserved memories of the Holocaust."[2] Because both phenomena are so intimately tied to stories of mass degradation, dispersion, and death, they elicit not only scholarly analysis but tempt philosophers, theologians, and politicians into competitions over comparative victimization.

In an early comparison, a historian of American slavery attempted to analogize the psychology of Nazi concentration camp inmates with the trauma of enslavement in order to explain what was considered to be the cultural annihilation and long-term infantilization of blacks in America. Subsequent research and discussion of this putative analogy indicated that the original comparison had been premised on deficient knowledge about both systems. Since the 1970s, the research on both subjects has, if anything, widened the distance between the Holocaust and New World slavery. A generation of slavery scholarship has increasingly demonstrated the ability of slaves not only to sustain themselves but to create systems of culture, family, community, enterprise, and consumption from the sixteenth to the nineteenth centuries.[3]

Histories of slavery in the Americas now routinely devote much of their pages to such themes as the development of religion, family life, women and children, leisure and the arts, independent economic activities, consumption patterns, and individual and collective forms of resistance. The whole scholarly enterprise now focuses on a system that endured and expanded for almost four centuries and produced an enormous variety of human interaction. Slaves created patterns of human relationships as complex as any to be found outside the distinctive economy of the Atlantic system. African Americans were part of a durable system in which the enslaved played key roles as actors in "an ever-widening social and economic space."[4]

By contrast, historians of the Holocaust must analyze human behavior, thought, and institutional development within a time-frame of years, not centuries. Analytical questions about intergenerational patterns of production and reproduction, modes of family- and community-building, and the evolution of economic activity over many generations are irrelevant. There were, of course, rapidly changing patterns of work, culture, and even artistic expression, but they unfolded in terms of months and years, not decades, generations, and centuries. Except for isolated individual fugitives hidden by gentiles and pockets of Jewish armed partisans, the Holocaust is a tale of rapidly *narrowing* economic and social space, physical concentration, immiseration, and annihilation.[5] A recognition of the divergence of the two "institutions" was quickly grasped in the wake of the initial comparison. It remains the starting point in any contrast of slavery in the Americas with the Holocaust in Europe.

If there is one aspect of African slavery that might be fruitfully linked to an analysis of the Holocaust, it is probably the process of initial enslavement. Coerced transfers of sub-Saharan Africans fed slave systems of the Mediterranean, Atlantic, and Indian Ocean basins for ten centuries. The largest component of this forced migration after 1500 was the transatlantic slave trade. During three and a half centuries, from the early 1500s to the 1860s, up to 12 million Africans were loaded and transported in dreadful conditions to the tropical and subtropical zones of the Americas. In the process, probably twice as many were seized in the African interior.

One historian has estimated that in the peak century and a half of the intercontinental forced migration from Africa (1700–1850), "twenty-one million persons were captured in Africa, seven million of whom were brought into domestic slavery [within Africa itself]." The human cost of sustaining the combined slave systems to the west, north, and east of sub-Saharan Africa between 1500 and 1900 was an estimated "four million people who lost their lives as a direct result of enslavement," plus others who died prematurely.[6] Of the nearly 12 million in the Atlantic slave trade, around 15 percent, or up to 2 million more, died on the Atlantic voyage—the dreaded "Middle Passage"—and the first year of "seasoning." In the Americas, the death rates dropped gradually to levels approximating those projected in Africa.[7] Averages offer only an inkling of the intensity of suffering in particular regions, communities, barracoons, and slave ships or in the diverse situations to which slaves were delivered in the Americas. In terms of conditions of life as well as of death, the long journey from the African interior was the peak period of pain, discomfort, psychological dislocation, and degradation in the Atlantic system. Within the parameters of the slave trade, comparisons with the Holocaust may, therefore, be more meaningful, even if the differences remain overwhelming.

Market Versus Nonmarket Forces

A fundamental comparison may begin with the terms given by those who organized the two systems. The Holocaust was envisioned as a "final solution" to a problem: Jews were beings whose very existence was a threat and whose physical disappearance was regarded as one of the highest priorities of the Nazi leadership. The success of the enterprise required rapid institutional innovation and was measured in a time frame calculated in months and years. The Atlantic slave trade developed incrementally with millennia of institutional precedents. The initial age of European transoceanic expansion from the fifteenth to the seventeenth centuries slowly added a new dimension to the expansion of African slavery. Europeans discovered by stages that they could best tap the mineral and agricultural potential of the Atlantic basin with massive rearrangements of labor. The rapid depletion of New World populations led to experiments in various forms of imported, coerced labor from both Europe and Africa. In large parts of the New World, as in Africa, slaves proved to be an economically optimal form of labor for slaveholders. The context of the development of the slave trade was, therefore, both long-term and incremental. For hundreds of years, the Americas presented enormous tracts of sparsely populated land and subsoil minerals suitable for profitable production and overseas export. During the same period, Europeans developed capital and communications networks capable of directing the transportation of American production to all parts of the Atlantic world. Simultaneously, Africans expanded and intensified their internal networks of enslavement, and Europeans tapped into those networks of enslavement for long-distance, coerced migration.[8]

Historians of slavery intensely dispute the slave trade's long-term effects on each region of the Atlantic system—whether and how much slavery stimulated or constrained development in Europe, the Americas, and Africa.[9] There is, however, a generally shared consensus about two points. First, there was no single collectivity, whether defined in political, geographical, religious, or racial terms, that dominated the entire trade complex at any point. Indeed, it is the fragmentation of power that assured the system was sustained as a competitive system. Second, whatever groups entered into and departed from this vast complex of human and material transfers, the central mechanism driving its general expansion for well over three centuries was the economic gain accruing to those who remained in it. Economic considerations and the attempt to bend economic outcomes to advantage by additions of political constraints define the terms in which participants entered or exited from the trade.[10]

Almost every scholarly work on the slave trade also acknowledges or infers the primacy of economics or political economy as the nexus of the flow of forced labor within the system.[11] Only the captives, transferred from owner to owner in a network of exchanges that often extended for months from the interior of Africa to the interior of the Americas, had no bargaining power in the stream of transfers. What drove the movement of human beings along the network was the value-added potential at the end of the process and the ability of individuals and states to tap into that delivery system. If the slave trade was what some historians have termed an "uncommon market," *uncommon* is clearly the modifier; *market* is the noun. What ensured that the trade continued was the dream of wealth flowing back into the system as returns on previous investments in human beings. And though the slave trade epitomized the reduction of human beings to the category of things, it was also the slaveholder's conception of the enslaved as potentially *valuable* things that sustained the system of exchange. From the perspective of all those involved in the traffic, the longer that all able-bodied slaves remained alive, the greater was their potential to add to the wealth, status, and power of the traders and slaveholders. The slaves' status as property and as productive instrument, analogous to "laboring cattle," ensured that their disablement or death registered as costs to their owners.[12]

The Holocaust of 1941–1945 developed in a different context and was driven by different motivations. It was confined to a single continent. It reached its greatest intensity in European areas and against populations that had been least directly involved in the Atlantic slave trade. Unlike the latter, it was dominated by one hegemonic political entity: the Nazi regime. It functioned most effectively, according to its own directors, where the Nazis had unimpeded institutional authority to implement their plans. Where Nazi political power was less direct and more limited, the system worked less effectively or thoroughly.[13] Rather than attempting to convert underpopulated or underexploited areas into optimal producers of wealth, the perpetrators conceived of the areas under their influence as already overrun with undesirable populations afflicted with human pollutants. Even before the decision for the Final Solution, the Nazis assigned a very high political priority to methods of quarantine and expulsion of Jews into zones far beyond Europe. Africans, Europeans, and Americans in the Atlantic slave trade measured their success in terms of the numbers of captives landed and sold alive. In the Nazi system, every Jew destroyed was a gain in "racial" security and a once-for-all economic gain in confiscated goods.[14]

The slave trade was an open-ended process. Its voluntary participants (the traders) wished to perpetuate it. As a forced migration, it devastated areas of Africa and changed the balance of population groups within the Americas. Regarding the impact on the population of Africa, a major historical debate revolves around the question of whether the population of western or west-central Africa would have been substantially larger in 1700 or 1850 in the absence of the transatlantic branch of the slave trade. However, it never so depleted western and west-central Africa as to threaten the Atlantic system.[15] By contrast, the Holocaust was directed against specific groups within Europe and had very specific effects on those groups. Millions of Jewish deaths were so concentrated in time and place that the impact of overall and short-term depletion of the target population was dramatic and definitive.

As a "way of death," the slave trade was kept in being by the maintenance of a continuous flow of living human bodies who were a means to the production of labor. The Holocaust was kept in motion by the production of dead human bodies. The two systems, therefore, reveal dramatically different tempos of mortality. Joseph Miller, a historian of the Angolan slave trade, has drawn a profile of "Annualized Mortality Rates Among Slaves from Capture Through Seasoning." He depicts a typical trade cycle extending over four years (fourteen months in transit and almost three years of seasoning in the New World).[16] For African slaves, the highest rate of loss would have occurred in the first fourteen weeks of captivity: on the journey through Africa, within the coastal holding quarters (the barracoons), and during the Atlantic Middle Passage. Ironically, one of Miller's four-year cycles is as long as the whole period of the Holocaust.

The mortality profile of the Holocaust victims is dissimilar from that of Angolan slaves. In some areas, whole communities were massacred on the spot. In the wake of the invasion of Russia in 1941, the *Einsatzgruppen*, or special killing squads, and their auxiliaries rounded up and slaughtered tens of thousands of Jews in open areas near their homes.[17] For one stage of the slave trade, Miller notes that annualizing the death rate in the slave barracoons "would produce a preposterous annual rate" of 1,440 per 1,000 per year. Raul Hilberg also notes the futility of offering annualized infant mortality rates of over 1,000 per 1,000 in the ghetto experience. At Auschwitz between July 1942 and March 1943, even among those Jews and non-Jews not immediately killed on arrival, the "annualized" death-rate was more than 2,400 per 1,000. It would be even more absurd to speak of the series of mass slaughters during the early months of the Nazi sweep through the various regions of the Soviet Union in terms of "annual" mortality.[18] What is clear is that in this opening phase of the Final Solution in the East, the primacy of on-the-spot maximum annihilation was manifest in the documentary reports making their way back up through the Nazi chain of command.

For the millions of Jews who resided elsewhere in Nazi-dominated Europe, the Holocaust proceeded rapidly, from late 1941 to early 1945, through stages of identification, concentration, and deportation.[19] Short of death for victims of the Atlantic slave trade, one peak of collective suffering came early in the process of enslavement: the trauma of uprooting, family disintegration, and physical restraint (shackling). A fresh set of afflictions accompanied the march to the sea, including attrition from epidemic disease, hunger, and thirst. In this African side of the process, large numbers of slaves were siphoned off into local populations. Others, however, were added to the enslaved caravans along the line of travel as criminal and "tribute" slaves. Captives were sometimes used as beasts of burden, carrying other commodities down to the coast, thereby offsetting some of the costs of transportation for their captors. At the coast there would be some respite from shortages of food and water experienced en route. However, the slave would have exchanged the conditions of forced marches in shackles for the dangers and discomfort of sedentary imprisonment. Concentrations of people from different disease environments increased the appalling toll of disease. The "slave pens" in Benguela, Angola, "were about 17 meters square with walls three meters or more in height." With "two square meters per individual," the barracoons contained 150 to 200 slaves, often enclosed together with pigs and goats.[20]

Few aspects of the trade expressed the valuelessness of dead slaves more clearly than the slave merchants' habit of dumping bodies of the dead in a heap in a small cemetery or depositing them in shallow graves in great numbers as food for scavenging birds and animals. On the western shore of the Atlantic in Rio de Janeiro, slave traders heaped up their decomposing losses in a mountain of earth awaiting weekly burials. On those occasions when slaves died too quickly for burial, the decomposing corpses were partially burned, giving off a terrible odor.[21]

Transit

For those captives not retained in Africa who survived the barracoons, the most distinctive part of the Atlantic slave trade was the transoceanic journey. The Middle Passage was a voyage lasting from weeks to months in an environment that none of the enslaved had ever experienced in their lives. In the Holocaust, there is no precise counterpart to the Middle Passage. For European Jews, a completed *seaborne* voyage actually represented redemption. During the Nazi period, one transatlantic voyage of Jews illustrates the contrasting contexts of the two systems. In the famous case of the aborted journey of the *Saint Louis* to Cuba and the United States in 1939, passengers' forced return to the Old World meant captivity and destruction.

For enslaved Africans, the boarding process often signaled their transfer to the authority of Europeans. The state, the church, and the owners might affix their own seals of ownership upon each boarding victim through the repeated application of hot irons to their bodies. Europeans branded slaves as marks of ownership exactly as they branded their cattle or horses or as goods clearing customs. In addition to the marks of capitalist ownership, some states might add their separate brand of royal arms, denoting vassalage to the crown. Representatives of the Church could add a cross branding to the royal arms as a mark of baptism. Under certain jurisdictions, the branding process might continue in the Americas where slaveowners affixed their own signs and renamed their new human properties or designated them as runaways.[22]

For deported Jews, the passage to the death camps in boxcars was also like nothing they had ever experienced before. Lack of food, water, heat, or sufficient air circulation created a human environment rife with futile disputes—by "curses, kicks and blows . . . a human mass extended across the floor, confused and continuous, sluggish and aching, rising here and there in sudden convulsions and immediately collapsing again in exhaustion." The journey of two or three days ended when the crash of opening doors and barked orders forced the passengers out onto platforms.[23] The closest analogue to the branding of Africans was the tattooing of inmates at Auschwitz after selection. They were not renamed but numbered, signifying their transition to the condition of anonymous state property. Only by showing one's "baptism" (number) could an inmate get his or her daily ration of soup.[24]

For Africans, the ordeal of oceanic transit could last from weeks to months. Many of the Africans were sick, and all must have been terrified boarding an object that they had never seen, heaving upon a medium they had never experienced. The passengers were arranged in tightly packed horizontal rows lying shoulder-to-shoulder along the length of the ship and were even curled around the mast. The males were linked together in irons, making it difficult for them to "turn or move, to attempt to rise or lie down," without injuring each other. The collisions and curses that accompanied the crowding were further intensified by fights at feeding times and during attempts to relieve themselves. Overflowing lavatory buckets and the effluvium of digestive tract diseases added to the discomfort of stifling air. From the beginning of the voyage, the holds were covered with blood and mucus and were so hot that the surgeons could visit the slaves only for short periods at a time. To the many incubating intestinal diseases that the slaves had brought on board with them were added the nausea of seasickness.[25] Accounts of the pervasive sensory impact of excrement on the slave ships correspond to Holocaust reports of the wall of feces three feet high in one ghetto lavatory and a concentration camp latrine at Auschwitz where a system with a capacity for 150 was used each morning by 7,000 people. With many inmates stricken with diarrhea and dysentery and with no more than ten minutes allowed for bodily functions, people were knee-deep in excrement.[26]

Cruelty and arbitrary abuse added to the toll of hunger, thirst, and disease in both systems, but most slaves who died of hunger and thirst did so as the consequence of unanticipated long voyages. The railroads to Auschwitz moved relatively close to a schedule, the precision of which was the pride of the German railway bureaucracy. Trains rolled when they had been cleared for through passage to their destination. What one historian calls the "floating tombs" of the African trade had their literal equivalents during the Holocaust. Trucks in transit to death camps sometimes served as gas chambers.[27]

Crews of African ships were at much greater risk than were the Nazi guards and their auxiliaries. Slave crews faced considerable danger from tropical disease, hunger, and thirst. They had no recourse to reinforcements in the event of a slave uprising when slaves were released from their hold below deck for daily exercise. Above all, ship's captains in the slave trade had a stake in the survival of their human cargo. Every sale at the end of the voyage meant revenue for the state and profits for the traders. Every dead body meant some loss on invested capital.

Nothing better illustrates the legal difference between the two systems than one of the most bizarre slave trade cases ever heard in an English Court—the *Zong* case, argued in Britain in 1783. The slave ship *Zong* had sailed from Africa to the Caribbean in 1781 loaded with 470 slaves bound for Jamaica. After twelve weeks under sail, it had already lost over sixty Africans and seventeen crew members. In order to preserve the rapidly dwindling water reserves, save the remaining "cargo," and allow the investors to claim a loss under their insurance policy, the captain threw 131 of the sickest slaves to their deaths. (Unlike losses due to capture or insurrection, losses of slaves due to death by suicide or sickness were routinely uninsurable.) Designated victims were selected in daily batches by the *Zong*'s crew. They were pushed overboard in sight of the remaining slaves. Consequently, ten more slaves, witnessing the selections, threw themselves overboard.

The underwriters refused to pay for those cast into the sea. A civil suit was brought by the investors. The case was argued in the court of Lord Chief Justice Mansfield, famous for having declared in 1772 that colonial slave law did not apply within England. Counsel for the slavers logically brushed aside the whole question of murder, on the ground that in terms of the suit the *Zong* slaves were goods and property. The only question before the court was whether some property had been rationally jettisoned at sea in order to preserve the rest. Mansfield agreed: "Though it shocks one very much . . . the case of the slaves was the same as if horses or cattle had been thrown overboard."[28]

Nothing like the *Zong* case came before a German court over the disposal of captive Jews—nor could it in Nazi "actions" or shipments. No one who engaged in either the authorized killing of or who *refused* to kill Jews was the object of legal action. There was no property over which such a case could have arisen— no acknowledgment of the monetary value of persons, no contract for the sale of persons, no description of the sex and age of the deceased at the point of loading, no lawful insurance upon the human cargo, and no inquest into reasons for the deaths of any or all of a transported group. The passengers' fares were payable to the railway system whether or not they arrived alive (one-way for Jews, round-trip for their guards). The fares were paid for by funds previously confiscated from the victims themselves. No suits were filed for uncompleted journeys due to death en route. There was literally no "interest" in the survival of the passengers en route.

Both captive Africans and Jews were designated as "pieces," but Africans were more highly differentiated goods because an African's status was derived from the exchange value of an adult male for a piece of imported textile. A set of categories designated slaves who were less than full "pieces," in order to indicate their lower exchange value, ranged according to age, health, and strength. The "use-value" of the ideal African piece was clear. By contrast, all Jews who were not deemed of "full" immediate labor value were immediately sent to the furnace. Their only use-value was that of certain "pieces" of their bodies.[29]

Divergence

At journey's end, the fate of the captives diverged. In the transatlantic slave trade, landfall marked the end of the seaborne horrors. Slaves very often arrived disabled, covered with sores, and suffering from fevers, but the sight of land and the removal of shackles excited a transient feeling of joy. The captives were offered fresh food. They were bathed, "bodies cleansed and oiled," and given gifts of tobacco and pipes. In some ports, a priest might come aboard to reassure the terrified passengers that they had not been transported in order to be eaten on disembarkation. The next stage of the process involved further psychological humiliation. Captives had to endure long and repeated physical inspections by prospective buyers. Slaves were offered for sale almost naked to prevent deception. The healthiest and strongest went first. The remaining ("refuse") slaves were sometimes taken on to other ports or sent onshore to taverns and public auctions. Further separations from relatives or shipboard companions at this point added to the trauma of sale. If slaves survived this series of traumas, they might enter a period of relative recovery ("seasoning"), along with the imposition of a new name, instruction in a new language, and coercion in a new work discipline.[30]

For Jews in transit, the moment of arrival marked not a lessening but the most dangerous, single moment of their collective suffering. As they arrived, they were unloaded onto a vast platform. Compared to the purchase of African slaves, the railside inspection of Jews was extraordinarily casual. SS men or other agents of the state moved quickly through the silent crowd interrogating only a few: "How old? Healthy or ill?" Mothers who did not wish to be separated from children were told to remain with their children. The SS decided, often in a fraction of a second, between life and death. In a few minutes from the opening of a railway car, the overwhelming majority were on their way to the gas chamber. A mentality of superfluity enveloped the whole process. Only in this context can one fully appreciate Primo Levi's opening phrase in *Survival at Auschwitz*: "It was my good fortune to be deported to Auschwitz only in 1944, that is, after the German

Government had decided, owing to the growing scarcity of labor, to lengthen the average life span of the prisoners destined for elimination."[31]

The slave trade was always predicated on the value of the captives as potential laborers. Well before the decision for the "Final Solution" to the "Jewish question" by mass murder in 1941, the Nazi regime had also realized the potential utility of coerced Jewish labor following the captives' pauperization. In Germany, a series of decrees between 1938 and 1941 mobilized all able-bodied Jewish labor within the Reich and occupied Poland, sustained at a standard of remuneration and nutrition far below that of the non-Jewish populations around them. On the eve of the invasion of Russia, more than 100,000 had been conscripted in Germany alone.[32] In the occupied Polish territories between 1939 and 1941, a running debate ensued between attritionists (favoring accelerated starvation) and utilitarians (favoring temporary use of Jewish labor for producing at least the equivalent of their temporary upkeep). The debate revolved around local policy options while awaiting decisions from above about the disposition of the Jewish population. Some ghettos briefly succeeded in achieving the status of short-term economic (not long-term demographic) viability. By the end of 1941, a portion of ghettoized adult able-bodied Jews was contributing to the Nazi economy and war production at minimal survival levels. Had the Nazis decided in favor of exploitation rather than liquidation of the Warsaw ghetto in the summer of 1942 and had the harsh living conditions and the high death rate remained at levels of the first half of that year (i.e., over 1,000 percent of the prewar monthly rate), "it would have taken eight years for all of Warsaw's Jews to die out."[33]

The German invasion of Russia was accompanied not only by a moving frontier of massacre to its east but by the creation of death camps. The decision for mass annihilation in the already conquered territories was taken at a moment when the Nazis looked forward to total victory in the East. In such a context, the Slavic populations under Nazi control were also perceived to be superfluous—one more obstacle to the movement of an Aryanized frontier to the east. Enormous numbers of Russian prisoners of war were allowed to starve to death during this early period of the Holocaust. The Nazis, therefore, anticipated no major economic impediments to their twin ideal of general racial reorganization and accelerated Jewish annihilation. By stressing the parasitic concept in relation to both economic and racial development, the Nazis could also formulate the annihilation of Jews in terms of accelerated economic modernization. In addition to its public health dimension, the Final Solution would eliminate petty bourgeois impediments to the growth of large-scale industrial organization. This "imagined economy" of some Nazi bureaucrats drew on both capitalist and Communist visions of the industrial future.[34]

The division of "visions of labor" between slave traders and Nazi officials illustrates another divergence between the Holocaust and the transatlantic slave trade. Jews were of demographically negative value to the Nazi New Order. To the sponsors of the slave trade, Africans were indispensable, or at least optimal, to economic and imperial development. The failure of slaves to achieve a positive reproduction rate in the tropical Americas (thereby requiring continuous infusions of Africans for sustained economic growth) was perceived as a shortcoming, not a virtue, of the Atlantic system.

Labor

In policy terms, these divergences between the two systems are even more marked for the period of the Holocaust after the stalling of the German blitzkrieg against the Soviet Union. By the end of 1941, the conflict had settled into an extended struggle. German economic mobilization for war was intensified. As more Germans were required for military service, massive inputs of new labor were needed to fuel the German war machine. At that critical moment, the Nazis finalized the Final Solution into a rational bureaucratic annihilation. German industrialists began scrambling for alternative sources of labor, including the remnants of the Russian prisoners of war. The moment that killing operations against the Jews accelerated, the economic pressure increased. Thus, by 1944 there were more than 7.5 million coerced laborers in the heart of Europe, compared with less than 6 million African slaves in the Americas in 1860 after more than three centuries of the Atlantic slave trade.[35]

However, the rising number of Germany's slave laborers failed to boost productivity. The disciplinary habits and indifference to human suffering, developed during the era of superfluity, hindered the introduction of rationalized allocation or management of labor and precluded the development of incentives among prisoners. "Until the very end the Nazis pursued the policy of maximum results with minimum investments." The system was most effective not in raising productivity but "in squaring the economic postulates of German industrial circles with the plans to exterminate the Jews and certain categories of slaves, which had been outlined in the first years of the war by Nazi leaders and put into practice by the SS."[36] Primo Levi's opening phrase about his own "good fortune" in arriving at Auschwitz in May 1944 was, therefore, also an obituary on the fate of his fellow Jews. When Levi was arrested, the overwhelming majority of Jews in Nazi-controlled Europe had already been murdered.

The labor shortage caused a small slowdown in the killing process. For three years, individual Jews engaged in desperate attempts to ensure themselves against deportation to the death camps by retaining their status as slaves. Even small children grasped the significance of labor qualification as a final, frail barrier between death and brief survival. "How deeply this labor-sustained psychology had penetrated into the Jewish community is illustrated by a small incident observed by a Pole. In 1943 when an SS officer (Sturmbannführer Reinecke) seized a three-year-old Jewish girl in order to deport her to a killing center, she pleaded for her life by showing him her hands and explaining that she could work. In vain."[37]

The comparative figures on enslavement and annihilation between 1941 and 1945 show that the ideology of Jewish elimination took precedence over the ideology of production in Nazi policy. Time and again Jews were deported before requested replacements arrived. At the highest political levels, economic reasoning was treated with condescension or contempt. Even when grudging concessions were made to urgent requests for the temporary retention of Jewish slave labor, it was understood that "corresponding to the wish of the *Führer* the Jews are to disappear one day."[38] Hitler personally overruled a request by the bureaucrat responsible for labor supply to postpone the removal of Jews from German soil in vital armaments factories. Josef Goebbels rejoiced that the arguments of "economic experts and industrialists, to the effect that they cannot do without so-called Jewish precision work, do not impress him [Hitler]."[39]

In Nazi Europe, it was usually capitalists and bureaucrats in direct control of Jews who tried to rationalize labor mobilization on the road to elimination. This underlines the difference between the two historical processes that we emphasized at the outset. In the Atlantic system, political rulers—both African and European—tapped into and tried to manipulate a competitive market that they could never hope to fully master. They failed in their attempts to control the flow of slaves to or at the coast or to monopolize the seaborne transit of slaves. If they succeeded temporarily, the effect was either to stifle the slave trade to their own zones of power, to draw new competitors into the trade, or to stimulate the formation of new networks of trade and production.[40] In the Holocaust, the power relationship between state and capitalists was reversed. It was the political leadership that literally controlled the switches governing the flow of captive populations into war industry or death factories.

Europeans in both systems converged in acquiring adult males as slaves. This group was heavily overrepresented among those boarded on the African coast. It also was overrepresented among those selected for survival at Auschwitz and elsewhere. (One must note, however, that adult males were the *first* group targeted for mass killing by the Nazi *Einsatzgruppen* in the East during the summer of "superfluity" in 1941.)[41] The Nazis, however, chose their labor force from a full demographic range of human beings. Mothers, children, and the aged were transported in the same shipments as young males and were usually designated for death on arrival. In the slave trade, African captors and traders substantially altered the sex and age distribution of captives offered for sale to European traders. Among Africans, captive women and children had considerable value.[42] Women and children in the slave trade who died from hunger, nutritional deficiencies, thirst, exposure, and disease perished for reasons beyond the determination of their captors. Under the Nazis, Jewish children who died in large numbers for these same reasons perished because of Nazi decisions to withhold food and medicine available to the surrounding population.

If one turns from victims to perpetrators, one professional group appears to have played a significant role in both processes. Doctors in the British slave trade were rewarded for saving lives en route to the Americas. A recent economic historian specializing in the medical history of the slave trade has concluded that doctors, for all of their limitations, succeeded in reducing mortality on the slave ships. Moreover, in the end, the greatest contribution to Africans by some "Guinea surgeons" in the Atlantic system was their testimony about conditions aboard slave ships. Physicians enjoyed quite a different role in the Holocaust. In Auschwitz, conclude two historians, doctors presided over the killing of most of the 1 million victims of that camp. They chose between labor and death, decided when the gassed victims were dead, rationalized the selection and cremation process, and lent the prestige of their profession to the whole operation, converting mass murder into a medical procedure. Nazi doctors rationalized the public health ideology of annihilation. They spent more time and care in examining some of the dead than most of the living. They conducted ferocious experiments on the bodies of the living. Jews who never saw a Nazi doctor during the years of the Holocaust stood a far better chance of survival than those who did.[43]

Racism

Justification for the two systems also overlapped. "Race" was used as a rationale for sustaining both processes. "No other slave system," writes one recent historian of British slavery, "was so regulated and determined by the question of race."[44] Historians of slavery might make an equally strong claim about the rationale for collecting vast numbers of coerced laborers at work sites throughout Nazi-dominated Europe. Jews, Gypsies, and Slavs were not only ranked in racial "value" but their bodies were at the disposal of the state for experiments, as well as for labor brigades and brothels.

Ironically, race may have played a limited role as a justifying concept in the launching and early expansion of the Atlantic slave trade. This finding has generated a long and inclusive debate on the role of antiblack racism as a cause or consequence of the enslavement of Africans.[45] Slavery was hardly synonymous with Africans nor were Africans with slaves when the Portuguese first began to purchase Africans in the mid-fifteenth century. Africans did not regard themselves as a unitary "race," and Europeans continued to enslave people from other portions of the world well into the age of exploration. From their earliest transoceanic voyages down to the eighteenth century, various European groups continued to enslave people in the Mediterranean, Africa, the sub-Sahara, America, and Asia. At the beginning of the Atlantic slave trade, only peoples of European descent were considered nonenslavable in the full sense of becoming inheritable reproductive property. Many non-European groups were only gradually exempted from enslavement by Europeans. By 1750, sub-Saharan Africans and their descendants constituted the overwhelming majority of slaves in the Americas and the exclusive source of slaves for the transatlantic trade. As the African slave trade persisted, the racial link embedded itself ever more deeply in the ideological fabric of European consciousness, especially in the Americas. In the process of dehumanization, European holders of African slaves intrinsically linked them to domestic animals or pets. Inventories consistently listed the value of slaves first and that of livestock second. Unlike Jewish captives, however, Africans "were not generally likened to predators, or to vermin," or to invisible carriers of disease.[46]

At no time, moreover, was the linkage between Africans and slaves fully congruent. European states and slave traders were fully aware that their slave-trading partners in Africa (princes, warriors, and merchants) possessed some of the same distinctive physical features as the enslaved. Treaties were signed and contracts were made by Europeans with Africans. Europeans paid tribute and customs to Africans. Military, economic, and marital alliances were formed with Africans. Africans were educated in European schools. Legal and administrative precautions were taken against wrongful seizures or enslavements of Africans. General characterizations of Africans as being more uncivilized or barbarous than Europeans, therefore, did not preclude an enormous range of political, economic, family, and cultural exchanges with Africans as equals in those relationships.[47]

Whatever the constraints against enslaving non-Africans, the identification of slavery with Africans in the Americas was a residual result of centuries of experimentation with various African and non-African groups, not the outcome of an imagined racial selection before the beginning of the Atlantic slave trade. Considerations of race came to define the outer limits of enslavability, not the designated status of Africans as slaves. The color-coded racial hierarchy was designed by Europeans to stabilize an asymmetrical distribution of transatlantic power over the long term. Given the indispensability of the slaves, renegotiations of master-slave relationships began almost from the moment slaves arrived in the New World. If racism undergirded the African slave trade, it was an effect rather than a cause of that system.[48]

Ironically, the closest analogue in European culture to a "racially" defined fear of contamination during the early period of the transatlantic slave trade was the Iberian obsession with "purity of blood." For two centuries after 1500, Spanish and Portuguese authorities conducted ongoing hunts for "Judaizing" descendants of Jews converted to Christianity. Such *conversos* or "New Christians" were indefinitely branded by their ancestral link to the Jewish tradition. In the Iberian settler societies, racial legislation was primarily concerned with the regulation of nonslave groups, including New Christians, Indians, and free people of "mixed" race. For slaves, legal codes inherited from *pre-Atlantic* Roman law constituted the primary juridical nexus for grounding master-slave, free-slave, and slave-slave relationships.[49]

Racism fulfilled a different systemic function during the Holocaust. The difference was not that Jews were defined primarily by the religious affiliation of their grandparents rather than by ancestral geographic origin or by color. For the Nazis, a racial revolution was needed to unravel past legal and social integration. Racial legislation also prescribed a new system of individual classification in order to unravel the results of religious intermarriage. The regime intended that one precisely designated group would, one way or another, disappear. Nazi racial policy was, in this sense, committed to *a* final solution—a policy of "disappearance"—long before the particular physical implementation that began in 1941.[50] Thus, if European statesmen and merchants measured success in the slave trade in terms of ships and colonies increasingly filled with aliens, success for National Socialists was measured in terms of body counts and empty horizons. Rudolf Höss, the commandant of Auschwitz, not only arranged to return to his killing center in 1944 so that he could personally oversee the destruction of Hungarian Jewry but claimed credit for annihilating 2.5 million, rather than the 1.25 million, people actually murdered there.[51]

The slave trade and the Holocaust are characterized by another striking difference. For the first three centuries of the transatlantic slave trade, only isolated voices—no government—attempted to prohibit slaving by its own citizens. There was no need for concealment and no international declaration against the Atlantic slave trade until more than three centuries into the duration of the system. Every European state with ports on the Atlantic participated in the trade at one time or another. Participants in the Atlantic system operated within the comforting context of doing or seeing ordinary and customary things, even at times when they expressed personal revulsion or reservation about some particularly brutal action within that system.

The Holocaust differed from the slave trade in that it was not described by its perpetrators as conforming to some ancient and universal practice. The Nazis were cognizant that they were radical innovators and directors of an operation that they themselves had begun and that they alone were capable of seeing through to completion. Their commitment was crucial to the process. Indeed, they knew that they had bet their lives on a project that would be considered a war crime were they to be defeated.

Conclusion

This brief overview emphasizes the difficulty of comparing two events so disparate in space, time, intention, duration, and outcome. Yet the urge to find analogues to one's suffering is unquenchably human. What could be more encouraging than to see the recent surge of historical interest in the Holocaust as a model for calling attention to other human catastrophes? The African slave trade had, in its turn, served Jews as a means of making sense of catastrophic oppression, for apprehending the disorienting cruelty of the world. It was reflexive for Anne Frank to draw upon Europe's dark chapter in Africa in order to come to terms with her own terrifying present: "Every night people are being picked up without warning and that is awful particularly for old and sick people, they treat them just like slaves in the olden days. The poor old people are taken outside at night and then they have to walk . . . in a whole procession with children and everything. . . . They are sent to Ferdinand Bolstraat and from there back again and that's how they plague these poor people. Also they throw water over them if they scream." Beyond the evocation of comprehensible and distant past horrors lay only fragments of other incomprehensible and distant present horrors: "If it is as bad as this in Holland whatever will it be like in the distant and barbarous regions they are sent to? We assume most of them are murdered. The English radio speaks of their being gassed perhaps the quickest way to die."[52]

Anne Frank's successive entries should serve as a caution to scholars. In comparing historical catastrophes, there is a temptation to argue as though one could arrive at a hierarchy of suffering or cruelty or radical evil such that only one such process reaches the apogee of uniqueness. Systems of human action are like Tolstoy's happy and unhappy marriages, all alike in some ways but each different in its own.

NOTES

I wish to thank Stanley L. Engerman, George Mosse, and Alexander Orbach for their helpful comments.

1. James Walvin, *Black Ivory: A History of British Slavery* (Washington, D.C.: Howard University Press, 1994), p. ix. For a parallel and much more ambitious claim for the Holocaust, see Steven T. Katz, *The Holocaust in Historical Context*, 3 vols. (New York: Oxford University Press), vol. 1, p. 1.

2. *New York Times*, April 2, 1995, p. 1.

3. See Stanley Elkins, *Slavery: A Problem in American Institutional and Intellectual Life* (Chicago: University of Chicago Press, 1959), pp. 104–115; Earle E. Thorpe, "Chattel Slavery and Concentration Camps," *Negro History Bulletin* (May 1962):171–176; republished in *The Debate over Slavery: Stanley Elkins and His Critics*, ed. Ann J. Lane (Urbana: University of Illinois Press, 1971), pp. 23–42; Sidney W. Mintz, "Slavery and Emergent Capitalisms," in *Slavery in the New World*, ed. Laura Foner and Eugene D. Genovese (Englewood Cliffs, N.J.: Prentice-Hall, 1969), pp. 27–37; Laurence Mordekhai Thomas, *Vessels of Evil: American Slavery and the Holocaust* (Philadelphia: Temple University Press, 1993), esp. pp. 117–147. See the introduction to Martin A. Klein, *Breaking the Chains: Slavery, Bondage, and Emancipation in Modern Africa and Asia* (Madison: University of Wisconsin Press, 1993), pp. 11–12. In a reappraisal, Elkins did not seem inclined to defend the heuristic value of the analogy in comparison with other institutions such as asylums and prisons. See Elkins, "Slavery and Ideology," in Lane, *Debate over Slavery*, pp. 325–378; John Thornton, *Africa and the Africans in the Making of the Atlantic World, 1400–1680* (Cambridge: Cambridge University Press), pp. 152–182, 206–253.

4. See, most recently, the essays in Larry E. Hudson Jr., ed., *Working Toward Freedom: Slave Society and Domestic Economy in the American South* (Rochester, N.Y.: University of Rochester Press, 1994), p. viii; and Stanley L. Engerman, "Concluding Reflections," in ibid., pp. 233–241. See also the essays in *The Slaves' Economy: Independent Production by Slaves in the Americas*, a special issue of *Slavery and Abolition* 12(1) (May 1991); and Robert W.

Fogel, *Without Consent or Contract: The Rise and Fall of American Slavery* (New York: Norton, 1989), pp. 154–198.

5. See Raul Hilberg, *The Destruction of the European Jews*, rev. and definitive ed., 3 vols. (New York: Holmes and Meiers, 1985).

6. See Paul E. Lovejoy, "The Impact of the Atlantic Slave Trade on Africa: A Review of the Literature," *Journal of African History* 30 (1989):365–394, esp. p. 387.

7. Patrick Manning, "The Slave Trade: The Formal Demography of a Global System," in *The Atlantic Slave Trade: Effects on Economics, Societies and Peoples in Africa, the Americas, and Europe*, ed. J. I. Inikori and S. L. Engerman (Durham, N.C.: Duke University Press, 1992), pp. 117–141, esp. pp. 119–120; Philip D. Curtin, *The Atlantic Slave Trade: A Census* (Madison: University of Wisconsin Press, 1969); David Eltis, *Economic Growth and the Ending of the Transatlantic Slave Trade* (New York: Oxford University Press, 1987); idem., "Free and Coerced Transatlantic Migrations: Some Comparisons," *American Historical Review* 88(2) (1983):251–280; J. D. Fage, "African Societies and the Atlantic Slave Trade," *Past and Present* 125 (1989):97–115; David Eltes, David Richardson, and Stephen Behrendt, "The Structure of the Atlantic Slave Trade, 1597–1867" (unpublished typescript).

8. See, inter alia, Thornton, *Africa and the Africans;* Inikori and Engerman, *The Atlantic Slave Trade*; Herbert Klein, *The Middle Passage: Comparative Studies in the Atlantic Slave Trade* (Princeton: Princeton University Press, 1978); David Brion Davis, *Slavery and Human Progress* (New York: Oxford University Press, 1984); Orlando Patterson, *Slavery and Social Death* (Cambridge: Harvard University Press, 1982).

9. See Paul Lovejoy, *Transformations in Slavery: A History of Slavery in Africa* (Cambridge: Cambridge University Press, 1983); idem., "Impact of the Atlantic Slave Trade"; and Patrick Manning, "The Impact of Slave Trade Exports on the Population of the Western Coast of Africa, 1700–1850," in *De la Traite à l'esclavage*, ed. Serge Daget (Nantes, France: Société française d'histoire d'outre-mer, 1988), pp. 111–134. Compare, with David Eltis, *Economic Growth*, pp. 64–71; John Thornton, "The Slave Trade in Eighteenth Century Angola: Effects on Demographic Structures," *Canadian Journal of African Studies* 14(3) (1980):417–427; and Martin A. Klein, "The Impact of the Atlantic Slave Trade on the Societies of the Western Sudan," in Inikori and Engerman, *Atlantic Slave Trade*, pp. 25–47.

10. William A. Darity, "A General Equilibrium Model of the Eighteenth Century Atlantic Slave Trade: A Least-Likely Test for the Caribbean School," *Research in Economic History* 7 (1982):287–326; Hilary McD. Beckles, "The Economic Origins of Black Slavery in the British West Indies, 1640–1680: A Tentative Analysis of the Barbados Model," *Journal of Caribbean History* 16 (1982):35–56; Raymond L. Cohn and Richard A. Jensen, "The Determinants of Slave Mortality Rates on the Middle Passage," *Explorations in Economic History* 10(2) (1982):173–176; David W. Galenson, "The Atlantic Slave Trade and the Barbados Market, 1673–1723," *Journal of Economic History* 42(3) (1982):491–511; Herbert S. Klein, "Novas Interpretaoes do trafico de Escravos do Atlantico," *Revista de Historia* 120 (1989):3–25.

11. See, inter alia, Inikori and Engerman, *Atlantic Slave Trade*; Barbara L. Solow and Stanley L. Engerman, eds., *British Capitalism and Caribbean Slavery* (Cambridge: Cambridge University Press, 1987); Barbara L. Solow, ed., *Slavery and the Rise of the Atlantic System* (New York: Cambridge University Press, 1991); David W. Galenson, *Traders, Planters, and Slaves: Market Behavior in Early English America* (New York: Cambridge University Press, 1986); Janet J. Ewald, "Slavery in Africa and the Slave Trades

from Africa," *American Historical Review* 97 (1992):465–485; Julian Gwyn, "The Economics of the Transatlantic Slave Trade: A Review," *Social History* 25 (1992):151–162. On the contrasting meaning of humans as "things" in the Atlantic system and in the Nazi system, see Claudia Koonz, "Genocide and Eugenics: The Language of Power," in *Lessons and Legacies: The Meaning of the Holocaust in a Changing World*, ed. Peter Hayes (Evanston, Ill.: Northwestern University Press, 1991), pp. 155–177; David Brion Davis, *The Problem of Slavery in Western Culture* (Ithaca, N.Y.: Cornell University Press, 1966), ch. 2, pp. 31–35; and Sidney Mintz, ed., *Esclave = facteur de production: l'economie politique de l'esclavage* (Paris: Dunod, 1981).

12. See Henry A. Gemery and Jan S. Hogendorn, eds., *The Uncommon Market: Essays in the Economic History of the Atlantic Slave Trade* (New York: Academic Press, 1979), on the "Western" transoceanic trade; and *The Economics of the Indian Ocean Slave Trade in the Nineteenth Century* (Special Issue), *Slavery and Abolition* 9 (December 1988).

13. See, above all, Hilberg, *The Destruction*, vol 2, pp. 543–860.

14. See Claudia Koonz, "Genocide and Eugenics," pp. 162ff; Robert Jay Lifton and Amy Hackett, "Nazi Doctors," in *Anatomy of the Auschwitz Death Camps*, ed. Michael Berenbaum (Bloomington: Indiana University Press, 1994), pp. 301–316.

15. See David Eltis, "Free and Coerced Transatlantic Migrations: Some Comparisons," *American Historical Review* 88(2) (1983):251–280; Stanley L. Engerman and Kenneth L. Sokoloff, "Factor Endowments, Institutions and Differential Paths of Growth Among New World Economies: A View from Economic Historians of the United States," in *Why Did Latin America Fall Behind?*, ed. Stephen Haber (Stanford: Stanford University Press, forthcoming 1996). On depopulation in Africa, compare Manning, "The Slave Trade," in Inikori and Engerman, *Atlantic Slave Trade*, pp. 117–141, and Eltis, *Economic Growth*, pp. 64–71.

16. See Joseph C. Miller, *Way of Death: Merchant Capitalism and the Angolan Slave Trade, 1730–1830* (Madison: University of Wisconsin Press, 1988), p. 439, figure 11.1. Miller's data base is quite small and lower estimates have been suggested by other authors. For example, Miller estimates an average loss of 35 percent from the point of capture to arrival at the coast, with a further loss of 10–15 percent in the port towns, yielding a total depletion in Africa of 45 percent (ibid., p. 440). Patrick Manning estimates an interior loss of about 15 percent ("The Slave Trade," p. 121); as does John Thornton, "The Demographic Effect of the Slave Trade on Western Africa 1500–1850," in *African Historical Demography*, vol. II, *Proceedings of a Seminar* (Edinburgh: University of Edinburgh, 1977), pp. 693–720. Manning notes that population loss in Africa, though relatively less serious than the depopulations of the Americas and Oceania, was caused in large part by human agency. This characteristic would bring the slave trade closer to the Holocaust in terms of agency than other population catastrophes; Manning, *Slavery and African Life: Occidental, Oriental, and African Slave Trades* (Cambridge: Cambridge University Press, 1990), p. 87.

17. See Yitzhak Arad, "The Holocaust of Soviet Jewry in the Occupied Territories of the Soviet Union," *Yad Vashem Studies* 21 (1991):1–47.

18. Compare Miller, *Way of Death*, p. 401, n. 89, with Raul Hilberg, "Opening Remarks: The Discovery of the Holocaust," in *Lessons and Legacies*, pp. 11–19, esp. pp. 15–16; Yisrael Gutman, "Auschwitz–An Overview," in *Anatomy of the Auschwitz Death Camp*, ed. Yisrael Gutman and Michael Berenbaum (Bloomington: Indiana University Press, 1994), pp. 5–33. It is important to note that the Auschwitz mortality figure applies only to the 400,000 (of 1.5 million) who were given inmate status, registered, numbered, and left alive for some time. The majority of arrivals were killed immediately. See Franciszek Piper, "The System

of Prisoner Exploitation," in *Anatomy of the Auschwitz Death Camp*, pp. 34–49; and "The Number of Victims," ibid., pp. 61–76.

19. Hilberg, *Destruction*, vol. I.

20. Miller, *Way of Death*, pp. 379–401; Philip Curtin, *Economic Change in Precolonial Africa: Sengambia in the Era of the Slave Trade* (Madison: University of Wisconsin Press, 1975), pp. 168–173, 277–278.

21. Miller, *Way of Death*, pp. 391–392.

22. Miller, *Way of Death*, pp. 404–406; Walvin, *Black Ivory*, pp. 250–251, 284–292; see also Herbert S. Klein, *The Middle Passage: Comparative Studies in the Atlantic Slave Trade* (Princeton: Princeton University Press, 1978).

23. Levi, *Survival in Auschwitz*, pp. 17–20.

24. Ibid., pp. 27–28.

25. See Thornton, *Africa*, pp. 153–162. For eyewitness accounts by a slave and a surgeon, see Olaudah Equiano, *The Interesting Narrative of the Life of Olaudah Equiano*, 2 vols. (London, 1789), vol. 1, pp. 78–80; Alexander Falconbridge, *An Account of the Slave Trade on the Coast of Africa* (London: J. Phillips, 1788), p. 25.

26. Robert-Jan Van Pelt, "A Site in Search of a Mission," in *Anatomy of the Auschwitz Death Camp*, pp. 93–154, esp. pp. 130–132. See also Terrence Des Pres, *The Survivor: An Anatomy of Life in the Death Camps* (New York: Oxford University Press, 1976), p. 60, describing the "excremental assault" on the inmates. See also Hilberg, *Destruction*, p. 490.

27. Arad, "Holocaust of Soviet Jewry," p. 14.

28. Walvin, *Black Ivory*, pp. 16–20.

29. That captive Jews were more readily imagined to be criminals than slaves may also be inferred from the case of the Ukrainian who consented to find refuge for two Jewish children whose father feared an imminent Nazi "action" in his ghetto. When the children were discovered, Bazyli Antoniak was accused of complicity in harboring "criminals," not stolen goods. He was convicted and sentenced to death, despite the fact that the children, aged six and seven, were too young to be charged as criminals. Ingo Müller, *Hitler's Justice: The Courts of the Third Reich*, trans. Deborah Lucas Schneider (Cambridge: Harvard University Press, 1991), p. 164. Jews under Nazi control were, however, of value to Jewish groups outside the range of Nazi power. For details of the futile negotiations on the ransoming of Jews, see Yehuda Bauer, *Jews for Sale? Nazi-Jewish Negotiations, 1933–1945* (New Haven: Yale University Press, 1994). On the value of corpses, see Andrzej Strzelecki, "The Plunder of the Victims and Their Corpses," *Anatomy of the Auschwitz Death Camp*, pp. 246–266. Under the auspices of Breslau University, a doctoral dissertation was published in 1940, "On the Possibilities of Recycling Gold from the Mouths of the Dead"; Miller, *Way of Death*, pp. 66–69; Levi, *Survival*, p. 16.

30. Thornton, *Africa*, pp. 162–182; Walvin, *Black Ivory*, pp. 59–66; Miller, *Way of Death*, pp. 445ff.

31. Levi, *Survival*, pp. 9–21. See also Paul Hoedeman, *Hitler or Hippocrates* (Sussex England: Book Guild, 1991), pp. 187–193; Franciszek Piper, "Gas Chambers and Crematoria," in *Anatomy of the Auschwitz Death Camp*, pp. 157–182.

32. Konrad Kwiet, "Forced Labour of German Jews in Nazi Germany," in *Leo Baeck Institute: Year Book*, vol. 36 (London: Secker and Warburg, 1991), pp. 389–410, esp. p. 393.

33. Isaiah Trunk, "Epidemics and Mortality in the Warsaw Ghetto, 1939–1942," in *The Nazi Holocaust: Historical Articles on the Destruction of European Jews,* ed. Michael R. Marrus, 9 vols. (Westport, Conn.: Meckler, 1989), vol. 6; vol. 1, p. 43; Christopher R.

Browning, *The Path to Genocide: Essays on Launching the Final Solution* (Cambridge: Cambridge University Press, 1992), pp. 34–51, 130–141. For an alternative and detailed account of the Warsaw ghetto, see Charles G. Roland, *Courage Under Siege: Starvation, Disease, and Death in the Warsaw Ghetto* (New York: Oxford University Press, 1992).

34. Browning, *Path*, pp. 59–61; 111–122.

35. Ibid., pp. 73–74; Ulrich Herbert, "Labour and Extermination: Economic Interest and the Primacy of *Weltanschauung* in National Socialism," *Past and Present* 138 (1993): 144–195; Peter Hayes, "Profits and Persecution: Corporate Involvement in the Holocaust," in *Perspectives on the Holocaust: Essays in Honor of Raul Hilberg*, ed. James S. Pacy and Alan P. Wertheimer (Boulder: Westview Press, 1995), pp. 51–73.

36. Franciszek Piper, "The System of Economic Exploitation," p. 47. For an extended discussion of the role of utilitarian and nonutilitarian rationalizations of the Holocaust, see the essays by Susanne Heime and Götz Aly, Dan Diner, David Bankier, and Ulrich Herbert, in *Yad Vashem Studies*, vol. 24, ed. Aharon Weiss (Jerusalem: Yad Vashem, 1994), pp. 45–145. However configured, the Holocaust frame of reference assumed a "surplus" of people. The slave trade frame of reference assumed a deficit of laborers.

37. Hilberg, *Destruction*, p. 529.

38. Himmler, quoted in Kwiet, "Forced Labour," p. 403 (October 1942).

39. From J. Goebbels, *Tagebuck*, 2 March and 30 September, 1943, quoted in Kwiet, "Forced Labour," pp. 403–404.

40. Thornton, *Africa*, pp. 53–71.

41. Arad, "Holocaust of Soviet Jewry," p. 23.

42. Miller, *Way of Death*, pp. 159–163. On attitudes toward women and children in the African slave trade and in Auschwitz, compare Claire C. Robertson and Martin A. Klein, eds., *Women and Slavery in Africa* (Madison: University of Wisconsin Press, 1983), esp. the introduction, "Women's Importance in African Slave Systems," pp. 3–25; Irena Strzelecka, "Women," in *Anatomy of the Auschwitz Death Camp*, pp. 393–411; and Helena Kubica, "Children," ibid., pp. 412–427.

43. See Richard B. Sheridan, "The Guinea Surgeons on the Middle Passage: The Provision of Medical Services in the British Slave Trade," *International Journal of African Historical Studies* 14 (1981):601–625; idem., *Doctors and Slaves: A Medical and Demographic History Slavery in the British West Indies, 1680–1834* (Cambridge: Cambridge University Press, 1985), pp. 108–126; Robert Jay Lifton and Amy Hackett, "Nazi Doctors," p. 303. On the role of Nazi medicine in the process of mass murder, see also Robert Jay Lifton, *The Nazi Doctors: Medical Killing and the Psychology of Genocide* (New York: Basic Books, 1986); Götz Aly, Peter Chroust, and Christian Pross, *Cleansing the Fatherland: Nazi Medicine and Racial Hygiene* (Baltimore: Johns Hopkins University Press, 1994); Paul Hoedeman, *Hitler or Hippocrates* (Sussex, England: Book Guild, 1991).

44. Walvin, *Black Ivory*, p. ix; Anna Pawelczynska, *Values and Violence in Auschwitz: A Sociological Analysis* (Berkeley: University of California Press, 1979), pp. 54–55.

45. See, inter alia, William A. Green, "Race and Slavery: Considerations on the Williams Thesis," in Solow and Engerman, *British Capitalism*, pp. 25–50; Thornton, *Africa*, pp. 137–138; 143–151.

46. Winthrop D. Jordan, *White Over Black: American Attitudes Toward the Negro, 1550–1812* (Chapel Hill: University of North Carolina Press, 1968); David Eltis, "Europeans and the Rise and Fall of African Slavery in the Americas: An Interpretation,"

American Historical Review 98 (1993):1399–1423; Philip D. Morgan, "Slaves and Livestock in Eighteenth-Century Jamaica: Vineyard Pen, 1750–1751," *William and Mary Quarterly* 52 (1995):47–76.

47. See, inter alia, Philip D. Curtin, *The Image of Africa: British Ideas and Action, 1780–1850* (Madison: University of Wisconsin Press, 1964); William B. Cohen, *The French Encounter with Africans: White Response to Blacks, 1530–1880* (Bloomington: Indiana University Press, 1980).

48. Magnus Morner, *Race Mixture in the History of Latin America* (Boston: Little Brown, 1967).

49. Albert A. Sicroff, *Les Statutes de pureté de sangre en Espagne, au XVI, et XVII siècles* (Paris, 1955).

50. Koonz, "Genocide and Eugenics"; George L. Mosse, *Toward the Final Solution: A History of European Racism* (New York: Harper and Row, 1978), pp. 215–231.

51. Franciszek Piper, "The Number of Victims," an essay in *Anatomy of the Auschwitz Death Camp*, pp. 61–76, esp. p. 64.

52. *The Diary of Anne Frank: The Critical Edition* (New York: Doubleday, 1987), pp. 265, 273, 316: entries of October 6, 9, and November 19, 1942.

❀ **5** ❀

The Armenian Genocide as Precursor and Prototype of Twentieth-Century Genocide

ROBERT F. MELSON

Twentieth-Century Genocide

During this century, the world has experienced four tidal waves of national and ethnic conflict and genocide in the wake of collapsing states and empires. These were punctuated by the First and Second World Wars and by the postcolonial and post-Communist eras. During the First World War and its aftermath the Ottoman empire collapsed, and it committed the first total genocide of the twentieth century against its Armenian minority.[1] In the same period, the disintegration of the German and Austro-Hungarian empires set off *Volkisch*, nationalist and fascist movements that repressed minorities and precipitated the Second World War. In the context of that war, the Nazis attempted to exterminate the Jews and Gypsies and committed partial genocide against other peoples. Following the Second World War, as former European colonial empires—notably Britain and France— withdrew from their possessions, they left behind fragile regimes that lacked legitimacy. Such "Third World" governments frequently ruled over culturally plural societies and tried to impose the hegemony of one ethnic group over the rest. In reaction, minorities rebelled and sought self-determination. This led to ethnic wars and genocide in places like Indonesia, Burundi, Sri Lanka, Nigeria, Pakistan, Ethiopia, Sudan, and Iraq. In the wake of the recent collapse of Communist regimes in the Soviet Union and former Yugoslavia, we are experiencing the fourth wave of nationalist upsurge, ethnic conflicts, and genocide. Meanwhile, as in contemporary Rwanda, it should be noted that the third wave of postcolonial genocide has not yet spent its force.

This chapter puts forth the position that the Armenian genocide was not only the first total genocide of the twentieth century but that it also served as the prototype for genocides that came after. In particular, the Armenian genocide approximates the Holocaust; but at the same time its territorial and national aspects, which distinguish it from the Holocaust, make it an archetype for ethnic and national genocides in the Third World, as well as in the post-Communist states.

This chapter offers a brief historical overview of the Armenian genocide, then compares that event first to the Holocaust and also to the Nigerian and Yugoslav genocides. The second set of cases represents contemporary instances of genocide in the Third World and the post-Communist states, respectively. The chapter concludes by raising a number of questions about the Armenian genocide and about genocide in general.

The Armenian Genocide

In traditional Ottoman society, Armenians—like other Christians and Jews— were defined as a *dhimmi millet*, a non-Muslim religious community of the empire. Their actual treatment by the state varied to some extent with the military fortunes of the empire, with the religious passions of its elites, and with the encroachment upon their land of Muslim refugees from the Balkans and the Caucasus and of Kurdish pastoralists.

Although by and large *dhimmis* (religious minorities) were free to practice their religion, they were considered to be distinctively inferior in status to Muslims.[2] However, in the nineteenth century, the Armenians challenged the traditional hierarchy of Ottoman society as they became better educated, wealthier, and more urban. In response, despite attempts at reforms, the empire became more repressive, and Armenians, more than any other Christian minority, bore the brunt of persecution.[3]

Throughout the nineteenth century, the Ottoman sultans were caught in the vise between great power pressures on the one hand and the demand for self-determination among their minorities on the other. By the time Abdul Hamid II came to power in 1876, he had set a course of political and social repression and technological modernization. Nevertheless, he could not halt the military and political disintegration of his regime, and he was replaced in 1908 by a political revolution of Young Turks with new and radical ideas of how to address the Ottoman crisis.

In the first instance, the Committee of Union and Progress (CUP), the political organization formed by the Young Turks, attempted radically to transform the regime following liberal and democratic principles that had been embodied in the earlier constitution of 1876. They hoped for the support of the Great Powers for their reforms, but neither the European powers nor the minorities reduced their pressures. On the contrary, they took the opportunity of internal Ottoman disarray and revolutionary transformation to press their demands, and between 1908 and 1912 they succeeded in reducing the size of Ottoman territory by 40 percent and its population by 20 percent.[4]

Concluding that their liberal experiment had been a failure, CUP leaders turned to Pan-Turkism, a xenophobic and chauvinistic brand of nationalism that sought to create a new empire based on Islam and Turkish ethnicity. This new empire, stretching from Anatolia to western China, would exclude minorities or grant them nominal rights unless they became Turks by nationality and Muslim by religion.

This dramatic shift in ideology and identity, from Ottoman pluralism to an integral form of Turkish nationalism, had profound implications for the emergence of modern Turkey.[5] At the same time, Pan-Turkism had tragic consequences for Ottoman minorities, most of all for the Armenians. From being once viewed as a constituent *millet* of the Ottoman regime, they suddenly were stereotyped as an alien nationality. Their situation became especially dangerous because of their territorial concentration in eastern Anatolia on the border with Russia, Turkey's traditional enemy. Thus, the Armenians, at one and the same time, were accused of being in league with Russia against Turkey and of claiming Anatolia, the heartland of the projected Pan-Turkic state.

This was the situation even before the First World War. When war broke out, however, the Young Turks, led by Talaat Pasha, the minister of interior, and Enver Pasha, the minister of war, joined the German side in an anti-Russian alliance that would allow Turkey to expand at Russia's expense. It was in this context of revolutionary and ideological transformation and war that the fateful decision to destroy the Armenians was taken.

By February 1915, Armenians serving in the Ottoman army were turned into labor battalions and were either worked to death or killed. By April, the remaining civilians were deported from eastern Anatolia and Cilicia toward the deserts near Aleppo in an early form of ethnic cleansing. The lines of Armenian deportees were set upon again and again by Turkish and Kurdish villagers who were often incited and led by specially designated killing squads, *Teshkilat-i Makhsusiye*. These units had been organized for their murderous purposes at the highest levels of the CUP.[6] Those Armenians who escaped massacre were very likely to perish of famine on the way. In this manner, between 1915 and the armistice in 1918, some 1 million people—out of a population of 2 million—were killed. Later, a half-million more Armenians perished as Turkey sought to free itself of foreign occupation and to expel minorities. Thus, between 1915 and 1923 approximately one-half to three-quarters of the Armenian population was destroyed in the Ottoman empire.

The Armenian Genocide and the Holocaust

The Armenian genocide and the Holocaust are the principal instances of total domestic genocide in the twentieth century. In both cases, a deliberate attempt was made by the government of the day to destroy in whole an ethno-religious community of ancient provenance. When one compares the situation and history of the Armenians in the Ottoman empire to the Jews in Europe, a pattern leading to genocide becomes apparent. It is a pattern that also reveals some significant differences, and it is those differences that link the Armenian genocide not only to the Holocaust but to contemporary instances of that crime. Let us first consider the similarities between the Armenian genocide and the Holocaust:

1. Under the prerevolutionary regimes in the Ottoman empire and Germany, Armenians and Jews were ethno-religious minorities of inferior status that had experienced rapid social progress and mobilization in the nineteenth century. These circumstances helped to create what came to be known as the "Armenian question" and the "Jewish problem." Armenians raised a "question" and Jews created a "problem," because neither the Muslim Ottoman empire nor Christian Europe were prepared to deal with low-status religious minorities that had become increasingly assertive and successful in the modern world.

2. Under the prerevolutionary regimes, Armenians may have suffered massacres, and Jews may have experienced discrimination in Germany as well as pogroms in Russia; but in none of these cases was a policy of total destruction formulated or implemented to resolve "questions" or to solve "problems." Genocide followed in the wake of revolutions in the Ottoman empire and Germany.

3. Following the reversals of 1908–1912, the CUP rejected Pan-Islam and Ottomanism as legitimating ideologies linking state to society and turned to Turkish nationalism and Pan-Turkism. The CUP identified the Turkish ethnic group as the authentic political community on which the Turkish state could and should rely, and by implication it excluded the Armenians from the Turkish nation.

The Armenians were in danger of being conceived as enemies of Turkey and of the Turkish revolution once Ottoman Turks came to view themselves not in religious terms but in ethnic terms. What made the Armenian situation significantly more dangerous than that of other minorities was the Armenian *millet*'s concentration in eastern Anatolia, an area that Turkish nationalists claimed to be the heartland of the Turkish nation. Moreover, the eastern *vilayets* (provinces) of Anatolia were on the Russian border, Turkey's traditional enemy, casting the Armenian presence in a sinister light.

In a similar fashion, a revolutionary situation in Germany allowed the Nazis to recast German identity and ideology. The German revolution destroyed the Weimar Republic, undermined democratic and socialist conceptions of legitimacy, and enabled the Nazis to come to power. Once the Nazis controlled the apparatus of the state, they set about recasting German political identity in terms of their racial and antisemitic ideology. They did this by excluding and expelling those whom they defined as "non-Aryans" and "Jews" from the newly valued and invented "Aryan" community.

4. When the First World War broke out, the CUP enthusiastically joined the Ottoman empire to the Germans against the Russians. This permitted Talaat and Enver to claim that the internal Armenian enemy was in league with the external

Russian foe. Wartime circumstances then were used to justify the deportation and destruction of the Armenian community.

Similarly, the Nazis launched the Second World War in order to carve out an
empire for Germany, and it was under wartime circumstances that they implemented their policies of partial genocide against Poles, Russians, and others and
their extermination against the Jews. In particular, they viewed the Soviet Union
as their principal foreign foe, and they assumed that it was ruled by a "world
Jewish conspiracy." Thus, in 1941, at the same time that they invaded the Soviet
Union, they launched the "Final Solution."

Thus did ideological vanguards use the opportunities created by revolution
and war to destroy ancient communities that had been judged to be "problematic" under the prerevolutionary regimes and "enemies" under revolutionary and
wartime circumstances. These elements—the prerevolutionary statuses of the victims and revolutionary and wartime circumstances—may be said to account for
some of the essential similarities between the two genocides. There were, however, significant differences as well.

The perpetrators of the Armenian genocide were motivated by a variant of nationalist ideology, the victims were a territorial ethnic group that had sought autonomy, and the methods of destruction included massacre, forced deportation,
and starvation. In contrast, the perpetrators of the Holocaust were motivated by
racism and antisemitism and ideologies of global scope; the victims were not a
territorial group, and so, for the most part, they had sought integration and assimilation instead of autonomy, and the death camp was the characteristic
method of destruction. A word needs to be said about these factors that differentiate the Armenian genocide from the Holocaust. It will be shown, however,
that it is precisely these differences that link the Armenian genocide to contemporary events.

Differences Between the Armenian Genocide
and the Holocaust

Like these similarities, the differences between the Armenian genocide and the
Holocaust may be plotted along the same dimensions: Jews and Armenians differed in status in the two empires; Nazi racist antisemitism differed significantly
from the Pan-Turkist nationalism of the Young Turks; and the killers of the
Armenians relied mostly on massacre and starvation rather than the death camps.

Like the Armenians in the Ottoman empire, the Jews were an ethno-religious
community of low status in Christian Europe. Unlike the Armenians, however,
who were the subject of contempt for being non-Muslims, the Jews of feudal
Europe became a pariah caste stigmatized as "killers of the Son of God." Thus,

Jews were not only despised in most parts of Europe, they were also hated and feared in a way the Armenians in the Ottoman empire were not.

In the nineteenth century, to the extent that the state became bureaucratic, the society meritocratic, and the economy capitalistic, Armenians and Jews began to advance in status and wealth. Indeed, it has been suggested that Armenian and Jewish progress was viewed as illegitimate and subversive, which precipitated antagonistic reactions both in the Ottoman empire and in imperial Germany.[7]

Here at least two variations may be noted. Whereas Armenians were a territorial group that increasingly made known its demands for greater autonomy and self-administration within the Ottoman system, Jews were geographically dispersed and thus, with the exception of the Zionists who sought a Jewish state in Palestine, most made no territorial demands on the larger societies in which they lived.[8] Instead, to the extent that they accepted the modern world, most Jews sought assimilation to the culture and integration into the wider society.

The reaction against Jewish progress, assimilation, and attempts at integration became a wide movement of European antisemitism, a form of racism that set up unbridgeable obstacles to Jewish inclusion. According to antisemites, Eugen Dühring, for example, not even conversion would allow Jews to become the equals of Germans or other Europeans. Already in 1881, he wrote:

> A Jewish question would still exist, even if every Jew were to turn his back on his religion and join one of our major churches. Yes, I maintain that in that case, the struggle between us and the Jews would make itself felt as ever more urgent . . . It is precisely the baptized Jews who infiltrate furthest, unhindered in all sectors of society and political life.[9]

According to Wilhelm Marr (another nineteenth-century antisemite), for example, Jews were not only an alien race, they constituted an international conspiracy whose aim was the domination of Germany, Europe, indeed, the whole world. Thus, antisemites founded not only a movement that opposed Jewish progress and assimilation, they formulated a far-reaching ideology that helped them to explain the vacillations and crises of the modern world. It was an ideology that came to rival liberalism and socialism in its mass appeal.

By way of contrast, no such ideology of anti-Armenianism developed in the Ottoman empire. Armenians may have been popularly despised for being *dhimmis*, or *Gavur* (infidels), and later, under the Young Turks, they may have been feared as an alien nation supposedly making claims to Anatolia, the heartland of the newly valued "Turkey." However, even Pan-Turkism left the door open to conversion and assimilation of minorities, something that racism and antisemitism explicitly rejected.

Moreover, though the Young Turks may have claimed that the Armenians were in league with their international enemies, especially the Russians, there was no equivalent in the Pan-Turkish view of the Armenians to the Nazis' hysterical struggle against the "Jewish spirit" that was said to linger in Germany and Europe even after most of the Jews had been murdered. Saul Friedländer has noted:

> It was the absolutely uncompromising aspect of the exterminatory drive against the Jews, as well as the frantic extirpation of any elements actually or supposedly linked to the Jews or to the "Jewish Spirit" . . . which fundamentally distinguished the anti-Jewish actions of the Nazis from their attitude toward another group.[10]

Thus, the Holocaust became centered not only in Germany but evolved into an international policy of mass murder and cultural destruction that included Europe and even the whole world. Finally, the death camp, a conception of the Nazi state, was an extraordinary organization, not seen before or since. It was a factory managed by the SS but staffed at all levels by the inmates themselves. Its primary aim was to dehumanize and kill its prisoners after confiscating their property and making use of their labor. Although Jews, like Armenians, perished in massacres and by starvation, the use of the death camp as a method of extermination differentiates the Holocaust from the Armenian genocide.

At the same time that these differences—the nationalist ideology of the perpetrators, the territoriality of the victims, and the methodology of destruction, especially expulsion and starvation—differentiate the Armenian genocide from the Holocaust, they link that earlier genocide to contemporary destructions in the Third World and in the post-Communist states. In that sense, as has already been noted, the Armenian genocide predates and partly encompasses both kinds of genocide and is, thereby, a prototype for genocide in our time. We now turn to an examination of the Nigerian and Yugoslav genocides and to their comparison to the Armenian prototype.

Nigeria

Genocide has been committed throughout the Third World. Following are a few examples: Indonesia, Burundi, Rwanda, Sudan, East Pakistan, and Iraq. In all of these instances, a shaky and hardly legitimate postcolonial state ruling over a culturally plural society attempted to establish the hegemony of a leading ethnic group over other ethnic segments of society. This attempt at domination provoked movements of resistance and self-determination, which the postcolonial state then tried to halt by force, including massacre and partial genocide.

Nigeria gained its independence from Great Britain in 1960. It was organized as a federation of three states, each centering on a major ethnic group. The northern state was dominated by the Hausa-Fulani, the western by the Yoruba, and the eastern by the Ibos. The major ethnic groups jockeyed for power at the federal level, but each had its "minorities" that felt discriminated against at the state level of the federation. The postindependence government, dominated by Hausa-Fulani Muslims, was resisted by southern, largely non-Muslim groups, especially the Ibos. In 1966, after a failed military coup, thousands of Ibos were massacred in northern Nigeria. In 1967, a year after the massacres, the Ibos tried to secede. They called eastern Nigeria "Biafra" and fought a war of self-determination until 1970, when their secession attempt collapsed.

During the war, over 1 million Biafrans starved to death as a result of the deliberate Nigerian policy of blockade and disruption of agricultural life. Thus, between 1966 and 1970, a "genocide-in-part" occurred in Nigeria, following the United Nations (UN) definition. It is important, however, to recall that what happened in Biafra differed from the Holocaust and the Armenian genocide in that the policies of the Nigerian Federal Military Government (FGM) did not include extermination of the Ibos.

Yugoslavia

A definitive history of the recent conflict in former Yugoslavia does not yet exist, but it is possible to render a provisional sketch. The Yugoslav disaster stems from the failure of the Communist regime to establish legitimate political institutions, a viable economy, and a compelling political culture. After Marshal Tito's death in 1980, ethnically based nationalist movements started to mobilize and to demand greater autonomy if not yet self-determination. The process of dissolution and disintegration was drastically accelerated with the rise of Slobodan Milosevic, who articulated an integral form of Serbian nationalism and irredentism that called for the creation of a Yugoslavia dominated by Serbia such as had existed after the First World War. This frightened the other nationalities and encouraged intransigent elements.

Milosevic's integral Serbian nationalism, in a context of Yugoslav and Communist institutional decay and insecurity, helped to sharpen ethnic enmities, strengthen centrifugal forces throughout the federation, and accelerate the processes of disintegration. Thus, on September 27, 1989, the parliament of Slovenia adopted amendments to its constitution giving the republic the right to secede from Yugoslavia. Thousands of Serbs demonstrated in Novi Sad, fearing for their status in an independent Slovenia. On July 3, 1990, the Slovenian parliament declared that the laws of the republic took precedence over those of Yugoslavia; on December 22, 1990, Slovenia reported that 95 percent of the voters supported a plebiscite on independence; and on June 25, 1991, Slovenia declared its independence from Yugoslavia.

A similar march of events occurred in Croatia, which declared its independence on the same day. The big difference between Slovenia and Croatia, however, was the presence of a large Serbian minority in the latter. Moreover, no sooner was independence declared in Croatia than the Franjo Tudjman regime launched an anti-Serb campaign that would have alarmed the Serbs, even if nationalist elements among them had not been earlier mobilized by Milosevic. Now that their kin were being threatened in Croatia, Milosevic and other Serbian nationalists could call forth the terrible history of the Ustasha genocide of the

Second World War to mobilize the Serbs against Croatian independence and in support of Serbian irredenta.

After June 25, 1991, when Slovenia and Croatia, in declaring their independence, thereby created Serbian minorities—especially in Croatia—the Serb radicals, using the cover of the Yugoslav army, launched an attack intended to incorporate Serbian-populated Croatian territory. To this end, Serbian forces not only initiated hostilities but set out on a path of terrorism and massacre in order to drive Croats out of areas that they desired to incorporate into Greater Serbia.

This policy of terrorism and ethnic cleansing accelerated with even greater ferocity against Bosnia when it declared independence on March 3, 1992. Indeed, in time, both Serb and Croat forces descended on Bosnia with the clear intention of carving up and destroying a state that initially had tried to stand aside from ethnic nationalism and had opted for a pluralist society. However, both Serb and Croat nationalists were intent on either carving up and destroying Bosnia or making it a rump state that would in time collapse. To this end, the Bosnian Serbs, led by their leader, Radovan Karadzic, a psychiatrist of Montenegrin origin, especially practiced massacre, ethnic cleansing, and cultural destruction against those they called the "Turks." Taken together, such policies of destruction on a wide scale are called genocide.[11]

Keeping Nigeria and Yugoslavia in mind, it is also important to note the great fear and insecurity that possess everyone when a government is challenged and a state begins to disintegrate. This great fear, especially in culturally plural societies, leads people to seek the shelter of families and kin and persuades various groups to band together for protection and to view one another as potential enemies.

Indeed, before a culturally plural state like Nigeria or Yugoslavia disintegrates, its politics may revolve about various ethnic issues of group status and the distribution of scarce goods; but once a state crashes, for whatever reasons, ethnic groups begin to fear for their lives, as well they should. Once a political order disintegrates, who can guarantee an ethnic group that its mortal enemies won't come to power and try to dominate it or even destroy it? It is this great fear that has seized all the groups in Yugoslavia, including those Serbs who are the main perpetrators of partial genocide.

The Armenian and Nigerian Genocides

In both the Nigerian and Bosnian cases, we can see some parallels to the Armenian genocide. A dominant ethnic group in a culturally plural society attempted to establish its hegemony. It was resisted by minorities that attempted to gain some form of autonomy or self-determination. In reaction, the dominant group perpetrated repression and genocide. Yet there are significant differences that may be even more instructive.

The crucial difference between a total domestic genocide, as occurred in the Armenian case, and a partial one, as occurred in Nigeria, can also be seen by comparing the two. Unlike the Armenians, once Biafra was defeated and the danger of secession passed, the Ibos were not massacred or further expelled from Nigeria. On the contrary, there was a genuine attempt to reintegrate the Ibo population into Nigeria when the war ended.

This difference may be due to two reasons. First, although the FGM was dominated by Hausa-Fulani elements, it included minorities in its leadership; indeed, General Yakubu Gowon, its commander, was a Christian from the north. Thus, the FGM never developed an ideology of "northernization" or "Muslimization" the way the Young Turks relied on Turkification and sought to create an ethnically homogeneous Turkey.

Second, the territorial issue, a crucial element in the Armenian case, was present in the Biafran case, but it worked in favor of the Ibos. The Ibos of the north were "strangers" and not "sons of the soil"; thus, they could not make a legitimate claim to northern territory.[12] Moreover, it is significant that the Ibos had their own area, which, except for its oil, the north did not covet. Once the Ibos were driven from the north back into their space and the Biafran secession was defeated, the northern elements in the army and elsewhere had succeeded in their major aims. Further massacre and starvation of the Ibos was unnecessary for ideological, territorial, or any other reasons, and the partial genocide ceased.

The Biafran state was never claimed as the "homeland" of the Hausa-Fulani in the manner that Anatolia had been staked out by the Turks. Thus, a federal solution to ethnic conflict could be implemented in Nigeria the way it could not in the Ottoman empire. The Armenians could not be driven back to "their" lands, since their lands were claimed to be the heartland of Turkey. Indeed, it may be suggested that this Turkish claim to Armenian lands was a major reason why the Armenian genocide, unlike the mass death of Biafra, became total in the manner of the Holocaust.

The Armenian and Bosnian Genocides

Two major similarities between the Armenian genocide and the partial genocide occurring in Bosnia should be apparent. Like the Young Turks, the Serbian—and to some extent the Croat—nationalists are also dreaming of a large state that would include their peoples and exclude other ethnic and national groups. Like the Armenians, the Bosnian Muslims, an ethno-religious community making claims to land, were being massacred and driven out by Serb and Croat nationalist movements that sought to incorporate their lands, "cleanse" the area of their presence, and destroy their culture.[13]

However, the status of Bosnia as an independent state recognized by the international community marks a significant difference between the situations of Ibos in Nigeria and of Armenians in the Ottoman empire. Neither Armenians nor Biafrans were widely recognized as members of independent states while their destructions were in process.[14]

Armenians were largely abandoned to their fate, in part because the genocide occurred in the midst of a world war. During the cold war, both the Eastern and

Western blocs discouraged movements of self-determination, fearing superpower involvement; and the African states did the same, fearing their own disintegration along ethnic lines. This may explain, in part, why Ibos, like Armenians, were also abandoned, except for some humanitarian relief.

That "partial" and not "total" genocide occurred in Bosnia, unlike Armenia, should be very cold comfort for the world community. Eighty years after the Armenian genocide and fifty years after the Holocaust, a European state practiced genocide while Europe, the United States, and the United Nations seemed unable or unwilling to halt the slaughter. If genocide cannot be halted in Europe, it cannot be stopped or prevented anywhere else, certainly not in places like Rwanda or Burundi. This, then, is the "New World Order" we face as we stand at the threshold of the third millennium.

Conclusion

The Armenian genocide was a precursor and prototype for the Holocaust in that a minority of traditionally low status that had successfully begun to enter the modern world was set upon and nearly destroyed in the context of revolution and war. However, the Holocaust was not an identical replay of the Armenian genocide. The Armenian case differed from the Holocaust in three dimensions: First, the Young Turks were largely motivated by an ideology of nationalism, whereas the Nazis were moved by an ideology heavily influenced by social Darwinism and racism. Second, the Armenians were a territorial group concentrated in the eastern *vilayets* of the empire, and they had historical claims to the land. In contrast, the Jews were not a territorial group. To destroy the Jews, the Nazis had to formulate a policy of genocide that transcended Germany and even Europe. Lastly, the method of destruction of the Armenians centered on their deportation, shooting, and starvation, whereas in the Holocaust the majority of Nazi victims perished in death camps. This is not to deny that a large percentage of Nazi victims also perished by shootings and starvation in the manner of their Armenian predecessors.

It should be noted, however, that it is precisely these differences that enable the Armenian genocide to be a precursor and prototype for contemporary genocide. Indeed, one conclusion we can draw from this analysis is that the Armenian genocide is a more accurate archetype than is the Holocaust for current mass murders in the postcolonial Third World and in the contemporary post-Communist world. In Nigeria and Yugoslavia, for example, as in the Armenian case and unlike the Holocaust, the perpetrators were driven by a variant of nationalism, the victims were territorial ethnic groups aiming at some form of autonomy or self-determination, and the methods of destruction involved massacre and starvation.

I have tried to show that the Armenian genocide was a precursor and prototype both for the Holocaust and for contemporary nationalist genocides. In no case was it an exact template for later genocides, nor were these duplicates of the Armenian case; nevertheless, the Armenian pattern of destruction set a terrible precedent for our century and for the future.

NOTES

This chapter was first delivered as a paper at "The Armenian Genocide: An Eighty Year Perspective, 1915–1995," a conference held at the University of California–Los Angeles, April 7–8, 1995. An earlier version of this paper was presented at "Remembering for the Future International Conference on the Holocaust," held at Berlin, Germany, March 13–17, 1994.

1. On the basis of the United Nations definition, it is possible to distinguish between "genocide-in-whole" and "genocide-in-part." In this chapter, a "total domestic genocide" is a genocide-in-whole directed against a group of a state's own society, whereas "partial" genocide is a genocide-in-part. Total genocide implies extermination and/or massive death of such order that a group ceases to continue as a distinct culture and collectivity. Partial genocide stops at extermination and the annihilation of culture. For further discussion concerning these distinctions, see Robert F. Melson, *Revolution and Genocide: On the Origins of the Armenian Genocide and the Holocaust* (Chicago: University of Chicago Press, 1992), pp. 22–30.

2. See Roderic H. Davison, "Turkish Attitudes Concerning Christian-Muslim Equality in the Nineteenth Century," *American Historical Review* 4 (1954):844–864.

3. See Melson, *Revolution and Genocide,* pp. 43–69.

4. See Feroz Ahmad, *The Young Turks* (Oxford: Clarendon Press, 1969), p. 153.

5. See Bernard Lewis, *The Emergence of Modern Turkey* (New York: Oxford University Press, 1961).

6. See Vahakn N. Dadrian, "Genocide as a Problem of National and International Law: The World War I Armenian Case and Its Contemporary Legal Ramifications," *Yale Journal of International Law* 2 (Summer 1989):221–334.

7. See Melson, *Revolution and Genocide,* p. 137.

8. For discussions of the ideological crosscurrents that affected Jews in this period, see Jonathan Frankel, *Prophesy and Politics: Socialism, Nationalism, and the Russian Jews, 1862–1917* (Cambridge: Cambridge University Press, 1981), and Ezra Mendelsohn, *The Jews of East Central Europe Between the World Wars* (Bloomington: Indiana University Press, 1983).

9. Cited in Paul R. Mendes-Flohr and Jehuda Reinharz, *The Jews in the Modern World: A Documentary History* (New York: Oxford University Press, 1980), p. 273.

10. See Saul Friedlander, "On the Possibility of the Holocaust: An Approach to a Historical Synthesis," in *The Holocaust as Historical Experience,* ed. Yehuda Bauer and Nathan Rotenstreich (New York: Holmes and Meier, 1981), p. 2.

11. According to a Helsinki Watch *Report,* genocide is taking place in Bosnia and other former areas of Yugoslavia. Although all sides have been accused of atrocities, it is the Serbian side, especially in Bosnia, that is charged with genocide. See *War Crimes in Bosnia-Hercegovina* (New York: Human Rights Watch, 1992), p. 1.

12. See Donald L. Horowitz, *Ethnic Groups in Conflict* (Berkeley: University of California Press, 1985), for discussions of how groups validate their claims to status and power. A basic distinction lies between those who have historically dominated an area and migrants who are new arrivals. The first, the "sons-of-the-soil," make their claims on the basis of ancestral privilege; the second cannot. Thus, Armenians in Anatolia could make a claim to the land, the way Ibos in the north could not.

13. As of this writing (January 1996), Bosnian Muslims and Croats are part of a shaky confederation. In the recent past, however, Croat and Bosnian Croat troops, like their Serbian counterparts, were equally intent on dismembering Bosnia and expelling Muslim populations from territories they claimed for Croatia.

14. See Richard G. Hovannisian, *Armenia on the Road to Independence* (Berkeley: University of California Press, 1967), and John J. Stremlau, *The International Politics of the Nigerian Civil War* (Princeton: Princeton University Press, 1977).

❀ **6** ❀

The Comparative Aspects
of the Armenian and Jewish
Cases of Genocide:
A Sociohistorical Perspective

VAHAKN N. DADRIAN

Introduction

This chapter is an attempt to interrelate, within the confines of a few written pages, the two principal genocides of this century in order to encourage emerging efforts to shift attention from case studies to comparative studies of genocide. Case studies by nature are narrowly conceived undertakings, no matter how unusual the event they may cover. They are self-contained discourses, and as such they have limited value for science and scholarship. Yet nations that have been victimized by genocide tend, by the very nature of that victimization, to inflate their experiences to the level of historical uniqueness. Actually, there is some validity to this stance. Wholesale and exterminatory massacres do constitute unique experiences, but they are not necessarily exclusive experiences. It is this aspect of the argument that renders the issue problematic; the idea of uniqueness does not need to be entwined with that of exclusivity.

The reason for this is as logical as it is simple. Although genocidal victimization may be a unique experience for the victim group in question, in a broader perspective, one that transcends the confines of the victim experience, that uniqueness may be superseded by conditions of comparability, that is, elements suggesting commonality in relation to the experience of other victim nations. Moreover, the sense of uniqueness belongs to the domain of emotive self-images intruding into the functions of analysis. It is in the nature of things that the universal significance of a case of genocide becomes diminished to the extent that it may be portrayed as a singular case. This inverse relationship is intrinsic to the canons of analytical reasoning and methodology; in principle, singularity simply precludes universality.

In the case of genocide, unlike other crimes, the ramifications are global and devastating for humanity at large. Therefore, the importance of the task of analyzing genocide is matched and even exceeded by the importance of the task of preventing it. But the notions of singularity and exclusivity impede rather than facilitate such analysis, which is a prerequisite for prevention. The pitfalls of this emphasis on singularity were recently underscored by a noted author in the field of genocide studies, who also happens to be a Holocaust survivor. I refer to Robert Melson, who wrote:

> Some of us who have turned to the Holocaust as a reference point for comparison have done so in order to keep its message alive. Indeed, I would suggest that if the Holocaust is not compared to past and contemporary instances of genocide, its message and significance will wither. In time, its history will become like the Crusades or the Chmielnitski massacres, for example, the preserve only of Jewish mourners, narrow specialists, and Holocaust deniers.[1]

Comparison is essentially an analytical task, whereas case studies, in their general thrust, are descriptive because their texture disallows the depiction of common denominators among several cases. The determinants of genocide are to be discerned in the interplay of such common denominators. In brief, only comparative studies can yield carefully delimited generalizations about the nature and mechanics of genocide as a general problem of humanity. Generalizations of this type constitute the core of scientific endeavor affording progress toward the ultimate goal of averting genocidal cataclysms. The conditions under which Auguste Comte, the founder of the modern discipline of sociology, relinquished his involvement in mathematics and statistics and initiated that new discipline are instructive in this respect. As a contemporary of the French Revolution, he was aghast at the explosion of brutality and lethal violence under its banner ideals; as he acutely felt the need to avert such explosions in the arena of human conflict, he postulated his maxim about social engineering, *Voir pour prévoir, prévoir pour prévenir.* Translated broadly, it means, "It is necessary to understand in order to be able to anticipate, and it is necessary to anticipate in order to be able to prevent."

Even though generalizations, which are distilled from comparative studies, reflect the common features and characteristics among the cases being compared, their elaboration does not need to exclude other features that are not common. One may not limit oneself to the quest for common denominators in order to do justice to the comparative method. By taking into account those factors that are rather uncommon, one may in fact underscore the importance of the common features. In other words, the depiction of certain dissimilarities among two or more cases of genocide may serve to enhance the significance of the similarities yielding a set of generalizations. Precisely for this reason and in preface to our discussion, below I single out and review a number of dissimilarities between the Armenian and Jewish cases of genocide.

I
The Incidence of Dissimilarities in the Two Cases

Important dissimilarities come to the fore when one tries to apply the victimological perspective. How did Armenians and Jews become victims for dissimilar rather than similar reasons? The first thing to consider is their status as victim populations, for it is here that they emerge as victims for opposite reasons. The Armenians were destroyed in their natural homeland—their ancestral territories—in historic Armenia. Consequently, the devastation enveloped the very fabric of the Armenian nation in terms of its social, religious, and cultural institutions. An indigenous civilization with its legacy of antiquity was torn asunder by a nation that had secured possession of these territories through invasion and conquest. In the Jewish case, the victims were destroyed as an immigrant population by the rulers of the host country. The cultural losses sustained thereby involved the treasures of a diasporan subculture.

A similar condition of victimization for dissimilar reasons concerns the matter of the religious status of the two victim groups. The Armenians were essentially destroyed on account of their identification with Christianity in general; the Jews were mainly destroyed for a diametrically opposite reason, namely, for their dissociation from Christianity and for all that such dissociation implied. Granted that neither the Nazis nor the Young Turks, the Ittihadists, were in any significant way religious people, but vast segments of the populations they controlled allowed themselves to be swayed by the animus of religion and, accordingly, either assisted in the process of destruction or condoned it.

One should not underestimate the ballast of Martin Luther's legacy of anti-Jewish animosity in Protestant and even Catholic Germany. In the Turkish case especially, Muslim fanaticism was ignited through the manipulation of religious hatred that reached its acme by the proclamation of "holy war" against "the infidels." As in the case of Nazi Germany, so in the case of the Turks, the exterminatory massacres were somehow an extension of the legacy of religiously fueled anti-Armenian sentiment prevalent in the era of Sultan Abdul Hamit. The massacres of this period were framed in terms of Muslims pitted against infidel Armenians. There was hardly any reference to Turks being described as confronting Armenians. It may be argued in this context that another significant difference is this very fact of antecedent massacres. Whereas the Armenian genocide may be considered as the culmination of a cumulative process of decimation of the Ottoman Armenian population through episodic massacres, there are no comparable antecedents in the history of German-Jewish relations. The historical evolution of antisemitism in modern Germany never found expression in pogroms that erupted, for example, in tsarist Russia in the decades preceding World War I.

This very fact of a history of past massacres in the case of the Armenians is another dissimilarity. Total helplessness had rendered the Armenians exceedingly vulnerable in the 1894–1896 and 1909 massacres, thereby amplifying the scale of their decimation, which is estimated to involve about 200,000 victims. Consequently, small bands of Armenian patriots—identified with Armenian political parties—had stockpiled arms and ammunition in the years following these massacres in anticipation of future massacres against which they intended to defend themselves and their communities. This condition, coinciding with the conditions of World War I, in which Turkey had intervened, particularly aggravated the plight of the general Armenian population targeted for destruction. At the rudimentary stages of the genocide, the leadership of the Armenian nation throughout the length and breadth of the Ottoman empire was subjected to an array of tortures as their tormentors held them responsible for the creation of these stockpiles. In his memoirs, U.S. Ambassador Henry Morgenthau describes the fiendishness of the methods used to torture the victims.

> One day I was discussing these proceedings with Bedri Bey, the Constantinople Prefect of Police. With a disgusting relish Bedri described the tortures inflicted. He made no secret of the fact that the Government had instigated them, and, like all Turks of the official classes, he enthusiastically approved this treatment of the detested race. Bedri told me that all these details were matters of nightly discussion at the headquarters of the Union and Progress Committee. Each new method of inflicting pain was hailed as a splendid discovery, and the regular attendants were constantly ransacking their brains in the effort to devise some new torment. Bedri told me that they even delved into the records of the Spanish Inquisition and other historic institutions of torture, and adopted all the suggestions found there. Bedri did not tell me who carried off the prize in this gruesome competition, but common reputation throughout Armenia gave a pre-eminent infamy to Djevdet Bey, the Vali of Van, whose activities in that section I have already described. All through this country Djevdet now became known as the "marshall blacksmith of Bashkale," for this connoisseur in torture had invented what was perhaps the masterpiece of all—that of nailing horseshoes to the feet of his Armenian victims.[2]

Obviously there was no comparable resort by the Jewish victims to such stockpiling of weapons, as they had no reason to anticipate comparable massacres and, hence, felt no need. This Armenian resort to anticipatory defense measures was and still is being used by the advocates of "the Turkish viewpoint" as a principal ground for justifying governmental anti-Armenian measures. These are portrayed as intended to quash rebellion while blaming the victims as guilty of stabbing Turkey in the back in her struggle of life and death.

Another dissimilarity relates to the diverseness of the mechanics of genocidal mass murder. Given the primitive conditions and level of technology in Turkey in World War I, in the Armenian case the operations of mass murder were particularly harrowing, as dying was made a prolonged and agonizing experience for most of the victims, especially the old, the women, and the children that made up the deportee convoys. In his narration of the mechanics of the Armenian genocide, Ambassador Morgenthau gives an example of a massacre in which a "mob of Turkish peasants" used "clubs, hammers, axes, scythes, spades and saws."

> Such instruments not only caused more agonizing deaths than guns and pistols, but, as the Turks themselves boasted, they were more economical, since they did not involve the waste of powder and shell. . . . Bodies, horribly mutilated, were left in the valley, where they were devoured by wild beasts. After completing this destruction, the peasants and gendarmes gathered in the local tavern, comparing notes and boasting of the number of "giaours" that each had slain.[3]

As if to emphasize the inordinate significance of this mode of killing the victims, Morgenthau decried "the utter depravity and fiendishness of Turkish nature, already sufficiently celebrated through the centuries."[4] Despite diverse circumstances, even though victims of mass murder share a common fate, the incidence of dissimilarity in the use of techniques of killing has some significance in itself. It not only brings into relief the disparities of the levels of culture and civilization of the perpetrator groups but may differentially accentuate the memories and the pain of remembrance of future generations identified with the victim populations.

Closely allied to this notion is the issue of the implementation of the genocide as distinct from such other issues as decisionmaking, supervision, and control. In the Jewish case, the bulk of the victim population was destroyed within the confines of concentration camps where the killing operations were streamlined, mechanized, and systematic through the use of advanced technology. Therefore, through the method of division of labor, special cadres were selected and trained to carry out the actual killing operations. In the case of the Armenians, however, there was no similar specialization of perpetrator groups. By Turkish admissions, large segments of the provincial population in particular willingly participated in regional and local massacres.[5] These acts were made relatively easy because the killing fields were not concentration camps but the remote valleys, gorges, hills, mountaintops, rivers, and lakes of Turkey and the Black Sea littoral.

Two types of mass murders especially punctuate the harrowing character of the Armenian genocide. Tens of thousands of Armenians, by special maritime arrangements, were taken to and drowned in the high seas that enveloped the many districts of the province of Trabzon constituting a narrow littoral on the Black Sea.[6] Similar drowning operations were conducted in areas through which run the Euphrates River and its tributaries. As Ambassador Morgenthau wrote, "The most terrible scenes took place at the rivers especially at the Euphrates.

... In a loop of the river near Erzinghan ... the thousands of dead bodies created such a barrage that the Euphrates changed its course for about a hundred yards."[7] The other type of mass murder underscores the holocaustal dimensions of the Armenian experience. Nearly the entire population of Muş city, Muş plain, in Bitlis province, consisting of about 100 villages with a total population of 80,000–90,000, was burned alive in stables, haylofts, and farm yards. The commander of the Ottoman 3rd Army, one General Mehmed Vehib, in his testimony to the Inquiry Commission that was attached to the Turkish military tribunal investigating the wartime massacres, described the procedure involved with particular reference to Tchreeg, one of those villages.[8] There were many instances of such holocaust in the provinces of Van and Aleppo. A case in point is the holocaust at Deir-Zor. "On October 9, 1916, Moustafa Sıdkı [Deir Zor's police chief from 1914 to 1918] ordered great stocks of wood to be piled and 200 cans of petroleum spilt on to the whole stock; he then lit it and had 2,000 orphans with bound hands and feet thrown into the pyre." This is the statement of an Armenian lawyer, a surviving eyewitness who, in a memorandum dated January 31, 1921, informed the Armenian patriarch of Istanbul of this instance of a holocaust.[9] In his postwar memoirs, German Colonel Ludwig Schraudenbach, the commander of the 14th German-Turkish Division fighting in the area of these massacres, confirms this "most shocking atrocity. . . . Children pressed between wooden planks, tied to them, and burnt to death."[10]

The types of atrocities detailed in the memorandum sent to the Armenian patriarch represent the memories and images that Armenians continue to harbor, assigning to their genocide the attribute of singularity. But types of atrocities belong to the category of the mechanics of genocide; they are but details in the overall scheme of genocide in which the experience of victimization is lethal, massive, and terminal insofar as the process of extermination is concerned. In this process, victim differences involving nationality, gender, socioeconomic class, and age dissipate and collapse as the engine of genocidal mass murder functions to level these differences with swift finality. The degree of importance one may attach to the method of destruction is, therefore, eclipsed by the overriding significance of the genocidal character and outcome of that destruction. Singular or unique deaths do not necessarily yield a singular or unique genocide. Victim nations may be drawn and, therefore, respond primarily to these particular aspects of the genocide, defining it as a unique experience. But as far as scholarship is concerned, what matters most is the common genocidal fate in which these particular aspects of such victim nations tend to configure.

A signal dissimilarity attaches to the level of genocidal decisionmaking involving actual intent. Even though Holocaust literature is dominated by the argument that Hitler and his cohorts were totally and unconditionally committed to the extermination of the Jewish race immediately upon their seizure of power in interwar Germany, the historical evidence is indicative of a different pattern of behavior by these Nazi leaders. What is discernible in this pattern is the gradual evolution of an attitude where actual genocidal intent appears developmentally to be crystallizing itself.

Apart from sporadic and general statements advocating the destruction of the Jews, by all accounts there is no definite and firm decision at the outset to exterminate them wholesale; there seems to be no clear sign of focusing on a signal lethal option, preempting all other options, to "solve" the "Jewish question." In fact, evidence demonstrates that the Nazis eventually opted for the Holocaust largely by default. In the initial stages of the initiative to get rid of the Jews, the Nazi concern was mainly economic. Indeed, as the plenipotentiary of the Four-Year Plan, Hermann Göring, in November 1938, assumed control of the planning and implementation of Jewish policy, and that policy was defined as "the Elimination of Jews from the German *Economy*" (emphasis added). In relaying Hitler's respective order, Martin Bormann, head of the Nazi Party Chancellery, chose to define the respective measures as "the beginning of the final solution to this problem."[11]

The subsequent draft plans revolved around the central issue of Jewish immigration from Germany, Austria, and other incorporated areas. The coercive aspects of this policy reduced emigration to expulsion, which, however, at times was staggered to allow the victim émigrés and their families to join the workforce and integrate into the economy of the host countries, even though they were being subjected to thorough expropriation by the Nazis themselves. After the German invasion and victory in Poland, emigration gave way to organized deportations to various localities in the newly formed *Generalgovernment* in the occupied center of Poland. Yet this was considered an intermediary stage for the long-range plan of resettling "millions of Jews," perhaps in Madagascar, a jungle island lying in the Indian Ocean about 250 miles off the southeastern coast of Africa.

Involved in all these arrangements were the Jewish Emigration Section of the Gestapo, Section III of the Foreign Office, and the central security bureau of the SS (the *Reichssicherheitshauptamt*, or RSHA), all eager to streamline the procedures for purging Germany of the Jewish element through emigration rather than extermination. Moreover, as late as September 21, 1939, Reinhard Heydrich, the head of the RSHA, defined the "ultimate goal" as the "emigration of the Jews [which] must be completed later." The absence of a genocidal policy—as distinct from genocidal thought—in the treatment of the Jews by the antisemitic Nazis up to the period ushering in the war against the Soviet Union is described by Raul Hilberg:

> As a plan for administrative actions, the idea [of genocide] was not yet obvious or even feasible; but as a thought of something that could happen, it was already ingrained in German minds. . . . Hitler did not order the annihilation of the Jews immediately upon the outbreak of the war. Even Hitler shrank from such a drastic step. Even Hitler hesitated before the "final solution." Even Hitler had to be convinced that there was no other choice.
>
> . . .

From 1938 to 1940, Hitler made extraordinary and unusual attempts to bring
about a vast emigration scheme. The biggest expulsion project, the Madagascar plan,
was under consideration just one year before the inauguration of the killing phase.
The Jews were not killed before the emigration policy was literally exhausted.[12]

Notwithstanding the sporadic pronouncements of Hitler (including those in
Mein Kampf) and of his cohorts, it is clear that Nazi antisemitic activities were not
necessarily on a genocidal track. However coercive and brutal, the measures of expropriation and expulsion were not exterminatory. In a recently publicized document, it is revealed that even beyond the year 1940 the Nazis, led by Hitler, were
intent on resettling rather than literally exterminating the Jews. Here is a portion
of that document explained; the event described refers to December 1941.

> Heydrich revealed that the Führer had authorized Himmler to resettle Jews from all
> German-controlled territories into certain Russian areas in the northeast. Bühler be-
> lieved that Heydrich had spoken of eleven million Jews. To accomplish this task,
> Heydrich said, Himmler would need exclusive control of resettlement, and he would
> forbid any interference with the task given him by the Führer. Bühler wanted to know
> if this new policy meant that there would be no more dumping of Jews into the
> *Generalgouvernement,* and that those Jews already brought there would soon be re-
> moved. Heydrich said that he hoped so. Apparently mollified, Bühler agreed to re-
> port this information to Frank.[13]

No such options were considered by the Young Turk Ittihadists for the emigration of the Armenian population. In discussing the doom of "two million or more
Armenians" slated for wholesale "deportation," Ambassador Morgenthau observed, "As a matter of fact, the Turks never had the slightest idea of reestablishing
the Armenians. . . . When the Turkish authorities gave the orders for these deportations, they were merely giving the death warrant to a whole race; they understood this well, and, in their conversation with me, they made no particular attempt to conceal the fact."[14] In other words, at the very outset the genocidal intent
was there; the respective decision was firm and implacable. The German state
archives, containing a vast amount of wartime confidential and secret reports from
German ambassadorial, consular, and military officials stationed in Turkey during
the war as that country's allies, amply and unmistakably attest to this fact.[15]

This feature of dissimilarity is critical in the sense that it allows an examination into the conditions under which Nazi measures against the targeted Jewish
population changed direction, ultimately acquiring a genocidal thrust. In other
words, the Holocaust was an emergent rather than a firmly shaped and prefixed
undertaking; it evolved and became a by-product of the dynamics of war and its
consequences. Involved here are such developments as intensification of the existing conflicts, new opportunities to reduce inhibitions and increase the temper
for boldness in action, and a significant change in the nature, dimension, and

composition of the potential victim population. These developments were due to both the swift military successes of the Wehrmacht in the initial stages of the campaign against the Soviet Union and the attendant, vast aggregation of the potential victim population. The inclusion in that population of millions of eastern Russian Jews, as opposed to European and German Jews, qualitatively and quantitatively altered the equation as far as Nazi designs of victimization of the Jews were concerned.

There is another aspect to this problem that arises out of the contentions of most, if not all, Holocaust scholars who insist on the exclusivity of the tragedy of the Holocaust. In differentiating the Armenian genocide from the Holocaust, many of these noted Holocaust scholars assert, for example, that even though the Armenian genocide comes closest to the Holocaust, still, in one major respect, it cannot be compared to it. The core of their assertion is the argument that the Nazi genocide against the Jews was not only total and unconditional but also had a generic thrust in that it aimed at the obliteration of the Jewish race on a global rather than on a regional scale. In support of this argument, these scholars invariably refer to the fate of the Armenian populations of Istanbul and Smyrna, who are portrayed as people who, in fact, were spared and, therefore, escaped deportation and eventually survived. In recently rejecting the inclusion in a text describing the Armenian genocide (intended for Israeli high school students slated to be educated about other cases of genocide), the commission in charge of examining that text, with a view to making appropriate recommendations to the Israeli Ministry of Education, added to these cities Jerusalem and Aleppo. In other words, since so many Armenians escaped destruction, there could not be a design to eradicate the Armenian people as a whole. Hence, or so goes the argument, it is even questionable whether the term "genocide" applies to the Armenian experience. The inaccuracies and misinterpretations associated with these contentions epitomize the pitfalls of cursory or defective knowledge on the subject.

First of all, Istanbul Armenians were not spared deportation and destruction, as has been maintained for so long by Turks and non-Turks alike. In addition to the 2,345 intellectuals, businessmen, clergymen, teachers, and others who had been rounded up and mostly destroyed at the initial stage of the genocidal enactment,[16] subsequently, and in stages, 30,000 other Istanbul Armenians were quietly but systematically seized and eliminated, as indicated by confidential German reports. Ambassador Morgenthau further stated that the Ittihadists had plans to eliminate the rest of the Armenian population of Istanbul. Only the Turkish military setbacks and ancillary handicaps prevented the perpetrators from completing this task. As to Smyrna (Izmir), here again faulty information led to the inaccurate belief that the Turkish authorities, on their own volition, spared the Armenians of that port city. The fact is, however, that Liman von Sanders, the German general in charge of the military security of that zone, threatened the Ittihadist governor of the province with the use of military force to block the deportation of the rest of that city's Armenian population after one contingent was already deported; as the German Foreign Office in Berlin supported the stance of the German general, the Turkish governor felt constrained to oblige.[17]

This raises the issue as to how thorough or complete the Nazi sweep was of the destruction of the targeted Jewish population. Were there no clusters of Jewish groups that escaped or were allowed to escape the lethal clutches of that sweep? In other words, is it warranted for students of the Holocaust to differentiate the Jewish victims from other victim groups, such as the Armenians, by the yardstick of the optimal scale of destruction avowedly characterizing the Holocaust? Given the vastness of the subject, only a few illustrations may be offered to question this line of thought. Out of the total 515,000 German Jews, the Nazis allowed 165,000 of them to emigrate to other countries. In 1939, the combined German-Austrian Jewish population had "shrunken to half of its original size" for the same reason.[18] In the Armenian case no person was allowed to emigrate or to leave the country under any circumstances following the initiation of the empire-wide anti-Armenian measures. Moreover, out of a total population of 330,000 Jews in France, "around 80,000 were victims of the Final Solution."[19]

Do these facts on incomplete instances of mass murder diminish the severity of the Holocaust taken in its totality as a genocidal undertaking? If mitigating circumstances are adduced to explain away these instances of incomplete mass murder or to call them mere aberrations, do they only apply to the Holocaust? The leeways through which the Nazis allowed exceptions to certain categories of Jews to be exempt from mass murder are evident. Hilberg cites Heydrich's "old-age ghetto" in Theresienstadt as a "reservation for old and sick Jews." However dubious in purpose this arrangement was, the old and sick Armenians, slated for destruction, were afforded no such exemption, not even on paper. As late as February 1943, Himmler ordered his subordinates "to permit the Jews in the old people's ghetto of Theresienstadt to live and die there in peace." Change of administrative personnel and dramatic changes in the fortunes of war were factors, however, to the aggravation of the plight of these Jews, many of whom subsequently ended up being transported to death camps to share the fate of their conationals.[20] There were similar cases of aberrations with respect to children and young females in the Armenian victim population. They escaped destruction through compulsory proselytizing, induced conversions, adoptions, concubinage, slave labor, bribery, and isolated instances of pity and compassion by individual Turks, Kurds, and other Muslims. As in the case of the Young Turks, so in the case of the Nazis, as far as official policy was concerned, exceptions and exemptions were more often than not either indulgences meant to deflect from the capital crime of genocide or tactical adaptations to pressing needs and exigencies. One can afford to neglect certain parts of an organism after having targeted and succeeded in destroying the core of that organism. In this sense, it is the ultimate outcome of the operation that counts, not the aberrant details of the operation.

Finally, reference may be made to the aftermaths of both genocides, marking diametrically opposite end results. In the Jewish case, there was retributive justice to a significant degree; it was attended by widespread German contrition, the payment of indemnities on a massive scale, and correlative atonement. The entire process culminated in a new drive for political regeneration that ushered in the establishment of the state of Israel. In a macabre yet auspicious way there was an attempt at redemption for all the losses and ordeals the Holocaust entailed for the victim population. One may say that, obversely, all these measures of remorse, reparation, and redemption were denied the surviving Armenian population, whose genocidal victimization is still being denied with persistence and truculence by the perpetrator camp. This can only serve to compound the effects of the genocide. Instead of the appearance on the scene of a residual and liberated new Armenian nation, the surviving Armenian population was in part dissolved in a number of host nations through dispersal or endured seven decades of new hardships under the heels of an oppressive Communist regime. In terms of future developments, this is perhaps the most crucial aspect of the problem of dissimilarity under review here.

II
The Elements of Convergence of the Two Cases

As stated in the introduction to this chapter, the primary purpose of comparing cases of genocide is to distill from them certain common characteristics on the basis of which one may be able to offer some limited generalizations. Such a methodology requires, however, a statement in which genocide is defined as a concept. For the present purposes, it may, therefore, be suggested that three major components are discernible in the definition of genocide. First and foremost, genocide presupposes an intergroup conflict with a history of growth and escalation. Second, genocide serves as a radical device to resolve that conflict; in this sense, genocide is functional. Third, genocide is afforded by a critical disparity of power relations obtaining between the parties to the conflict. In the final analysis, genocide is, therefore, an exercise of power with lethal consequences for the weaker party being victimized by the overwhelming power of the perpetrator group. Within this framework, the mutual relations between a potential perpetrator and a potential victim group—and especially the conflictual aspects of these relationships—emerge as the central problem in the occurrence of genocide. Accordingly, the discussion below focuses on these relationships in the quest for similarities that may lend themselves to the drafting of a modest set of generalizations.

The Historical Ballast of Persecution

Jews and Armenians are two distinct peoples of antiquity. Their histories span millennia punctuated by episodes of sustained persecution. The cumulative effect of this exposure to persecution could not fail to impact upon the collective psyche of these peoples and contribute to the cultivation of defense mechanisms geared to the need for survival as ethnic-national entities. As a result, there developed an ethos of submissiveness intended to mollify the agents of persecution and, thereby, avoid confrontation and peril. With respect to Jewish survival techniques, Hilberg calls this phenomenon "compliance" syndrome, which is anticipatory and often automatic. "The Jews anticipated the force and complied . . . in advance."[21] Extending this notion to his explanation of Jewish behavior during the Holocaust, Hilberg refers to "a two-thousand-year-old experience. In exile . . . the Jews had always been in danger; but they had learned that they could avert danger and survive destruction by placating and appeasing their enemies."[22] Identical patterns developed among the Armenians as a subject people. Yielding completely to their subjugators was a technique for ethnic-national survival, but such submissiveness had consequences that thrust the condition of survival to the threshold of permanent peril. Indeed, when submissiveness becomes predictable for a potential perpetrator group, the submissive group automatically becomes a potential target for abuse; it becomes fair game for victimization because its submissiveness can be taken for granted.

Throughout their histories it is in this sense that Jews and Armenians earned a reputation as tested targets for an assortment of methods of victimization. In a perverse twist of labeling, both peoples acquired a notoriety as ideal objects of persecution, akin to the notoriety of some perpetrator groups. By the same token, both peoples developed an inner toughness that served to preserve their sense of ethnic identification but that was masked by their functional submissiveness. The cultivation of ethnocentrism under such circumstances was conducive to the maintenance by both peoples of a minority status among a host of dominant groups, a status that was portentous in several respects.

The Ramifications of a Minority Status

In sociological terms, the concept of minority has less to do with the criterion of numbers of people and has more to do with that of domination; in this sense, it has reference primarily to quality of status rather than to quantity of people. The logical counterpart to minority is, therefore, not majority but the dominant group. In some instances, a numerically inferior group may have the status of dominant group, and a numerically superior group may be relegated to a minority status. In the genocidal victimization of the Armenians and the Jews, their unchanging minority status in relation to the perpetrator groups, possessing a dominant status, played a major role. It is, therefore, important to understand the specifics of the relevance of this dominant group-minority relationship.

One of the by-products of minority status in societies that have no democratic tradition, are nonpluralistic, or are mainly nominally pluralistic, is the exposure of a given minority to the practice by the dominant group of prejudice and discrimination. Such a practice, as a rule, entails a variety of disbarments, exclusions, and even legal disabilities imposed upon the minority directly or indirectly, overtly or covertly. No minority can escape the psychological and social-psychological effects of such an exposure. Interactive mechanisms in the evolution of mutual relations begin to shape up in such a way as to reflect the consequences of such prejudice and discrimination. In important respects, the behavior of the minority is conditioned by the treatment it is accorded by the dominant group. In this sense, such behavior becomes a function of that treatment. In a pilot study of German Jews who were confined to a ghetto in Frankfurt am Main in the pre–World War II years in Germany, Louis Wirth, one of the pioneers of the Chicago School of Sociology, came up with the following conclusion: When a group of people is treated differentially over a period of time, in due course they will begin to think of themselves as being, in fact, different and may even end up acting differently.[23]

This is an allusion to the by-products of ghettoization and to the rise of an allied ghetto mentality. As such, it is an allusion to obstacles of assimilation through the creation of walls of separation from the mainstream of society. The transition from a condition of denial of the means of assimilation to that of eventual unassimilability is one of the major issues straining dominant group-minority relations. The more the Armenians were degraded by the dominant Muslims for their Christian faith and debarred from many spheres of social and national life, the more they clung to that faith and to all that is implied by it. The ethnocentrism of the Armenians that developed as a result in no small way contributed to the aggravation of the Turko-Armenian conflict, which always existed in an embryonic form. The same argument more or less applies to the Jews. One can hardly separate Jewish ethnocentrism from the tribulations that the Talmudic faithful endured throughout the centuries.

In both cases, the legacy of religion not only in some way preconditioned the minority status but, in the process, left its imprint upon the ethnic consciousness and subdued ethnic assertiveness of both peoples.[24] In brief, the religious identities of both peoples were pregnant with the rudiments of conflict, with a potential to erupt in major conflagrations. As Richard L. Rubenstein observes in this connection, "It is my conviction that the Holocaust can be understood with least mystification if we do not ignore the abiding elements of conflict characterizing the relations between the Jews and their neighbors throughout the entire period of their domicile in the European Christian world."[25] But the consummation of intergroup conflict involves power relations in which the factor of disparity in strength and leverage is likely to determine the outcome. Given the minority status of the Jews and the Armenians, their disadvantage emerges here as a structural problem. Their position of weakness or relative impotence was determined by the arrangements of the sociopolitical system in which they were pitted against dominant groups equipped with most of, if not all, the resources of power. This fact leads to the consideration of another common denominator.

The Vulnerability Factor

As minorities, Jews and Armenians have been frequent targets of persecution throughout history but especially in modern history. As noted above, this is a known fact. What needs to be emphasized, however, is the related fact that their having been recurrent targets, without the ability to counteract or retaliate, proved to be an experience that compounded their condition of vulnerability. When a group is subjected to repeated acts of victimization and the victimizers are not held accountable, for one thing the vulnerability of the victim group is confirmed through the fact of impunity accruing to the perpetrator. But beyond that, and all things being equal, the confirmation yields for the perpetrator, or other potential perpetrators, prospects of new levels of victimization; that confirmation, in fact, becomes a source of new incentives for victimization by way of sheer extrapolation on the part of the potential victimizer.

From a well-known fact, one does draw inferences and projects them into the future. In other words, the impunity accruing to a victimizer functions to amplify the vulnerability of the victim. Armenian and Jewish histories are punctuated by episodes of this type. The anti-Jewish pogroms of 1881–1882 and the 1903 Kishinev massacre in tsarist Russia in the decades preceding World War I are two such examples. They not only confirmed the vulnerability of the Jews, they portended developments capable of compounding that vulnerability. By the same token, one may argue that both the Abdul Hamit–era massacres in the 1894–1896 period and the 1909 Adana massacres dramatically exposed the vulnerability of the Armenians in the Ottoman empire.

The absence of any significant measure of retributive justice in the aftermath of all these massacres immensely aggravated the plight of the Ottoman Armenian population, rendering it an easy target for optimal destruction. In fact, one may even assert that the World War I Armenian genocide is foreshadowed in this series of untamed massacres. Two authors who personally examined the 1894–1896 massacres, by way of on-the-spot investigations, prophetically foretold at that time the demise of Ottoman Armenians through a major holocaust. One of them was an American—a student of the Civil War—who boasted of his "rather keen appetite for facts."[26] The other was noted British ethnographer William M. Ramsay, who in 1897 predicted the genocidal fate of the Armenians with these words: "The Armenians will in all probability be exterminated except the remnant that escapes to other lands."[27]

In discussing tsarist intentions about the Jews, Rubenstein allows that "the ultimate aim of Russian policy in the aftermath of the events of 1881 was the total elimination of the Jews."[28] He recognizes even a transfer of the condition of vulnerability from the Jews to the Armenians by the establishment of precedents, such as the tsarist pogroms that preceded the Abdul Hamit–era massacres. The impunity of one perpetrator group by way of contagion impinged upon the deadly motivations of another, thereby bringing into acute relief the vulnerability of Ottoman Armenians. It is in this sense that Rubenstein observes the existence of "an eerie parallel between the beginnings of the process which led to the destruction of European Jews and the one leading to the destruction of another 'elite minority,' the Armenians."[29]

Another aspect of the vulnerability syndrome has a paradoxical twist and is an extension of the effects of the structural barriers imposed upon the Jews and the Armenians. As degraded and often despised minorities, they were debarred from certain occupations and offices, most notably the military, the government, and the civil service. As preemptive and exclusionary as such arrangements were, they impelled—if not compelled—these two peoples to pursue other alternatives and forego the military and the government. The result was that appreciable numbers among them cultivated skills and aptitudes through which they prospered. Instead of being confined to the limited incomes of salaried employment in government, the military, and the civil service, they expanded and opened up new vistas offering possibilities for unlimited riches through the vehicles of trade, commerce, and industry.

The economic ascendancy that many of them thereby achieved and the wealth they had acquired proved a liability, however, especially in times of economic crises affecting the respective dominant groups. It did not matter that this type of ascendancy was made affordable in default, that is, mainly as a result of debarments described above. The ability to harness to advantage such debarments and attain relative affluence proved a liability in relation to the resentment of the dominant groups that might be struggling economically. In democratic and pluralistic societies, economic preponderance is a distinct source of power, impinging upon all spheres of life, including polity. But the societies enveloping the Armenians and Jews as minorities were apt to consider such preponderance as an unwarranted anomaly calling for remedies. It may, therefore, be proposed that when economic ascendancy is attended by political impotence, in times of acute national crises, the combination may prove perilous for the minorities. This represents an aberrant form of vulnerability that has plagued Armenian and Jewish efforts to coexist with antagonistic dominant groups. The vulnerability stems from the cardinal fact that because of their minority status they were denied access to resources of power within the sociopolitical systems of which they were a part.

The critical significance of this economic factor in the vulnerability syndrome of both peoples was cast in stark relief in the course of their genocidal victimization. It not only aroused the inveterate cupidity of the manifold casts of perpetrators, but, in several respects, economic considerations became codeterminants in genocidal decisionmaking and genocidal enactments involving both victim groups. (Hilberg has an entire chapter on this subject, subsumed under the title "Expropriation.")[30] This was even more so in the Armenian case. Not only German, Austrian, and American but authentic Turkish sources attest to the incidence of a genocide that was largely based on economic calculations, projections, and designs. The goal was to invest Muslim Turks with economic power and promote the formation of Turkish commercial classes to supplant those among the non-Muslim minorities, particularly the Armenians. It was a violent form of enacting a massive redistribution of wealth.

This fact was implicitly acknowledged by Halide Edib, a prominent Turkish feminist writer who had close ties to Ittihadist leaders. She wrote, "Besides this political argument . . . there was a strong economic one, morally supported by the Germans. This was to end the economic supremacy of the Armenians, thereby clearing the markets for the Turks and the Germans."[31] In his August 19, 1915, report to Ambassador Morgenthau, Aleppo's veteran American consul, J. B. Jackson—whose district was the scene of untold acts of plunder, robbery, and pillage by the Turks—characterized the ongoing Armenian genocide as "a gigantic plundering scheme as well as a final blow to extinguish the race."[32] In his memoirs, Morgenthau describes the economic animus in the enactment of the genocide. In the narration of one particular encounter with Mehmed Talât, the architect of the Armenian genocide, the latter is portrayed as having impetuously demanded that two American life insurance companies, New York Life Insurance and Equitable Life of New York, "send us a complete list of their Armenian policy holders, they are practically all dead now. . . . It of course all escheats to the State. The Government is the beneficiary now." This "most astonishing request . . . was too much, and I lost my temper," wrote the ambassador.[33]

There was one more element of vulnerability afflicting these two victim groups in particular. Neither the Armenians nor the Jews had a parent state to warn, threaten, counteract, or retaliate against the perpetrator groups. They had been, and at the time of their demise they were, virtually orphan nations. The perpetrators could, therefore, afford to discount a direct confrontation with any state entity with a high stake in their fates. This element of vulnerability was further accented by the passive attitude of the world powers. Pleading intense preoccupation with warfare and with the objective of ultimate victory, they allowed both genocides to run their course without any significant measure of preventive intervention on their part. This fact reinforced the assessment of the Nazis and the Young Turk Ittihadists that their targeted victims were fair game. Passivity and inaction by these powers were conditions that, in the minds of the perpetrators, were converted into a license for mass murder.

The inclination for such an inference is explained in American sociologist W. I. Thomas's notion of "definition of the situation." According to this notion, if men define situations as real, they are real in their consequences. The dismal failure of the Nazi efforts to induce the Western powers, especially France, to help resettle the Jews of Germany and Austria in their territories is underscored by the attitude of French Foreign Minister Georges Bonnet, who, in an exchange with German Foreign Minister Joachim von Ribbentrop in December 1938, rebuffed the latter on this issue. In fact, Bonnet asked Ribbentrop to prevent German Jews from coming to France, adding that France was thinking of shipping 10,000 Jews somewhere else, probably Madagascar; concluded Ribbentrop, "No country wished to receive them."[34] This kind of attitude prompted even Hitler to lament in January 1939 the plight of the Jews with these words: "It is a shameful example to observe today how the entire democratic world dissolves in tears of pity, but then, in spite of its obvious duty to help, closes its heart to the poor, tortured

Jewish people."[35] Three years later, when the destruction process was in high gear, Dr. Joseph Goebbels, a top Nazi leader, made the following entry in his diary on December 13, 1942: "At bottom . . . I believe both the English and the Americans are happy that we are exterminating the Jewish riffraff."[36] All this led to the suspicion "in the Jewish ranks" that "the Allies secretly approved" the Nazi campaign of annihilating the Jews.[37]

As to the Ittihadists, based on past experiences, they were convinced that they would again have a more or less free hand in bringing into play their anti-Armenian scheme, which this time involved the introduction of a "final solution" with regard to the Armenian population of the Ottoman empire. The exigencies of the war, in which practically all the Great Powers were embroiled, fortified that conviction. So much so, in fact, that they completely ignored the formal and ostensibly solemn warning of the Allies—England, France, and Russia—who, on May 24, 1915, when the genocide was being initiated, declared they would hold responsible all Turkish officials and other people implicated in the mass murder of the Armenians.[38] If anything, however, the tempo of the genocide was intensified and accelerated in the wake of this proclamation. The significance of the spirit of disdain and defiance, implicit in this sequential response, was exceeded only by the significance of the patent failure of the Allies to live up to their commitment when Turkey lay prostrate at the end of the war and sued for armistice.

In holding Turkey accountable for the atrocities against the Armenians, the Allies in 1915 had introduced the concept of "crimes against humanity," which was later adopted by the prosecutors at Nuremberg and subsequently incorporated into the Preamble of the United Nations (UN) Convention on Genocide.[39] The legal condemnation of the Holocaust and the conviction and sentencing of the Nazi perpetrators were acts that were essentially predicated upon this concept of "crimes against humanity." One of those who was thus convicted in Nuremberg allowed in his memoirs that the Holocaust and the related crimes were afforded due to the failure of the victors to exact retribution from those guilty of crimes against humanity in World War I. He maintained that such prosecution "would have encouraged a sense of responsibility on the part of leading political figures [i.e., Nazis] if after the First World War the Allies had actually held the trials they had threatened."[40] Nowhere is this more patently attested to than in a famous statement attributed to Hitler, who is quoted as saying, "Who after all is today speaking of the destruction of the Armenians" *(Wer redet heute noch von der Vernichtung der Armenier)*.[41] In other words, the impunity associated with the perpetration of the Armenian genocide not only highlighted the abiding vulnerability of the Armenians but had such repercussions as to bring into relief the analogous vulnerability of the Jews.

This is one instance where the principle of common features entwines with the principle of common links. In this sense, the Armenian genocide is not only a precedent but also a source of instigation for the enactment of the Holocaust; it incited the criminal instincts of the Nazi perpetrators by exciting their unbridled racist and nationalist ambitions.

For all these reasons, one should not underestimate this third element of vulnerability so gravely imperiling the survival of the Jews and Armenians. And that perilousness demonstrates how the internal vulnerability of a minority can be immeasurably magnified when combined with external vulnerability. It may best be described as the absence of external deterrence in face of internal threats of destructive designs against a vulnerable minority. That peril is aptly articulated by Hilberg who, speaking of the doom of the Jews, states, "The Jews of Europe had no allies. In its gravest hour Jewry stood alone."[42] Yet this is a statement that accurately describes a condition, without placing it in a context where one can relate to analogous phenomena, in order to achieve a deeper level of penetration. As noted at the outset, this is a problem intrinsic to all case studies, which are self-contained discourses lacking a transcendental, analytical bent by the exploration of the comparative method. The pathos for exclusive singularity undergirds the entire framework of Hilberg's monumental treatise, which, accordingly, ends with a lamentation reflecting that pathos. In explaining why the Jews became the prime targets of the Nazis, Hilberg maintains that "historical precedents . . . determined the selection [of the Jews], which for centuries had been the standby victim of recurring destruction" and prepossessingly concludes that "no other group could fill this role so well. None was so vulnerable."[43]

The Opportunity Structure

However motivated, tempted, or eager, no potential perpetrator can proceed from contemplation to action without suitable opportunities. This is a basic law of criminology encompassing many forms of criminal behavior. More often than not, the greatest restraining force for criminally inclined individuals or groups is not the penal codes of criminal justice but, instead, want of suitable opportunities. It is no coincidence that the two major genocides of this century were consummated in the vortex of two global wars. There is, therefore, an intrinsic, acute relationship between the concepts of modern warfare and the opportunity structure, in the sense that the exigencies and emergencies of warfare are pregnant with uncommon opportunities for illicit behavior by state apparatuses, governments, monolithic political parties, or military juntas. The utilization of vehicles for such behavior calls, therefore, for a brief revue.

The nature of warfare is such, for example, that as a rule it allows legislative authority to subside, if not to vanish entirely, with the executive branch of the government as the main beneficiary of the "emergency powers" accruing to it. In a war, the bastion of power is usually the executive branch. As the authority of the legislative branch either subsides or vanishes altogether, the power of the executive increases substantially. Emergency powers are expressive of the supreme opportunities that a war yields in this regard. In both systems, the Nazi and the Young Turk Ittihadists—the principal agents of these powers—have been the so-called "security forces" comprising a vast network of outfits; they were invested with levels of power that in most cases bordered on license for criminal abuse.

Perhaps the greatest source of power in an oppressive society in times of war is the military establishment that is identified with the authorities in charge. To the extent that the outcome of the war hinges on military performance, military authorities will acquire inordinate power and, accordingly, will be catapulted into relative predominance. Genocide not only requires opportunistic decisionmaking, its execution depends on functional efficiency. In addition to planning and administering the logistics involved, there has to be a command-and-control setup to ensure a reasonably smooth operation. The goal is optimal destruction at minimal cost. This is a task for which the specialized skills of the military are needed.

In both cases of genocide, the military played a crucial role. Involved were not just regular officers but officers who were intensely committed to the respective ideologies and goals of the Nazis and Ittihadists. Within this framework of loyalty and dedication, they performed critical staff work, maintained secrecy and discipline, and participated in field operations as commanders of killer bands. Such terms as "Nazi officers" and "Ittihadist officers" are descriptive of the potentially lethal process of indoctrinating military officers with political party credos and teachings and, in general, of politicizing the military or segments of it. War emerges here as an ideal opportunity for harnessing political power into military power as an instrument of genocide.

The dynamics of such a process of power amplification were such that the vulnerabilities of the Jews and Armenians as minorities increased in proportion to this growth of power; the stronger the victimizers became, the weaker became the victims. This is a mechanism that ultimately leads to what might be called "victim entrapment."

In the Armenian case, the Turks used four devices to amplify their power while increasing the vulnerability of the Armenians. First, they suspended the parliament; it was prorogued just before the initiation of the genocide and was reconvened when that genocide had all but run its course. Second, they introduced a system of temporary laws, the framing of which became the prerogative of the executive, that is, the Ittihadist power-wielders. Third, armed with these powers, they launched a program of massive arrests in all parts of the Ottoman empire. Nearly all community leaders, intellectuals, educators, ranking clergymen, and political activists were simultaneously rounded up in nightly surprise raids, deported; most of them were subsequently liquidated. Finally, in order to further emasculate the victim population and reduce it to easy prey for eventual annihilation, all able-bodied Armenian males were conscripted in three stages as part of the general mobilization. Very few of them survived the ensuing operations of summary executions or extirpation through other lethal measures. The resort to these measures was considerably facilitated by the continuation of the state of siege and martial law.

In the Jewish case, similar procedures were adopted. The emasculation of the Jewish community in Germany was more progressive in its course, as its initiation dated back to the interwar years. Its first stage—the promulgation of the

March 23, 1933, Enabling Act—had a general thrust and was not specifically directed against the Jews. As in the case of the Ittihadist initiative described above, the Nazis managed to institute an act through which they would be empowered to make laws without the approval of the German parliament, the *Reichstag*. The five articles of the act all but destroyed the German constitution. As in the case of the Young Turk Ittihadists, the Nazis subsequently embarked upon their deadly scheme of *Gleichschaltung*, whereby they substituted Nazi power for parliamentary power. With the outbreak of World War II, however, the Enabling Act acquired special significance for the Jews, as it was renewed in 1939 and 1942 in conformity with its article 5, which required renewal every four years. These renewals imparted a semblance of legitimacy to the array of anti-Jewish measures adopted by the various agencies of the Nazi-dominated government.

The principal rationale for targeting the Jews and Armenians during these two global wars was the designation and the decrial of both groups as "internal foes." This way, they could be considered as legitimate targets for destruction; after all, enemies in warfare are meant to be destroyed in pursuit of victory. Genocide thus becomes an integral part of warfare, an extension of the external war—internally. Here, the social-psychological mechanism of interactive behavior described above, involving the reliance on the mechanism of "definition of the situation," came into play. No matter how inaccurate, misperceived, or distortive, when a discordant or potentially harmful minority is defined as an "internal foe" by a dominant group waging an exhaustive war, the subsequent treatment accorded to that minority will be attuned to that definition. Definitions of situations, no matter how unreal or misleading, do indeed have consequences, and the standards used to fashion such definitions are determined by the more powerful party to the conflict, that is, the dominant group. Such power, indeed, yields manifold latitudes to contrive and impose arbitrary definitions, affording abusive or criminal actions against the group denounced, degraded, and targeted within the framework of the definition in question.

The exigencies of war provided another set of opportunities for the perpetrators. There is a need for methods and instruments geared to facilitating the process of destruction. In other words, as already noted, there is a need for functional efficiency. The standard mechanism in all these definitions that applied to the Armenians and Jews was the act of labeling them as actual or potential "traitors," "enemies of the state." For victimization to have an appearance of validity, if not legitimacy, the victims have to be stigmatized first; labeling is intended to serve that purpose.

At the level of actually implementing a scheme of genocide, the opportunity factor emerges as pivotal. The maxim employed here by the perpetrator is "optimal results at minimal losses." To achieve such a goal, the victim population must be trapped by methods of deception, deflection, and, when necessary, coercion. The element of surprise is part of this procedure. The most striking and, at the same time, the most functional method of trapping the targeted Jewish and

Armenian populations was the reliance on the use of the term "deportation." The term was easy to explain and defend in the context of wartime exigencies. It allowed the victims to acquiesce to what it denoted, without much pondering as to what it might connote to the perpetrators. To reinforce the imagery of a temporary inconvenience, the perpetrators contrived such ancillary terms as "relocation" (*Aussiedlung, Evakuierung, Wohnsitzverlegung, Umsiedlung*); in Turkish, the Ittihadists used the words *tehcir, tebdili mekân*.

In the Nazi case, if one disregards the operations of the *Einsatzgruppen*, the mobile killer bands, there were mostly the death camps. In the Ittihadist case, there were no such camps but open-ended traps of all kinds of death and destruction. Thus, the reliance on euphemisms, involving code words for genocidal killing operations, had a definite function. Once dislocated and removed from their cities, towns, and villages, the victim populations were totally defenseless. Coercive hardships, despair, and physical isolation combined to render them an easy prey for disposal. Deportation had the additional function of creating a condition where destruction became substantially facilitated; it created a temporary concentration and density of population that, for purposes of targeting, is an ideal condition. The cycle of trapping thus reaches its terminal and lethal stage.

This process of destruction by way of deportation was attended by a host of auxiliary measures endemic to wartime emergency conditions. They included control of nearly all channels of internal and external communications of those in the targeted victim populations who were placed under clandestine surveillance. The victim populations underwent fragmentation in the manner in which they were subjected to deportation, especially in the Armenian case. As a result, clusters of populations were kept in the dark as to one another's conditions and the overall fate of the entire population. Again, in the Armenian case, the process of destruction was immensely facilitated by two types of procedures. Due to a general mobilization, most able-bodied men were conscripted and removed from the fold of their families. As already described, they were then handled separately by military authorities. At the first opportunity, those remaining—the young and the old males—were separated from the deportee convoys and were then promptly liquidated, often in front of their female relatives.

The ultimate weapon that was forged and amply used by the Nazis and Ittihadists in connection with the opportunities afforded by the two global wars was the type of outfit most suited for the performance of inexorable killing operations. The Young Turk Ittihadist leadership called it the "Special Organization" (*Teşkilâtı Mahsusa*), which was largely, almost entirely, comprised of felons, convicts, and repeat criminals. They were released from the prisons of the Ottoman empire and carefully examined by teams consisting of medical experts, War Ministry staff officers, and representatives of the Justice Ministry in charge of the Ottoman prison system. After one week of training at the camp grounds of the War Ministry, they were put in special brigand (*çete*) uniforms and sent to the interior of the country to carry out their secret missions. They were deployed at remote and strategic spots through which the multitudes of deportee convoys were expected to pass. The standard procedure was to set upon these convoys and slaughter them on the spot, after robbing and plundering them. These killer bands were led by select army staff officers. The logistics and related aspects of planning were arranged by Department II at the Ministry of War and Ottoman General Headquarters in close cooperation with the secret Directorate of the Ittihad Party, often portrayed as the Central Committee of the party.[44]

The creation of special units to destroy the Jewish victim population is meticulously detailed by Hilberg.[45] The roles of *Einsatzgruppen* are of particular significance, underscoring the paramount role of the SS and police units affiliated with it, especially in occupied Russia.[46] But superseding in importance these roles, relative to this discussion, is the involvement in killing operations of convicts, mobilized and directed by the SS. This organization was branded a criminal organization by the International Military Tribunal in Nuremberg. Foremost in this connection were some of the units operating under the command of Erich von dem Bach-Zelewski, SS *Obergruppenführer*, and general of the Waffen SS and Police. The number of troops under his command was greater than that of the *Einsatzgruppen*. Von dem Bach had up to two divisions at his disposal. These divisions included the Dirlewanger Brigade, "which was composed of habitual criminals." Dirlewanger, the commander, was a convict in his own right. Among the victims of the von dem Bach killer bands were 363,211 Jews.[47] For his part, noted author Robert Jay Lifton emphasizes the role at Auschwitz of "hardened criminal psychopaths" joining the SS personnel there in killing operations.[48]

All these arrangements raise the question as to specifically how and by whom they were made. What is the source of authority in terms of ultimate instances and intermediary instances of authority involving a hierarchical structure? By what criteria and at what level have these authorities claimed legitimacy and, accordingly, tried to legitimize the entire lethal undertaking? These issues are addressed below.

The Decisive Roles of Two Monolithic Political Parties

Holocaust and genocide literature is dominated by a central theme about the fundamental problem as to who the ultimate authors of genocidal initiatives are. Due to the application of massive and lethal state force and the complex organization needed to mobilize such force through institutional channels, the vast majority of scholars involved in genocide studies depict the state as the supreme author in this respect. After all, the sovereign state is the embodiment of legitimate power that, at will, can be converted into coercive force by simply applying and exerting that power. Moreover, the levers of state organization are equipped to handle the task of streamlining the genocidal enactment. The works of noted author Irving Louis Horowitz epitomize this conceptual orientation.[49]

The flaw in this approach is that it issues from a perspective in which the relationship of formal authority to informal authority is not properly assessed. By definition, the state is simultaneously the locus and the expression of formal authority. Under more or less normal circumstances, that authority is predicated upon the principle of legitimacy, which not only serves to sanction the authority of the state but also circumscribes the parameters of that authority while conditioning the terms of its application. Even in times of war, there are limits as to the extent to which these parameters may be enlarged and the conditions—under which force may be used—may be relaxed. In other words, in origin, structure, and function, the state is not geared to conceiving, organizing, and implementing a monstrous crime such as genocide represents. As a rule, formal authority precludes such a recourse to criminality. In order for a state to get involved in the business of genocidal enactments, it has to undergo structural changes and transform itself into an engine of destruction. In other words, it has to be criminalized.

The only instrument capable of generating such a transformation is a type of informal authority that is in ascendance and in rivalry with the authority of the state. Driven by an inveterate urge for power, the agents of such authority compete for the resources of the state. In the two genocides under review here, these agents were none other than the combative and daring leaders of two monolithic political parties that were animated with revolutionary and radical designs. I refer, of course, to the Nazis (the National Socialist Party) and the Young Turk Ittihadists (the Committee of Union and Progress).

As they proceeded to entrench themselves in their respective positions as monolithic parties—in the course of which they had to overcome obstacles, resistance, and threats—they drifted into progressively more radical ideologies and postures. Their drive for supreme domination culminated in the seizure of the reins of power over the respective states. In the modern history of sovereign states, this is perhaps the most dramatic and portentous juncture, where the bearers of informal authority overwhelm the formal authority of the state apparatus. What is even more critical, however, is the fact that with seizure of power the informal authority of the party does not evaporate or subside. Merging with the formal authority of the state organization that the party now controls, it emerges in a reinforced mold of informal authority, holding sway over the key agencies of the government identified with that state. This is a process of intrusion in and permeation and domination of the state apparatuses, as a result of which the functions of the state are subverted for the benefit of the party and party programs and ideologies are superimposed upon governmental agencies. In brief, for all practical purposes, the state is reduced to a tool of the party and its ideological interests.

These considerations suggest, therefore, that the focus of attention be shifted from states to political parties capable of displacing state power and substituting for it party power and leverage. A state, thus divested of or impaired in the free use of its means of authority, can hardly be considered a determinant in the conception and enactment of the crime of genocide. It is a historical fact of paramount import that the architects of the genocides of the Jews and Armenians were placed in the highest leadership strata of the Nazi and Ittihadist parties. This means that in order to examine and comprehend the overt as well as covert aspects of both genocides it is necessary to examine the leadership, ideology, structure, and inner workings of the two political parties that, in fact, became substitutes for the governments they supplanted and usurped. As Ambassador Morgenthau observed, "The Young Turks were not a government; they were really an irresponsible party, a kind of secret society, which, in intrigue, intimidation, assassination, had obtained most of the offices of state."[50] Commenting on the Nazis in the same vein, a German author recently noted that the German "state apparatus was controlled by the staff of Hess and the party-chancellery of Martin Bormann."[51]

Nowhere is the convergence of the Jewish and Armenian cases of genocide so dramatically revealed as in the exposure of the crucial, initiatory roles the two parties played. The act of initiation was intimately connected with two analogous top-secret conferences in the course of which a final decision was reached to liquidate the two victim populations. The January 20, 1942, Wannsee Conference is a well-known fact. What is less emphasized, however, is that even though there were some professional civil servants and servile bureaucrats attending that conference it was the purest form of party decision reached by those potentates of the party whose prime and exclusive loyalty was not to the German state but to the *Führer*, Adolf Hitler. The deliberations took place in the central office of National Security, run by the SS.[52] The idea was to render Germany "free from the Jews" (*Judenfrei*).

An almost identical conference took place in Istanbul, then the Ottoman capital, shortly after Turkey unilaterally intervened in the war. It was a major link in the chain of secret party enclaves meant to radically resolve the Armenian question. As in the case of Wannsee, the five participants included the highest ranking party leaders, such as party boss Mehmed Talât; doctors Mehmed Nazım and Behaeddin Şakir, the most powerful two members of the party's Supreme Directorate; Seyfi Düzgören, the head of counterintelligence and guerrilla war at the Ottoman General Headquarters; and Ismail Canbolat, head of the National Security office (*Emniyeti Umumiye*). The blueprint that resulted from this conference outlined the measures to be taken and the methods to be used for the liquidation of Ottoman Armenians.[53] What is so remarkable about this document is the fact that the actual process of destruction and its outcome confirm the authenticity and operativeness of the blueprint, serving as it did as a basic directive for the organization of the Armenian genocide.

The distinct and nearly exclusively genocidal roles of the two political parties are underscored by the fact that the party executioners had sworn their oath of allegiance not to the state, nation, country, or any other symbol but to Adolf Hitler and national socialism, on the one hand, and to Ittihad and its mission on the other. In interpreting this ritual, Robert Jackson, chief counsel for the United States at Nuremberg, wrote this:

> The membership took the Party oath which in effect, amounted to an abdication of personal intelligence and moral responsibility. This was the oath: "I vow inviolable

fidelity to Adolf Hitler; I vow absolute obedience to him and to the leaders he desig-
nates for me." The membership in daily practice followed its leaders with an idolatry
and self-surrender more Oriental than Western.[54]

Likewise the Ittihadist operatives, agents, and killer-band leaders were sworn
party loyalists and felt hardly any obligation to the state. Their oath included the
commitment that should they ever reveal a party secret or disobey a command of
the central authorities of the party they would be targeted for destruction. Special
Organization Chieftain Major Yakub Cemil, who played a major role in the
Armenian genocide, openly declared: "If the party ordered me to kill my father, I
would not hesitate for a moment."[55] Informal authority has optimal scope for exercise, because, unlike a state organization, it does not have to observe fixed or
preordained rules and regulations. Precisely for this reason, it can afford to be irresponsible and dispense with the need for accountability. These are conditions
that not only allow but stimulate, if not encourage, deviant or criminal behavior.
The genocidal enterprises reviewed here were essentially the by-products and
consequences of the exercise of informal authority by political parties that held
the levers of power of a state but also had covert genocidal agendas.

The organizational makeup of the two parties was such as to allow the leadership strata to rely on a level of discipline on the part of the committed party faithful that exceeded the functionality of the most dutiful bureaucrats engaged by the
two respective states. Some illustrations are in order. The Third Reich of the Nazis
was administered and controlled by a network of *Gauleiters*, all of whom were devoted—if not fanatic—party luminaries. The entire system of internal security,
police, intelligence, and the rest was run by select and trusted party zealots. These
were the essential components of the gigantic machinery through which the destruction process was consummated with the help of a network of co-opting or
submissive functionaries of the state representing formal authority.

Similar patterns obtained in the Armenian case. Ittihad engineered and supervised the destruction process through three types of representatives who were
sent to the provinces to serve as party provincial commissars overseeing the details of the massacres. There were first the so-called Responsible Secretaries
(*Kâtibi Mes'ul*); then there were the delegates (*Murahhas*); and then the
Inspectors (*Müfettiş*). Many of these party commissars were former army officers
of different ranks who had resigned from the military to dedicate themselves to
the goal of serving the party. In the implementation phase of the genocide, they
proved themselves as most efficient executors of the covert party designs targeting the provincial Armenian population. All of them were invested with a level of
power that surpassed that of the provincial governors-general over whom they
exercised veto power.

Nor can one underestimate the reward system set up by the party organization
to promote its designs and goals. As in the case of the Nazis, so in the case of the
Ittihadists, a system of adroitly arranged rewards elicited a high level of compliance from party members to requests and commands that were such as to com-

promise the integrity of the latter, reduce their capacity for compunction, and obviate guilt feelings. When guilt is shared with fellow partisans within the context of pressing party desiderata, inhibitions tend to attenuate themselves and guilt feelings are more or less smothered. There arise so-called emergent norms that elicit from the party faithful a deviant form of conformity.

To sum up, in the course of the genocides under review here, the state organizations in the Third Reich and the Ottoman empire were almost reduced to irrelevance as the Nazis and the Ittihadists gained optimal control of these organizations, including the key governmental agencies, such as cabinet ministries and legislative bodies. The analysis of the two genocides, therefore, has to be primarily anchored on the genesis, structure, leadership, reward system, and overt and covert designs of these two parties, considered to be the actual authors of these twin genocides.

Genocide as a Function of Social Restructuring

I stated at the beginning of this chapter that genocide presupposes an intergroup conflict that defies nonviolent settlement with a tendency to escalate and intensify. In line with this view, genocide can be regarded as a device to resolve that conflict radically and terminally. But the scrutiny of the two genocides in question clearly indicates that the resolution of the conflict itself may be considered as a means to still another end. The clue to this phenomenon is contained in the nature of the conflicts at issue. When a dominant group is bent on purging an ethnic minority from the fabric of its mainstream society, this is a reflection of a perception by that dominant group that there is an unacceptable incompatibility between itself and the minority; the conflict is expressive of this perceived incompatibility. The Nazis wanted to rid Germany of the Jews; the Ittihadists wanted to rid Turkey of the Armenians. The watchwords, "Germany for the Germans" and "Turkey for the Turks," encapsulated these sentiments. The implied common objective here was to reduce the heterogeneous complexion of German and Turkish societies toward the goal of optimal homogeneity. In other words, the underlying urge was to alter, for a variety of reasons, the ethnic-national makeup of the German and Turkish societies. This is a type of alteration that is best described as social restructuring.

This line of reasoning warrants a final conclusion with respect to the issue of the comparative similarities of the Armenian and Jewish cases of genocide; namely, in its ultimate thrust genocide is a function of social restructuring.[56] The destruction of the two victim populations was a means to the superordinate goal of recasting German and Turkish societies in the projected mold of integral nations. That function was afforded by conditions and developments in which the factors of minority status, vulnerability, opportunity, and the dictatorial ascendancy of monolithic political parties configured and pushed the genocidal process into channels for consummation. In recognizing the functional character of genocide, these factors need to be taken into account as contingency factors.

Comparative Aspects of the Armenian and Jewish Cases 127

The Sweep Beyond Domestic Genocide

One of the misconceptions of a number of holocaust scholars venturing to evaluate the Armenian genocide is revealed in their common argument that the Turkish drive to destroy the Armenians applied only to the Armenians of Ottoman Turkey. As such, so goes the argument, that drive was geographically confined as it was circumscribed by the territorial boundaries of Ottoman Turkey. In other words, it had a limited compass of destructiveness as compared with the Nazi drive culminating in the Holocaust. The facts are, however, at variance with this notion.

Following the outbreak of the Bolshevik Revolution in 1917 and the ensuing collapse of the Russian army that had occupied vast tracts of land in eastern Turkey, the Ottoman 3rd Army, which was on the verge of total defeat, was unexpectedly relieved of the perils of such defeat; it received a new lease on life. Taking advantage of this lifesaving opportunity, that army, after replenishing itself, launched a new offensive in the spring of 1918 and ended up occupying substantial portions of Russian Armenia in the Transcaucasus. As a result, the genocidal engine of destruction unleashed by the Young Turk Ittihadists was once more activated to decimate and destroy the other half of the Armenian population living beyond the established frontiers of Turkey. The horrors of this new drive of genocide were such that two German generals and a staff colonel, allies of Turkey and, at the time, on duty in the Transcaucasus, felt compelled to send to their superiors in Berlin a string of reports decrying the Turkish methods of annihilating the new victim population.

Major General Otto von Lossow, the German military representative at the Batum Conference, on May 15, 1918, informed Berlin that the Turks had embarked upon "the total extermination of the Armenians in Transcaucasia also" (*völlige Ausrottung der Armenier auch in Transkaukasien*).[57] On June 3, 1918, he sent a warning to the effect that "Talât's government party wants to destroy all Armenians [*alle Armenier ausrotten will*], not only in Turkey, but also outside Turkey."[58] For his part Major General Kress von Kressenstein, chief of the German imperial delegation in the Caucasus, on July 13, 1918, reported to Berlin about "the Turkish resolve to annihilate the Armenians" (*der Vernichtungswille der Türkei gegenüber dem armenischen Element*).[59] On July 31, the same general declared that "the Turks have by no means relinquished their intention to exterminate the Armenians" (*ihre Absicht . . . auszurotten*).[60] Colonel Ernst Paraquin, at the time the chief of staff of General Halil Kut (the commander-in-chief of the Turkish Army Groups East, which had invaded Russian Armenia) angrily declared, "With hypocritical indignation the Turkish government denies all barbarous conduct against the Armenians. The evacuation of Anatolia by the Russians furnished the desired opportunity to clear out also the Russian Armenians. . . . The annihilation campaign against the Armenians proceeded . . . with inexorable ruthlessness" (*mit geheuchelter Entrüstung jedes barbarische Verfahren gegen Armenier bestritt*).[61]

The two foremost military leaders of wartime Germany in their memoirs corroborate these charges of organized mass murder against Armenians in the Caucasus. General Erich Ludendorff, chief of staff in the German High Command, for example, declared, "Turkey plunged into a war of murder and looting in the Caucasus" (*Mord und Beutekrieg*).[62] Field Marshal Paul von Hindenburg likewise wrote: "Turkey wants to annex the Caucasus entirely and exterminate [*ausrotten*] the Armenians with all means available, massacres and bloodbaths are in the order of the day."[63] All these indictments and condemnations were formally and officially verified by Richard von Kühlmann, former ambassador to Turkey (1916–1917) and Germany's foreign minister at the time of the Turkish invasion of the Caucasus. He denounced the authorities, declaring "In violations of their promises the Turks systematically are pursuing their plan of annihilation of the Armenians in the Caucasus" (*die Vernichtung planmässig betreiben*).[64]

As if these exterminatory operations were not enough,[65] the new Kemalist regime, which on every occasion publicly had distanced itself from the previous Ittihadist regime on account of its criminal activities, after a lapse of sixteen months resumed the genocidal onslaught against the Armenians. Without declaring war, Turkish General Kâzım Karabekir in September 1920 attacked the fledgling Republic of Armenia in the Transcaucasus after having secured the formal authorization from Mustafa Kemal and his government in Ankara. Ill-equipped, ill-trained, and ill-prepared, and additionally fractured by the infusion of bolshevik propaganda that described the invading Turks as comrades and liberators, the untested army of the Republic folded rather quickly. Two factors considerably influenced the new Turkish élan to resume the genocidal drive. The victorious Allies were set to punish vanquished Turkey for wartime crimes, especially for the massacres against the Armenians, and concomitantly compensate the Armenians. They proceeded to redraw Turkey's boundaries for the benefit of a new Armenian state entity to be created in such a way that it was to bestride eastern Turkey and Russian Armenia in the Transcaucasus. More important, many of the leaders of the invading Kemalist army were those Special Organization leaders who during the war had played a key role in organizing and executing the genocide in Turkey proper. They were now reengaged as "freedom fighters" but actually resumed their genocidal task performance in the new occupied territories.[66] By all accounts that performance yielded what might be called a mini-genocide against the Armenians in the region of Gümrü (Leninakan). According to Soviet and Armenian sources, in five months of Turkish conquest and occupation about 200,000 Armenians of the region perished.[67]

That mini-genocide was enacted in compliance with top-secret instructions issued by Ankara. Turkish General Karabekir was ordered to initiate measures aiming at "the political and physical obliteration of Armenia" (*siyaseten ve maddeten ortadan kaldırmak*).[68] Only the prompt intervention of the 11th Red Army, stationed nearby, and the concomitant sovietization of Armenia averted the all but certain extirpation of the remnants of the Armenian nation by preventing the oc-cupation of the rest of Armenia by Karabekir's troops.

The similar aspect of the two cases in terms of the Nazi and Turkish Ittihadist drives to go beyond domestic genocide has within its structure, however, a very important dissimilar element. In contrast to their periodic indulgencies through which the Nazis vowed to destroy the Jews as a race, the Young Turk Ittihadists rarely, if ever, allowed themselves to lapse into such indulgencies. For them, the destruction of the Armenians was and remained a hidden agenda, a top-secret plan. They skillfully conspired for it, knew how to bide their time, and, when the opportunity presented itself, that plan was carried out swiftly and implacably. Turkish archival documents demonstrate, for example, that this pattern was fol-lowed in the execution of the 1920 mini-genocide in the Transcaucasus described above. On the very same day that Ankara, through a cipher telegram, secretly or-dered General Karabekir to wipe out Armenia through appropriate means (November 8, 1920), it sent to the Armenian government in Yerevan a parallel telegram. In it the Kemalist government expressed its "profound and genuine friendship" (*amik ve samimi*) toward the Armenian people, invoked the ideals of "humanity" (*insaniyet*), and promised assistance to help Armenia recover eco-nomically and achieve "complete independence and security."[69] Consistent with this proclivity for cunning and trickiness, Ankara, in its order to obliterate Armenia, had advised the Turkish general to "deceive the Armenians" (*Ermenileri iğfal*) and "fool the Europeans through an appearance of peacelovingness. In re-ality, however, [*fakat hakikatde*] the purpose of all this is to achieve the objective [stated above]."[70]

In trying to interpret the parallel character of the Nazi and Ittihadist mass-murder sweeps beyond domestic genocide, one is struck with a paramount fact that may be viewed as a condition transcending in significance the factors of per-petrator ideology and an allied perpetrator motivation. In both cases, the decisive motor force was military conquest resulting from warfare. In conditions of mili-tary occupation, associated with an ongoing war, it is far more easy to sustain the momentum of a successfully launched initial genocide than under almost any other condition. The objective element of opportunity and the subjective element of opportunism combine here to generate an inveterate urge in the mind-set of a perpetrator to be consequential in task performance; it is most tempting to try "to complete the job." In this sense, it may be argued that the extension of a do-mestic genocide beyond territorial boundaries is primarily a function of military conquest resulting from warfare. By virtue of such a conquest, the dispersed ele-ments of the original victim population can be readily targeted as well, especially in the aftermath of such a conquest and occupation, absent changes in the lead-ership of the perpetrator group or the onset of new domestic or external imped-iments or constraints.

The postulate that emerges from this comparative perspective is that the evo-lution and transformation of a domestic genocide into a territorially transcendental holocaust is not an intrinsic process but one that depends upon the effects of extrinsic factors acting as catalysts. No matter how powerful the ideological animus of such a transcendental drive may be, the actualization of the ideology hinges on the operational effectiveness of such catalysts. In brief, the phenomenon of holocaust, contrary to prevailing assumptions, is not a sui generis phenomenon but one bound up with extra-ideological contingencies.

NOTES

This is a revised and expanded version of a lecture delivered at the University of California–Los Angeles, on October 31, 1993.

1. Robert Melson, "Response to Professor Dadrian's Review," *Holocaust and Genocide Studies* 8(3) (Winter 1994):416.
2. Ambassador Henry Morgenthau, *Secrets of the Bosphorus* (London: Hutchinson, 1918), p. 202. It is significant that, in the American edition of this book, the name of Bedri, the chief of police in the Ottoman capital, whose position and rank were comparable to that of minister of police, is deleted. Instead, he is described as "a responsible Turkish official." Henry Morgenthau, *Ambassador Morgenthau's Story* (Garden City, N.Y.: Doubleday, Page, 1918), p. 307.
3. Ibid., p. 312.
4. Ibid., p. 328.
5. In using the general term "deportation," which, in practice—more often than not—meant massacres, wartime Turkish Foreign Minister Halil Menteşe (in his postwar memoirs) stated that "there are very few Turks in Anatolia who were not involved in this business of deportation" (*tehcir meselesi*) of the Armenians. "The Memoirs of Halil Menteşe: The Exile to Malta," *Hayat Tarih Mecmuası* 9(2) (September 1973):22. In his report to the State Department in Washington, D.C., Lewis Heck, the U.S. High Commissioner in the Ottoman capital from November 1918 through April 1919, declared that the deportation and massacre of the Armenians "were heartily approved at the time by the vast majority of the Turkish population of the country." The January 9, 1919, report, U.S. National Archives, R.G. 256. 867.4016/2, p. 2. The same statement is repeated in the January 20, 1919, report, R.G. 256. 867.00/59, p. 3.
6. For details on these drowning operations in and around the Black Sea port city of Trabzon, see the special issue of *Journal of Political and Military Sociology* 22(1) (Summer 1994), which contains collected essays by this author. The drownings are discussed at pp. 40–49.
7. Morgenthau, *Ambassador* [n. 2], pp. 317, 318.
8. The text of General Vehib's affidavit in original Ottoman script is deposited in the archives of the Jerusalem Armenian Patriarchate, Series H. 17, File nos. 171 and 182.
9. Ibid., Series L. 13, File nos. 323–239. Following is another portion of the Armenian lawyer's affidavit (pp. 5–6):

II. THE BEHEADING OF 500 CHILDREN

Only few days had passed from the burning of the 2,000 orphans, when Moustafa Sıdkı and his men tried to devise other means of torture.

They took 500 children to a part of the desert near the German Wireless Telegraph Station. He had them tied two by two by their feet and afterwards had them placed in a line on the ground. Then Moustafa Sıdkı sat in a heavy cart which was driven on this line of lying children in such a way that the wheels crushed the necks of these unfortunate children. Their heartrending shrieks resounded in the whole vicinity.

III. 2,000 ORPHANS DROWNED IN THE EUPHRATES

The annihilation of these helpless orphans was giving Moustafa Sıdkı and his accomplices such profound joy that soon other means of torture were found. On October 24, 1916, 2,000 orphans were carried to the banks of the Euphrates hands and feet bound. Moustafa Sıdkı after having sitted himself at ease, ordered to throw the orphans into the water two by two and enjoyed thoroughly the sight of their drowning.

IV. THE VICTIMS OF THE BRIDGE

On August 10, 1916 a caravan set on its journey to Mossoul. While passing over the bridge on the Euphrates, Moustafa Sıdkı, who was waiting there, ordered to bring the prettiest girls under the bridge. There these poor girls served to the lusts of Moustafa Sıdkı and his accomplices and were after that thrown into the Euphrates.

10. Ludwig Schraudenbach, *Muharebe* (War) (Berlin: Drei Masken Verlag, 1924), p. 352.

11. K. A. Schleunes, *The Twisted Road to Auschwitz: Nazi Policy Toward German Jews, 1933–1939* (Chicago: University of Illinois Press, 1970), pp. 215 and 225.

12. Raul Hilberg, *The Destruction of European Jews* (Chicago: Quadrangle, 1969), pp. 230–232.

13. Jerry Sawicki, *Vor dem Polnischen Staatsanwalt* (Berlin: Deutscher Militaerverlag, 1962), p. 198, quoted in Richard Breitman, "Additional Remarks," to Yehoshua Büchler's "Document: A Preparatory Document for the Wannsee 'Conference,'" trans. Yehuda Bauer, *Holocaust and Genocide Studies* 9(1) (Spring 1995):128. See also Yehuda Bauer's review of Richard Breitman, *The Architect of Genocide: Himmler and the Final Solution* (Hanover, N.H.: University Press of New England, 1992), in *Holocaust and Genocide Studies* 6(3) (1991):307–312.

14. Morgenthau, *Ambassador* [n. 2], p. 309.

15. See Vahakn N. Dadrian, "Documentation of the Armenian Genocide in German and Austrian Sources," *Widening Circle of Genocide: A Critical Bibliographic Review*, ed. Israel Charny, vol. 3 (New Brunswick, N.J.: Transaction, 1994), pp. 104–107.

16. Esat Uras, *Tarihte Ermeniler ve Ermeni Meselesi* (The Armenians and the Armenian Question), 2d ed. (Istanbul: Belge, 1976), p. 612.

17. In the case of Constantinople the facts are as follows: In the key indictment of the Turkish Military Tribunal, investigating the wartime massacres against the Armenians, there are repeat references to the sweeping compass of the deportation scheme, *Takvimi Vekâyi* No. 3540, pp. 6, 7; on p. 4 of the same document the procuror-general makes an allusion to the design of the Ittihadists involving a Final Solution of the Armenian question, and on p. 8 the same idea is expressed through an attribution to Dr. Nazım who uses a broader term, the "eastern question." In the ancillary indictment addressed against the re-

sponsible secretaries of the Young Turk Ittihad Party, the document makes a similar allusion about the empire-wide range of the anti-Armenian measures (*Memaliki Osmaniyenin
hemen her tarafında*). *Takvimi Vekâyi* No. 3571, p. 130.

The German documents found in the state archives of Bonn are corroborative in this
respect. In a major report on December 7, 1915, German Ambassador to Turkey Count
Paul von Wolff-Metternich informed his chancellor in Berlin that

A. already 30,000 Armenians have been deported from Istanbul;
B. 4,000 of them were dispatched only recently;
C. plans are made to remove the remaining 80,000 Armenians from the Ottoman
   capital;
D. the source of his information was the chief of the Istanbul police;
E. these bits of information should be kept secret (*die ich bitte geheim zu halten*)
   (this part of the report is deleted from the massive documentary tome compiled
   by J. Lepsius, *Deutschland und Armenien* [Potsdam: Tempelverlag, 1919], p. 202),
   German Foreign Ministry Archives (Bonn) A.A., Türkei 183/40, A36184. U.S.
   Ambassador to Turkey Henry Morgenthau, in a report to Washington on August
   11, 1915, stated that Talat "hints at drastic measures against all [Armenians] in
   Constantinople." U.S. National Archives. R.G. 59. 867.4016/90.

In a subsequent report on October 4, 1915, the same ambassador declared: "The greatest wealth of the Armenians is centered in Constantinople and I fear that it is but a question of time when the cupidity of some of the Turkish leaders and the desire of others to
complete their nefarious scheme of practically destroying Armenians in Turkey will be to
treat Constantinople Armenians as they have the others. Delay is being secured but entire
escape of Constantinople Armenians is doubtful if present general political conditions
here remain unchanged." Ibid., 867.4016/159. For a variety of reasons, that time was not
to come as Turkey was busy completing the exterminatory work in the provinces and subsequent military setbacks ultimately compounded the problems her leaders faced in the
task of completing the removal and annihilation of Istanbul Armenians. The documentary
thrust of this study leaves very little doubt about what Melson has called "total domestic
genocide." Robert Melson, *Revolution and Genocide. On the Origins of the Armenian
Genocide and the Holocaust* (Chicago: University of Chicago Press, 1992), pp. 2–4, 247–257.
Even more authoritative in this regard is the characterization of Tarık Zafer Tunaya, the
late dean of Turkish political scientists. When discussing the criminal proceedings against
the Ittihadist leaders in his third volume on the Turkish political parties, he saw fit to trans-
late the Ottoman word *taktil* into the modern Turkish equivalent of "genocide"
("*soykırım*"). The word *taktil* is the standard word the Turkish court-martial regularly used
to describe the thrust of the empire-wide massacres. Tarık Z. Tunaya, *Türkiyede Siyasal
Partiler* (Political Parties of Turkey), vol. 3, *Ittihad ve Terakki* (Istanbul: Hürriyet Vakfı,
1989), page 281.

As to Smyrna (Izmir), as stated in the text, the Turkish governor-general was personally
and directly threatened by the German General Liman von Sanders, who was then commander-in-chief of the Ottoman Fifth Army and whose zone of command encompassed
Smyrna and its environs. Upon the first act of deportation of 300 Armenians, signalling
subsequent wholesale deportations, General von Sanders informed Rahmi, the governor-
general, that in the case of any further act of deporting the city's Armenian population he
would use military units to arrest the teams of policemen assigned to deportation duties.

Von Sanders's objection to "massive deportations" was not meant to protect the Armenians, he said, but to secure and protect military interest, which, he argued, might be jeopardized by the turmoil the deportation measures were likely to create; and he prevailed. There were no further deportations from Smyrna. German Foreign Ministry Archives, Türkei 183/45, A31127, No. 703; Austrian Foreign Ministry Archives, P.A. 12/463, No. 89/P.-A; U.S. National Archives, RG.59.867.00/802.5. General von Sanders was supported in his move by then German Foreign Affairs Minister Arthur Zimmermann. German Foreign Ministry Archives (Bonn) Türkei 183/45, A30700. No. 1301.

18. Hilberg, *The Destruction* [n. 12], pp. 98 and 258.

19. Michael R. Marrus, "Coming to Terms with Vichy," *Holocaust and Genocide Studies* 9(1) (Spring 1995):24.

20. Hilberg, *The Destruction* [n. 12], pp. 278, 283, and 284.

21. Ibid., p. 62.

22. Ibid., p. 666.

23. Louis Wirth, *The Ghetto* (Chicago: University of Chicago Press, 1928).

24. Vahakn N. Dadrian, "The Convergent Aspects of the Armenian and Jewish Cases of Genocide: A Reinterpretation of the Concept of Holocaust," *Holocaust and Genocide Studies* 3(2) (Summer 1988):151–154.

25. Richard L. Rubenstein, *The Age of Triage* (Boston: Beacon Press, 1983), p. 130.

26. George H. Hepworth, *Through Armenia on Horseback* (New York: E. P. Dutton, 1898), pp. 146–147, 263, and 339–140.

27. William M. Ramsay, *Impressions of Turkey During Twelve Years' Wanderings* (New York: G. P. Putnam's Sons, 1897), pp. 156–157.

28. Rubenstein, *The Age of Triage* [n. 25], p. 142.

29. Ibid., p. 144.

30. Hilberg, *The Destruction* [n. 12], ch. 5, pp. 54–105.

31. *Memoirs of Halide Edib* (New York: Century, 1926), p. 386.

32. U.S. National Archives, R.G. 59. 807.4016/148.

33. Morgenthau, *Ambassador* [n. 2], p. 339.

34. Hilberg, *The Destruction* [n. 12], p. 259.

35. Ibid.

36. *The Goebbels Diaries*, ed. L. Lochner (New York: Doubleday, 1948), p. 241.

37. Hilberg, *The Destruction* [n. 12], p. 672.

38. Vahakn N. Dadrian, "Genocide as a Problem of National and International Law: The World War I Armenian Case and Its Contemporary Legal Ramifications," *Yale Journal of International Law* 14(2)(Summer 1989):262.

39. United Nations War Crimes Commission, *History of the United Nations War Crimes Commission and the Development of the Laws of War* (London: H.M.S.O., 1948), pp. 188–189; M. C. Bassiouni, *Crimes Against Humanity in International Criminal Law* (Dordrecht, Holland: Martinus Nijhoff, 1992), pp. 168–169 and 184–187.

40. Quoted In J. Willis, *Prologue to Nuremberg: The Politics of Diplomacy of Punishing War Criminals of the First World War* (Westport, Conn.: Greenwood Press, 1982), p. 173.

41. E. L. Woodward, R. Butler, and A. Orde, eds., *Documents on British Foreign Policy, 1919–1939,* 3d series, vol. 7, 1939 (London: H.M.S.O., 1954), Doc. No. 314, enclosure, pp. 258–260; Kevork Bardakjian, *Hitler and the Armenian Genocide* (Cambridge, Mass.: Zoryan Institute, 1985), pp. 3–24.

42. Hilberg, *The Destruction* [n. 12], p. 671.

43. Ibid., p. 641.

44. Vahakn N. Dadrian, "The Role of the Special Organization in the Armenian Genocide During the First World War," in *Minorities in Wartime: National and Racial Groupings in Europe, North America and Australia During the Two World Wars*, ed. P. Panayi (Oxford: Berg, 1993), pp. 50–82. See also Ahmed Refik (Altınay), *Iki Komite–Iki Kıtal* (Two Committees–Two Mass Murders), Ottoman script (Istanbul: Orhaniye Press, 1919), p. 23; Falih Rıfkı Atay, *Zeytindağı* (Mt. Olive) (Istanbul: Ayyıldız, 1981), pp. 35–36. See also the respective testimonies (at the Turkish court-martial trials) of defendants Colonel Cevad Kıanlıklı, the wartime military commandant at the Ottoman capital, and Atıf Kamçil, one of the chief directors of the Special Organization headquartered in Istanbul. See *Takvimi Vekâyi*, the official gazette of the Ottoman government whose supplements (*ilâve*) published select portions of the proceedings of the military tribunal in the period from 1919 to 1921, No. 3543, pp. 26–30. Page 28 contains additional documents from Colonel Behiç Erkin, the deputy director in Department I of the Ministry of War in charge of the Bureau of Procurement (*Ikmal Şubesi*). During the war, when the legal authorization of the release of the convicts was being sought by the Ministries of War and Justice, the same Colonel Behiç testified in the Ottoman Upper House (the Senate) about the necessity for and usefulness of the Special Organization relative to special task performances. *Meclisi Âyan Zabıt Ceridesi*, 3d period, 3d sess., 15th sitting, December 12, 1916, vol. 1, p. 187. As to the testimony before the Chamber of Deputies' Fifth Committee investigating the wartime misdeeds of cabinet ministers, wartime Justice Minister Saib Mollazade Ibrahim stated that the number of convicts released from the empire's prisons for such a mission "amounted to a significant sum total" (*mühim bir yeküna balig*). *Harb Kabinelerinin Isticvabı* (The Hearings on Wartime Cabinets) (Istanbul: Vakit Publications, 1933), p. 537.

45. Hilberg, *The Destruction* [n. 12], ch. 7, "Mobile Killing Operations," pp. 177–256, ch. 9, "Killing Center Operations," pp. 555–635.

46. Ibid., pp. 242–243.

47. Leo Alexander, "War Crimes and Their Motivation: The Socio-Psychological Structure of the SS and the Criminalization of a Society," *Journal of Criminal Law, Criminology, and Police Science* 39 (September-October 1948):309.

48. Robert Jay Lifton, *The Nazi Doctors: Medical Killing and the Psychology of Genocide* (New York: Basic Books, 1986), pp. 224 and 388.

49. Irving Louis Horowitz, *Genocide, State Power, and Mass Murder* (New Brunswick, N.J.: Transaction, 1976); *Taking Lives, Genocide and State Power*, 3d ed. (New Brunswick, N.J.: Transaction, 1980), p. 11.

50. Morgenthau, *Ambassador* [n. 2], p. 11.

51. Peter Longerich, *Hitler's Stellvertreter: Führung der Partei und Kontrolle des Staatsapparates durch den Stab Hess und die Partei Kanzlei Bormann* (Münich: Saur, 1992).

52. The participants were: Reinhardt Heydrich and Alfred Meyer, Drs. Georg Leibbrandt, Wilhelm Stuckart, Roland Freisler, and Joseph Bühler, and Martin Luther, Karl Schöngarth, and Otto Lange; other security potentates, likewise present, were Erich Neumann, Gerhard Klopfer, Wilhelm Kritzinger, Otto Hoffmann, and Heinrich Müller. Hilberg, *The Destruction* [n. 12], p. 264.

53. Vahakn N. Dadrian, "The Secret Young-Turk Ittihadist Conference and the Decision for the World War I Genocide of the Armenians," *Holocaust and Genocide Studies* 7(2) (Fall 1993):173–201.

54. Robert H. Jackson, *The Nürnberg Case: Together with Other Documents* (New York: Cooper Square Publishers, 1971), p. 40.

55. Special Organization Chieftain Major Yakub Cemil. Quoted by Secret Service Administrator Galip Vardar, *Ittihad ve Terakki Içinde Dönenler* (The Inside Story of Ittihad ve Terakki), ed. N. Tansu (Istanbul: Inkilâp, 1960), pp. 279–280.

56. Vahakn N. Dadrian, "Towards a Theory of Genocide Incorporating the Instance of Holocaust: Comments, Criticism and Suggestions," *Holocaust and Genocide Studies* 5(2) (1990), pp. 129–143.

57. A.A. Türkei 183/51, A206981.

58. *Deutsches Zentralarchiv*, or DZA (Potsdam). Bestand Reichskanzlei, or BRK. No. 2458/9. Bl. 202.

59. A.A. Türkei 158/20. A31679.

60. DZA. BRK. No. 2458/9. Bl. 287.

61. Ernst Paraquin, "Politik im Orient," *Berliner Tageblatt* (January 24 and 28, 1920). See also A.A. Türkei 158/24, A1373 for a summary of the contents of this two-part article. The quotation is from part 1.

62. Erich Ludendorff, *Urkunden der obersten Heeresleitung über ihre Tätigkeit, 1916–1918* (Documents of the High Command on its Activities, 1916–1918) (Berlin: Mittler und Sohn, 1922), p. 500.

63. Paul von Hindenburg, *Aus Meinem Lebel* (From My Life) (Leipzig, Germany: S. Hirzel, 1934), p. 168.

64. A.A. Türkei 183/51, A28533. No. 1178. June 3, 1918.

65. For a full reproduction of these and other comments by German military and civilian officials on these operations, see Dadrian, "Documentation" [n. 15], pp. 122–125.

66. Vahakn N. Dadrian, *The History of the Armenian Genocide: Ethnic Conflict from the Balkans to Anatolia to the Caucasus* (Providence: Berghahn, 1995), pp. 367–370.

67. Ibid., p. 361. See also Dadrian, "Genocide as a Problem," [n. 38], p. 332.

68. Ibid., p. 358.

69. Ibid., p. 386.

70. Ibid.

❀ *7* ❀

Stalinist Terror and the Question of Genocide: The Great Famine

BARBARA B. GREEN

*T*he question of whether Stalin's terror was genocidal in intent has focused largely on the famine of 1932–1933 and the assertion that it was not only artificial and man-made but was an intentional act of genocide directed against the Ukrainian people. Although a thorough consideration of this question must take into account the fate of the Kazakhs during collectivization and the deportation of entire nations—the "punished peoples"—this essay will consider questions surrounding the 1932–1933 famine.[1]

What was perhaps the greatest social and economic revolution in history—the industrialization of the Soviet Union—was carried out from above against opposition not only from the masses but from much of the elite. It required the concentration of an enormous amount of power in the hands of one man, Stalin, and the unleashing of unprecedented terror. Every effort was expended to prevent the development of any autonomous centers of power that could act independently of the state. Stalin instituted a relentless struggle for rapid industrialization and total collectivization, which he carried out with unbridled coercion. Collective and state farms put the rural population under state control, thereby simplifying the task of extracting grain both to feed the workers and for export.

There is no question but that a famine of enormous proportions took place in 1932–1933, primarily in Ukraine, in which millions died of starvation and disease. Most U.S. and British reporters at the time failed to report the nature or extent of the famine.[2] The British, Canadian, and U.S. governments, though aware of the famine, took no action because of the impact of the Great Depression in their own countries and because of international considerations.[3] It is through the relentless insistence of Robert Conquest, James E. Mace, Marco Carynnyk, and others that the famine has been brought to public attention.

These writers have argued that Ukraine was a deliberate and intended target because the loyalty of all Ukrainians was suspect. They maintain that the famine of 1932–1933, in which millions died, was deliberately engineered by Stalin to crush the Ukrainian people, eliminate the peasantry as a force upholding Ukrainian national ideals, stifle Ukrainian culture, and eliminate any manifestation of independence. Charging Stalin with genocide, Mace has called the famine "a means used by Stalin to impose a 'final solution' on the most pressing nationality problem in the Soviet Union."[4]

In contrast, Robert Tucker, Adam Ulam, Martin Malia, and other scholars, in discussing the devastating impact on the peasantry of Stalin's forced collectivization and extraction of grain, speak more to the transformation of Russian society and the impact on Russian peasants. For the most part, they merge Ukrainians with Russians and then label them all "Russian." They tend to consider the famine as an outcome of Stalin's obsession with power or as a consequence of the effort to transform a backward peasant society by extracting a surplus from the peasantry in order to invest in rapid industrialization.[5] When Hannah Arendt writes of the liquidation of the Soviet peasantry—the "most powerful class in the Union"—she says that it "was more thorough and more cruel than that of any other group and was carried through by artificial famine and deportation." However, Arendt makes no reference to Ukrainians as the intended victims.[6]

In direct opposition to Mace and Conquest, Stephen Wheatcraft argues that the famine was not created to weaken Ukrainian nationalism. Rather, Ukrainian nationalism was weakened as a consequence of the famine.[7] The fact that nationality policy changed in the early 1930s does not in itself prove that the change in nationality policy was the impetus for Stalin to impose a "final solution" by means of an artificial famine. It is important to bear in mind that Stalinist measures, when viewed only in terms of their impact on Ukraine, may appear as if they were directed specifically at Ukraine and Ukrainians. These measures were, however, intended as a means of transforming peasant society and solving the Soviet Union's serious grain problem, rather than as a policy directed at Ukrainians for genocidal reasons. Millions died during the famine of 1932–1933, but not all mass deaths are genocide.

Collectivization was bound to have a particularly cruel effect on the population of the borderlands. The urban population of the Soviet Union was largely clustered in the center, whereas the periphery was populated by peasants and herdsmen. Even in the borderlands, Russian or Russian-speaking cities were surrounded by non-Russian countryside. Collectivization and the Five-Year Plan were intended to put the burden of industrialization on the peasantry and this meant that there would be a disparate impact on nationalities on the periphery. Collectivization, directed primarily by Russians, was implemented despite opposition—even open rebellion—from the nationalities of the periphery.[8] A policy designed to forcibly extract grain from peasants to feed urban workers was bound to be perceived as a policy directed against the nationality that was dominant in the countryside. In the case of Ukraine, forced collectivization was seen as a war by the non-Ukrainian urban population against the Ukrainian villagers. As peasants and as Ukrainians, they resisted collectivization by whatever means they could. Resistance was met by increased force. There was a disparate impact on Ukrainians—not because they were Ukrainians but because they were peasants.

In this chapter I will argue that the deaths of millions of Ukrainians and other Soviet peoples in the famine of 1932–1933 are directly attributable to Stalin's attempt to totally reconstruct society through rapid industrialization, an effort in which he was determined that nothing would stand in his way. In the process, he instituted a totalitarian system permeated by terror. There were mass deaths and overwhelming suffering as a result of excessive grain procurement, but this was not genocide. I will trace the reasons for the excess grain procurement in the context of Stalin's Five-Year Plan and forced industrialization. My intent is to establish that this effort to totally reconstruct society can in itself account for the excess grain procurement that led to mass deaths and the famine.

Genocide Defined

Before it is possible to discuss whether genocide has occurred in a particular case, a clear understanding of the meaning of *genocide* is essential. Michael Ignatieff argues:

> "Genocide" is a worn and debased term, casually hurled at every outrage, every violence, even applied to events where no death, only shame or abuse, occurs. But it is a word that does mean something: the project to exterminate a people for no other reason than because they are that people. Before the experience of genocide, they may believe it a matter of personal choice whether they belong or believe. After genocide, it becomes their fate.[9]

An article in *Economist*, after noting that the Ukrainian terror-famine of 1932–1933 may have claimed as many victims as the Holocaust, has this to say:

> Yet the peculiar circumstances of the Holocaust do make it unique. Never has the extermination of an entire people, coupled with the technology of industrialisation . . . been attempted so systematically as an end in itself. Never has mass murder been so efficiently, so scientifically, perpetrated. Never has the annihilation of a race been so central to an ideology.[10]

The meaning of genocide and the uniqueness of the Holocaust are revealed in a few characteristics. The Holocaust was aimed at the extermination of an entire people because they were that people. The extermination was not a means toward an end; it was an end in itself. It was not an act of demonstrative violence in which some were killed in order to terrify the other members of the people into submission. It was not intended to affect behavior. It was not a pogrom or the result of uncontrolled mass violence. It was, rather, an intentional, systematic effort to exterminate an entire people utilizing modern technology to ensure efficiency.

The Question of Numbers

There has been a great deal of debate over the number of people who died in the 1932–1933 famine from starvation or from diseases resulting from widespread malnutrition. When the population totals in the All-Union Census of 1937 fell far short of expectations, the three statisticians directly responsible for the census were arrested as "enemies of the people," and the entire census was suppressed. M. Maksudov uses 1939 census data to argue that not less than 4.4 million, or one-tenth of the population of Ukraine, perished between 1927 and 1938.[11] Mace asserts that the figure of 5–7 million deaths in the famine for Ukraine alone is a conservative figure.[12] Conquest gives a figure of about 11 million premature deaths between 1926–1937, of which approximately 7 million can be attributed to the 1932–1933 famine. He claims that 5 million of the famine deaths were in Ukraine.[13]

During the Mikhail Gorbachev era, materials from the 1937 census were published, and these confirm that millions of lives were lost. Between 1926 and 1936, the total population of the Soviet Union increased by slightly over 10 percent, from 147 million to 162 million, considerably less than predicted. The Russian population increased from 77.8 million in 1926 to 94 million in 1937, but the Ukrainians decreased from 31.2 million to 26.4 million. Population decreases or failures to increase at the expected rate, of course, cannot be attributed solely to excess deaths caused by the famine. These changes were also a consequence of changing birthrates, migration, and assimilation.[14] A Russian writer recently attempted to calculate the number of victims using data from the files of the USSR Central Statistical Administration and National Economic Records. She estimates that the total number of deaths in the USSR in 1933 was 6.7 million, of which half were victims of the famine. In 1933, the only year in which statistics reveal a net population loss for the Soviet Union, the European part of the USSR lost 1.7 million people, of which 1.5 million were in Ukraine. A slow recovery began only at the end of the summer in 1933, after crops were harvested.[15] Wheatcraft, using the 1937 census figures, argues that the scale of excess mortality for the Soviet Union as a whole in 1932–1933 might be as high as 4–5 million.[16] Alec Nove, using figures cited by V. Tsaplin, a Soviet scholar, in the April 1989 issue of *Voprosy istorii*, estimates that in 1933 there were 3.1–3.2 million famine deaths in Ukraine alone.[17]

The controversy over the number of Ukrainians killed in the 1932–1933 famine continues. The subtext of the controversy is the assumption that if it can be established that the Ukrainian terror-famine claimed as many victims as the Holocaust, then an equivalence between the two events will have been established.

Mace is explicit on this. After discussing census figures, he states, "The point is that the Ukrainian famine was a deliberate act of genocide of roughly the same order of magnitude as the Jewish Holocaust of the Second World War, both in the number of its victims and in the human suffering it produced."[18] However, the question of numbers, though it has provoked high levels of controversy, cannot resolve this issue.

War Communism and the New Economic Policy

Tracing the development of Soviet agricultural policy from 1917 to 1932 illuminates the conditions that led, tragically and inexorably, to the Great Famine of 1932–1933. War communism, the attempt to build communism and serve practical needs during the civil war, was prompted by ideological idealism and cold necessity. Faced with the task of feeding the army and the workers, the Bolsheviks had no choice but to institute "forcible requisitions," which amounted to sending raiding parties into the countryside to seize food. With money worthless and no consumer goods to purchase, there was no incentive for peasants to sell their produce—they produced only enough to feed themselves and their families. Although the raiding parties were supposed to take only surplus food, this was usually not adhered to. War communism, however, was not just a policy of necessity. There was a determined effort to destroy the market economy.

Once the civil war was over, Bolsheviks faced severe domestic problems. The country's industry, transportation system, and agriculture were in ruins after six years of war. The disastrous harvest of 1921 produced a famine costing 4–5 million lives and was alleviated only through Western assistance.[19] The half-starved workers and peasants were turning against the Bolsheviks. At the Tenth Party Congress of 1921–1922, Lenin introduced the New Economic Policy (NEP), intended as a temporary retreat from building communism. NEP involved abandoning the policy of forced requisitions and the encouragement of private farming. It allowed small private or cooperative industries to produce consumer goods, permitted private trade, and encouraged a free labor market. Although economic reality necessitated reliance on peasants, traders, and small-businessmen, Lenin had no intention of permitting them to block the advance of socialism. He envisaged only a temporary retreat in the economic realm, but a retreat that might last one to two decades.

The introduction of NEP improved agricultural production as peasants responded to incentives. By substituting a tax in-kind for forced requisitions and enabling peasants to dispose of their surplus on the free market, peasants had reason to produce a surplus. In 1924, as the country stabilized, the tax in-kind was replaced by a money tax. A mixed economy developed as agriculture and petty trade were conducted by private individuals and a new entrepreneurial class of Nepmen (private traders) emerged.[20] In 1925, peasants were even permitted to hire farm workers and lease additional land. However, the Bolsheviks were not reconciled to dependency on the peasantry. Adam Ulam speaks of the "superstitious and deep-seated fear of the peasantry as a whole, the feeling on the part of the Communists that a vast, inert, and yet somehow threatening mass of people barred Russia's path to industrialization, modernity, socialism; that a kingdom of darkness must be conquered before the Soviet Union could become the promised land."[21]

Economic differentiation developed during NEP, although the lines between strata were not clear. The Communists divided the peasant class into three ill-defined groups. Poor peasants, or *bedniaks*, were those with no land or insufficient land to support their families. Middle peasants, or *seredniaks*, were those who were able to meet the needs of their families through their own work and that of their families; they accounted for about 63 percent of the peasantry. *Kulaks* were the so-called rich peasants, who hired farm laborers. Although most of the peasantry lived at bare subsistence level, it was the kulaks who produced most of the farm surplus to feed the cities and for export. The prerevolutionary, prosperous kulaks had been eliminated by revolution and civil war. These were peasants who, through ability, luck, and hard work, became somewhat better off than their neighbors. They might own two or three cows, a plow horse, and about 25 acres of farmland. They accounted for less than 4 percent of the peasantry and produced about one-fifth of the grain.[22] In order to recover from the effects of war and famine, the kulaks had to be indulged. However, this risked putting control of the Soviet economy in the hands of the despised kulak, "*the class enemy . . . the personification of evil on the social scene.*" Ulam states, "For many Communists the kulak was a demonic force," and he adds that Stalin was "abundantly endowed with the Communist obsession about the kulak."[23]

The Procurement Crisis

The "procurement crisis" of 1927–1928 was a critical step in the march toward the disaster of 1932–1933. The price of food fell while consumer goods were in short supply. Although the harvest was normal, peasants began to hold back their surpluses, refusing to meet their quotas for sale to the state at low, state-determined prices. From October to December peasants sold official collection agencies only half as much grain as they had during the same months in the previous year. To get cash, peasants sold their surpluses on the free market at higher prices or sold industrial crops for which the state paid fairly high prices. Peasants also earned money through seasonal work in towns. They tried to keep their grain until spring in the expectation that procurement prices would rise; this endangered food supplies to urban areas as well as the army.[24] Grain exports virtually ceased, foreign currency earnings fell, and the government was unable to import machinery to industrialize. Stalin saw "not peasants trying to earn a few more rubles, but millions of class enemies trying to ruin his benevolent designs and overthrowing Soviet power."[25] He refused to capitulate to the kulaks by raising procurement prices. He was convinced that class enemies were carrying out deliberate sabotage. Stalin announced the policy of "liquidating kulaks as a class."

Although he denied that he was ending NEP or restoring forced requisitions, in a January 6, 1928, directive Stalin instituted a program of forced confiscation of grain. His primary concern was short-range: He was determined to make the peasants turn over their surpluses. Local officials were threatened if they failed to improve grain procurement. Thirty thousand party activists were sent to the countryside. Even members of the Central Committee and the Politburo went to Ukraine, North Caucasus, the Volga region, and Siberia to supervise procurement operations. Fixed delivery quotas were set for each individual household. House-to-house searches were conducted to find hidden grain, and any grain discovered was confiscated.

All peasants were required to hand over surplus grain, but kulaks were subjected to especially harsh treatment. Local authorities set arbitrary quotas; if these were not delivered by a fixed date, the offender was subject to fines, confiscation, and prison sentences. Kulaks who refused to sell their surplus grain at official prices could be treated as speculators and have their surplus confiscated. Since most grain was in the hands of the middle peasants, they too were subjected to arbitrary procedures. In an effort to secure the support of the poor peasants and drive a wedge between them and the better-off peasants, one-quarter of the grain confiscated from kulaks was sold to poor peasants at reduced prices. Private individuals were forbidden to buy from peasants, and most free markets in rural areas were closed. Militias were posted at district boundaries to prevent grain smuggling.[26] By April, the deficit in grain procurement had been largely made up. This confirmed Stalin's belief that the peasants had sufficient grain to feed the country and to export. The problem was to extract it from them. This experience helped to shape Stalin's actions in 1932–1933.

Peasants concluded that since surplus production would be confiscated it made no sense to sow as much grain as they had in the past. In short, their economic incentive was destroyed. Many kulaks, the most productive peasants, "liquidated themselves" by selling their farms, mills, machinery, and draft animals and hiding their money and valuables. Well-to-do middle peasants produced less out of fear of being labeled as kulaks. When the sale of grain to the state dropped off sharply during the spring of 1928, the government renewed its emergency measures, including house-to-house searches. Fedor Belov describes how the committees of the poor raided victims' households, seizing grain, agricultural implements, harnesses, livestock, furniture, and clothing.[27] When the grain they had stored for spring sowing and to feed their animals and their families was seized, peasants retaliated with violence against party agents with arson and looting of shops and warehouses. Even poor peasants turned against the regime. The sale of bread was restricted in most regions, and rationing was introduced in the Urals and several grain-consuming regions. Despite Stalin's vow not to give in to the peasants, procurement prices were raised 15 to 20 percent, the supply of manufactured goods in the countryside was increased, and searches and seizures of grain were halted. The Soviet Union imported 250,000 tons of grain during the summer of 1928. The fall 1928 grain procurement plan was underfilled, the regime had not ensured the necessary minimum grain reserves, and peasant mistrust and hostility were heightened.[28]

Stalin became increasingly certain that class enemies were out to wreck the Soviet economy. He declared that as the country got closer to socialism, the resistance of the class enemy would grow stronger and the class struggle more intense. From May to July 1928, Stalin staged the Soviet Union's first show trial, the Shakhty affair, a public trial of fifty-two "wreckers," primarily members of the old technical intelligentsia, charged with participating in a foreign-controlled conspiracy to wreck the coal-mining industry in the Donbas. Stalin used the trial to emphasize the dangers from hostile capitalist countries and the need to build an industrial base for defense of the country.

The regime introduced the "Ural-Siberian" or "social influence" method of grain collection in March 1929. The *skhod*, or village assembly, with kulaks excluded, levied grain quotas on peasant households, thereby putting the main burden on kulaks and well-to-do middle peasants. Thousands of party activists infiltrated the skhods and manipulated them to suit the regime's purposes. Both social pressure and severe economic penalties were exerted to ensure delivery. Those who failed to deliver the quota were subject to the *piatkratnika*, a fine equal to five times the quota. If this fine was not paid, a kulak could be imprisoned and subject to confiscation of tools and property. The intent was to mobilize the rural poor to assist the state in grain procurement.[29] This effort to create class struggle in the countryside was not entirely successful, as village solidarity often prevailed.

Industrialization and the First Five-Year Plan

Stalin became convinced of the need for rapid industrialization to overcome the Soviet Union's backwardness in the shortest possible time. In order for the Soviet Union to survive in an increasingly hostile international environment, a modern industrial economy was essential. Rapid industrialization would require huge expenditures to import foreign technology and machinery. Therefore, the Soviet Union needed to greatly expand exports, primarily grain. Stalin concluded that the free market in grain presented the regime with an unpredictable, expensive, and inefficient food supply that made it impossible to accumulate the capital needed for industrialization. For Stalin, collectivization was intended not only as a means to transform the countryside but as a means to carry out an industrial revolution from above. Since long-term foreign loans were not available for investment, the only alternative was to extract a surplus from the agricultural sector. This would necessitate lowering prices paid to peasants for agricultural goods, increasing the tax on peasants, and taxing kulaks more heavily. Stalin said industrial expansion had to be paid for by "tribute" exacted from agriculture. An independent peasantry would react to such measures by cutting output. This would make collectivization imperative, though by this time Stalin was also stressing the need for increasing the productivity of individual farms. The onset of the world economic depression would make achievement of Stalin's goals increasingly difficult. The Soviet Union launched its program of rapid industrialization requiring the importation of manufactured goods precisely when the price of grain, its principal export, was about to fall on the world market.

The introduction of the First Five-Year Plan reflected Stalin's determination to move toward rapid industrialization and put increased demands on the countryside. Nothing would be permitted to stand in the way. *Gosplan*, the State Planning Commission, developed two versions of the First Five-Year Plan. The Sixteenth Party Conference of April 1929 endorsed the optimal variant, which depended on a totally unrealistic set of assumptions. Fulfillment of the Plan depended upon an increase in agricultural productivity, despite the fact that it was inaugurated in the middle of a grain crisis and that grain procurement was below that of the previous year. It called for sizable increases in resources to be made available to the agricultural sector for mechanization and fertilizer. The main thrust was for an ambitious expansion of heavy industry, but it assumed that heavy and light industry could expand together and that both investment and consumption could increase. These assumptions proved overly optimistic.[30]

The Plan called for partial voluntary collectivization but assumed continued long-term reliance on the private sector. It was hoped that the collective sector would demonstrate its economic superiority and, thus, win over peasants for the collective sector. Twenty-three percent of peasant farms were to be collectivized in the following five years. Collective and state farms, which had accounted for less than 2 percent of grain production between 1927 and 1928, were to cover 17.5 percent of the total cultivated area and account for 43 percent of grain production for the market by 1932–1933. Although 23 percent of peasant households were to be collectivized over the life of the Plan, in the first year the level of collectivization was to be raised only from 1.7 to 2.2 percent.[31] There were three forms of *kolkhoz* (collective farm). The loosest form of collective, the *toz*, was to predominate during this period. In the toz, peasants retained their individual holdings but joined together to buy or rent tools and machinery and worked some land cooperatively. In the *artel*—which eventually became the standard form of collective farm—all land, except for small garden plots, was owned and worked in common. In the *kommuna*, the highest type, private property was completely abolished, and peasants worked and lived communally.[32]

The Plan was based on the expectation that the 1929 harvest would be substantially larger than that in 1928. Large increases were expected in grain collections without any increase in the prices paid to peasants by the collection agencies. However, a severe drought hit parts of Ukraine and areas of the North Caucasus in July 1929. Losses in the Ukrainian harvest exceeded the entire amount of grain procured by state collection agencies the previous year. At the

end of July, compulsory grain delivery quotas were allocated to districts and villages, not as an emergency measure but as regular policy. Essentially, this meant
a return to the grain requisitioning policies of the civil war period.

The peasants' first priority in sale of grain was in fulfillment of state obligations
as determined by skhods acting on instructions received through party channels.
Penalties were imposed for refusal to deliver grain, even if there was no evidence
the peasant actually had any. Grain collection officials and kolkhoz chairmen
could be tried if they failed to take adequate measures to ensure grain delivery.
Peasants felt cheated when they were forced to sell to government procurement
agencies for less than they could get on the free market. They hid grain in pits to
avoid the procurement or sold it on the black market. Speculators bought bread
on the free markets of towns and resold it in areas short of bread. The price of
food on the free market soared. By November 1929, the peasant population of
large areas of Ukraine moved north in search of food. James Hughes states that
"the specter of famine" endangered Ukraine and the industrial heartland. As the
price of food increased in cities and towns, worker dissatisfaction grew. Although
the regime had spent hard currency reserves to import grain the previous year,
the commitment to rapid industrialization made the regime unwilling to repeat
this. Nor was it willing to moderate the pace of industrial development.[33]

The regime reacted by sending in large numbers of party members and government officials to enforce grain collection. Merle Fainsod describes the actions
of these special emissaries in the Western Oblast of Russia. Although they were
supposed to enlist poor and middle peasants in requisitioning grain from the kulaks, many kulaks were respected village leaders. Often the villagers maintained
solidarity with the kulaks. Even local soviet and party officials often protected kulaks from the emissaries. Under pressure to procure grain, the emissaries often
seized grain not only from kulaks but from middle and even poor peasants. The
collection campaign thus undermined the official policy of driving a wedge between the kulaks and the rest of the village. When kulaks failed to meet their quotas, "workers' brigades" or village soviet forces raided households and confiscated
grain. Kulaks hid grain, offered bribes, and retaliated. Reports of killings and
arson multiplied and the emissaries pleaded for Unified State Political Administration (OGPU) reinforcements.[34] The entire campaign was confused; the
railroads had difficulty in transporting grain, and quotas were changed arbitrar-
ily. Grain continued to be collected in regions that had already fulfilled their
plans.[35] Despite warnings by Nikolay Bukharin and other party moderates that
continued use of forceful measures would lead to catastrophe, Stalin was convinced that peasants were hoarding grain and deliberately sabotaging the
regime.[36]

Rapid Collectivization

The tempo of collectivization began to accelerate rapidly during this period. By
July 1, more than 1 million households—nearly double the number anticipated—

had joined kolkhozes, but this still amounted to only 4 percent of all peasant households.[37] In August, the party approved rapid collectivization of entire regions and a stepped-up campaign of dekulakization. The already heavy tax burden on kulaks was sharply increased, and any resistance led to total expropriation. Kulaks were assigned high quotas for grain delivery. Although local practices varied, kulaks who failed to meet quotas were deprived of their property and expelled from villages. Part of the intent was to terrorize middle peasants into joining collectives rapidly to avoid the risk of being thrown in with the kulaks.[38] By September, a new slogan, "The Five-Year Plan in Four," was being proclaimed. By October 1, 7.5 percent of all households were collectivized, the figures for the major grain-producing regions being considerably higher.[39]

In November 1929, the party's Central Committee met to congratulate itself on its success on the agricultural front. Grain had been collected more rapidly and in larger quantities than in previous years. And though the socialized sector had failed to fulfill its plan, collections from individual peasants had more than made up the difference, leading to overfulfillment of the plan. Grain collection was 50 percent over that of the previous year. Not only was the government able to export substantial amounts of grain, it was able to create a grain reserve of more than 1.5 million tons to ensure that spring sowing would be favorable for collectivization. Vyacheslav Molotov spoke of the need for immediate collectivization to provide the state with agricultural products at low prices, thus enabling the state to finance industrialization.[40] The Central Committee emphasized the need for a new decisive offensive against the kulak. This produced a profound shift in party policy from the attempt at gradual transformation to the establishment of whole villages, districts, and even regions in which collectivization would be completed within a short time span. Party members believed that the goals of the Five-Year Plan could be achieved, that industrialization could be accomplished and agriculture transformed. However, for this to occur, the power of the kulaks would have to be broken.[41]

Brigades of party activists, worker battalions, Komsomol (the Communist Union of Youth), and OGPU detachments were sent to villages. The party mobilized 25,000 urban members, the so-called Twenty-Five Thousanders, to go to the countryside to "liquidate the kulaks as a class" and create collective farms. Party workers were supposed to ally with poor peasants, oust kulaks from the villages, and try to win over the middle peasants for the kolkhozes. In practice, any peasant who resisted was labeled a kulak and treated as an enemy. Party activists closed village churches, burned icons, and arrested priests.[42] From October to December 1929, collectivized households increased from 7.5 percent to 15 percent.[43]

Stalin now determined to move even more rapidly. A Central Committee decree of January 5, 1930, called for completing collectivization in all grain-producing areas by the fall of 1931, but the process moved much faster once it got under way. Machine Tractor Stations (MTS) were established to service the collective farms. In less than two months, the number of collectivized households doubled. The effort was to collectivize most peasants before sowing started in mid-April. To supervise local dekulakization and collectivization, special *troikas* were established, consisting of the first secretary of the district party committee, the chairman of the Soviet executive committee, and the head of the local OGPU. These local authorities were under unremitting pressure from the center to fill collectivization targets. Factory workers poured into the countryside along with party and local government officials. More than a quarter of a million agents were sent from the cities and towns. Mass terror and coercion were used against peasants reluctant to join collective farms.[44] In some areas, peasants' land and draft animals were expropriated for the collective, as were cows, pigs, and chickens. In other areas, even peasant homes and garden plots were merged into communes. The Central Committee declared that the artel, by now the dominant form of kolkhoz, was to serve as a transitional form toward a full kommuna, in which peasants would have no individual property. Kulaks, except for those with sons in the army, were not permitted to join collective farms.[45]

Dekulakization

Expropriation of kulaks was carried out simultaneously with collectivization. A reign of terror was unleashed in large areas of the countryside. Many kulaks were expelled from their homes, their land, and often their villages. A top-secret letter of February 12 divided all kulak households into three groups based on the danger they presented and the severity of the punishment they should suffer:

1. Active counterrevolutionaries who organized terror and counterrevolution: these were to be shot or sent to prison or corrective labor camps; their families were to be banished to remote regions. Fifty thousand households were to be included in this category.
2. Politically active rich kulaks: they and their families were to be banished to remote regions. About 112,000 households were to be included in this category.
3. Less powerful kulak households who would be permitted to remain in their own district but would be resettled outside the collectivized villages on the worst land. These kulaks, numbering approximately 5 million, were to be required to perform communal duties.

The letter prohibited deportation or resettlement of poor or middle peasants, but in practice, many more peasants than the recommended numbers were banished, sent to corrective labor camps, or shot.[46]

The definition of "kulak" was so broad that few were safe. A peasant could be deemed a kulak for once having hired a laborer. Any peasant who was uncooperative could be labeled a *podkulachnik*, or kulak henchman, and treated as a kulak. Raiding parties took clothing, warm underwear, hats, and shoes from the bodies of members of kulak and even seredniak households. Often the goods were shared out among members of the raiding party who ate the food and drank the alcohol on the spot. Fear became pervasive among well-to-do peasants. There was a wave of suicides. Kulaks orchestrated fictitious divorces in hopes of saving the lives of their wives and children. Some abandoned their property and went into hiding.[47] Peasants resisted in the only way they could: destroying crops and slaughtering and eating their livestock. Four million horses were slaughtered. But it was not just draft animals that were killed. In February and March 1930, one-fourth of all cattle, one-third of all pigs, and more than one-fourth of the sheep and goats were destroyed. Riots, arson, and terrorist killings of officials multiplied. The majority of attackers were peasant women wielding pitchforks, spades, and axes. When heads of households were imprisoned, wives and children were left with no means of support. Bands of beggar children roamed the countryside and wandered into towns. Although some poor peasants used dekulakization to pay off scores against kulaks and to share in the spoils, most sympathized with the fate of their neighbors. Armed peasant revolts broke out. Violent reprisals were taken against the peasants. Chaos threatened.[48]

Some estimates suggest that approximately 1.1 million households were expropriated and that about one-half of the resulting 7 million dislocated citizens were packed into unheated boxcars and deported to special settlements or labor camps in the far north and other distant areas of the country where, if they survived the trip, they provided forced labor for road building, lumbering, construction, and mining. The number in labor camps grew from about 30,000 in 1928 to nearly 2 million in 1931.[49]

A Respite

Stalin's article, *Dizzy from Success,* published in *Pravda* on March 2, called a temporary retreat to prevent the breakdown of spring sowing. Stalin blamed local party and government officials for violating the voluntary principle of collectivization. Fifty-eight percent of all peasant farms had been collectivized on March 1, but many were only paper organizations. Peasants began leaving collective farms in such numbers that by June 30 the bloated collectivization figure was down to 23.6 percent. More than half of those leaving were in Ukraine and the North Caucasus. The mass exodus from the collectives threatened to disorganize the spring sowing.

The Great Depression had caused grain prices to fall 49 percent in 1930, but the price of machinery that the Soviet Union needed to import remained stable. This meant that the country had to export twice as much grain per unit of machinery imported as it had in 1928.[50] There were highly optimistic expectations for the harvest of 1930–1931 and an ambitious grain collection plan. The village quota took absolute precedence over all other needs. Peasants who failed to meet individual quotas were fined or imprisoned and their property was sold.

Relentless pressure stripped the individual peasants of their grain. Although less grain was collected than anticipated in the plan, it was 6 million tons over the 1929–1930 collection and double the 1928–1929 collection. No less than 83.5 million tons of grain were harvested, 26.5 percent of which was procured by the state through obligatory deliveries at low prices. The country exported 4.8 million tons, but because of the depression, the price received on the world market in early 1931 was only 36 percent of that received the previous year. Since the prices for cotton and timber had not fallen as badly, grain was supplied to cotton- and timber-producing areas of the country so they could export their production, enabling the Soviet Union to import the machinery and industrial materials needed for industrialization. Although agricultural supplies to towns increased more slowly than did the urban population, workers in large capital goods factories received higher bread rations than those in less important industries. The rural population had an absolute decline in consumption per head in 1930.[51]

Renewed Collectivization

After the successful harvest of 1930, Stalin pushed for collectivization with renewed vigor and determination, particularly in the major grain-growing regions. This time, however, peasants were permitted to keep homes, garden plots, and some domestic animals. More farm machinery was available, concentrated in the MTS, each of which had a Communist Party police unit, the "political section," charged with supervising the countryside. The MTS became centers of power in the countryside. Many middle peasants who refused to enter collective farms were reclassified as kulaks. By June 1931, the number of households in collective farms was back to the March figure. By September, 60 percent of peasant households were collectivized. This time around, compared to the first collectivization drive, there were more instances of destruction of property and slaughter of draft animals.[52]

The harvest of 1931 was poor, especially in Ukraine, but Stalin was relentless. The proportion of the gross yield procured by the state increased from 27 percent in 1930 to 33 percent in 1931. Procurement quotas had to rise because of the increase in the urban population. In 1930, there were 26 million urban workers being provisioned by the state. This rose to 33.2 million by 1931.[53] Under collective farm rules, the first obligation of a kolkhoz after a harvest was to deliver grain to the state in accord with procurement quotas. The second priority was to create seed reserves, supplies of fodder, and grain reserves and to pay the MTS for work performed. Only then was grain distributed to collective farmers. About 10 to 15 percent of the *kolkhozniks'* anticipated earnings were distributed in advance, but the peasants had to wait until December for final distribution. The poor harvest and high procurements left little grain for the kolkhozes to distribute to their members in 1931. In some areas, as much as 60 percent of the harvest was taken, leaving the peasant with little incentive to produce.[54] Archives recently discovered at the Ukrainian Communist Party's Institute of Party History document severe food shortages in the Ukrainian countryside during the winter of 1931–1932.[55]

The 1932 Harvest and Grain Procurement

Proponents of the view that the Great Famine of 1932–1933 constituted an officially directed genocide—accomplished through procurement quotas—against the Ukrainians argue that the grain harvest of 1932 was not particularly low and should have been adequate to feed the population. However, Mark B. Tauger points out that recent data from Soviet archives demonstrate that the 1932 harvest was considerably lower than official statistics indicate, aggravating the serious food shortage that had struck the country in 1931 and making "famine likely if not inevitable in 1933." His calculations give a total Soviet harvest of 50.06 million tons, nearly 30 percent below the official figure of 69.87 million tons. He argues that the famine was primarily the result of a genuine shortage.[56]

The 1932 harvest, as Sheila Fitzpatrick points out, was only the third since collectivization, so there was no backlog of experience to draw on. The state was not yet sure how much it could extract from the peasantry. The peasants, for their part, were trying to figure out how little they could deliver. When the government established procurement quotas, it had to guess the size of the future harvest and then announce the quotas. At all levels of agricultural production, from the peasant up, all were motivated to argue that the quota was impossible to meet; and, at all levels of party and government, every official knew or suspected the others were exaggerating the difficulties of meeting the quota. The pressures of the Five-Year Plan and the demands of industrialization pushed Moscow to impose unrealistically high quotas. The urban population was growing rapidly, and the government wanted to increase grain exports to pay for foreign technology and machinery. And whereas unrealistic quotas for industrial output could mean unfortunate results, in agriculture the result could be fatal, leaving peasants without food to survive the winter.[57]

The procurement plan for 1932 was initially fixed at 29.5 million tons, though it was later reduced to 18 million. As the regime encountered difficulties in grain procurement, pressure was increased. In June 1932, raions (districts) in the Western Oblast of Russia were informed that grain supplies, even for basic industries, would be exhausted by July 1. No reserves were left to meet July commitments. In a desperate attempt to feed the cities and towns, additional emergency grain-delivery quotas were imposed. An additional 4–5 percent was added to the grain delivery plans for each raion to ensure plan fulfillment. Militia and OGPU units prevented all sale of bread in bazaars until the peasants had met delivery quotas.[58] Peasants went on "grain strikes," refusing to work unless advance grain payments were increased. Raids on kolkhoz fields and thefts of grain, often by members of the kolkhozes themselves, became increasingly common. Much of the stealing was a result of hunger, but some was out of anger and resentment.[59]

Desperately hungry peasant women called "barbers" scissored off spikes of grain from unripened fields to feed their children. Peasants carried off in their pockets small amounts of grain from threshing stations. Others slaughtered pigs and cattle. Seed grain set aside for sowing, fodder for draft animals, and grain already distributed to collective farmers were requisitioned to meet quotas. Thousands of collective farm chairmen, specialists, and even party and state officials were arrested and convicted of "connivance in kulak sabotage."[60] The main centers of resistance were in Ukraine, the North Caucasus, and parts of the Volga region.

Famine spread across the country, primarily in rural areas but affecting towns as well.[61] Urban workers deserted factories, and millions of peasants fled collective farms in search of food. Internal passports were issued to registered town dwellers to control movement. Since peasants were not given passports, they were prevented from moving to towns without authorization, even to take seasonal work. Starving bands of children roamed the streets of towns. Hungry peasants crowded railroad stations and begged in the streets, even in Moscow and Leningrad. In July 1932, All-Union Party Politburo members Vyacheslav Molotov and Lazar Kaganovich appeared at the Third All-Ukrainian Party Conference to take the Ukrainian leadership to task for jeopardizing fulfillment of the agricultural plan.[62] The Ukrainian party leadership argued that the plans imposed on Ukraine were unrealistic. They pleaded for lower quotas but to no avail.[63]

Reprisals Against Peasants

An August 7, 1932, decree declared kolkhoz property "sacred" and "inviolable." Those who pilfered it were labeled "enemies of the people." The stealing of kolkhoz property, even of crops in the fields, was punishable by a death sentence or, in mitigating circumstances, by a minimum sentence of ten years in a labor camp and confiscation of property. Police, military, paramilitary, and Komsomol patrols were established in the countryside to protect the grain against the peasants who had grown it. Harvesting now took place under armed guard. Zhores Medvedev states that even this draconian law had little effect. Grain collections continued to be low. To add to the pressure, the government set up roadblocks in parts of Ukraine, North Caucasus, and the Don region to prevent grain being smuggled out for sale and to prevent the delivery of salt, kerosene, and cloth until quotas had been fulfilled.[64]

Grain exports continued, albeit at a reduced rate. Exports fell from 4.8 million tons in 1930 and 5.1 million tons in 1931 to 1.8 million in 1932 and 1 million in 1933. Tauger argues that as a result of the fall in world market prices for grain the Soviet Union's indebtedness increased while its potential ability to pay decreased. The West contemplated seizing Soviet assets and denying future credits if the Soviet Union defaulted. This would have undermined fulfillment of industrialization plans.[65] Exports could not be halted without scrapping the Five-Year Plan, which Stalin was not willing to do.

Stalin believed that the peasants suffered as a consequence of their own mis-deeds—their earlier opposition to collectivization, their stealing of grain, and their slaughtering of animals. If grain procurement quotas could not be filled, Stalin assumed that this had to be the result of deliberate efforts by enemies to undermine Soviet socialism and him personally. Stalin blamed local party work-ers and kolkhoz chairmen for attending to the needs of collective farms before fulfilling obligations to the state. He blamed local authorities for their lack of vig-ilance in uncovering the kulaks who were responsible for the disaster. Feeding the army, OGPU troops, and urban workers and exporting grain took priority over alleviating the starvation of peasants.[66]

Ruthless reprisals were taken against peasants, particularly in the North Caucasus and Ukraine. In the fall of 1932, a special Politburo commission headed by Kaganovich was sent to the North Caucasus to quell a strike of Kuban Cossacks who refused to cultivate their land. The entire populations of sixteen Cossack vil-lages in the North Caucasus were deported to Siberia.[67] When grain procure-ments in Ukraine failed to meet the goals, procurement brigades were sent back again. These procurement brigades, which included members of OGPU, the local militia, and armed activists, moved from village to village threatening the peas-ants.[68] At the end of December, Moscow sent instructions that kolkhozes that had not met their quotas were to give up all their grain, including seed funds.[69] Fedor Belov speaks of the "red brooms," the name given to groups of party members, primarily from the cities, who searched kolkhozes and individual plots for food peasants might have hidden, taking "surplus" grain from barns and corncribs.[70]

A Ukrainian decree of December 6, 1932, assigned six villages to a *chorna doshka,* or black list, for sabotaging grain procurements. Other villages were soon added to the list. This came close to constituting a collective death sentence. All state and cooperative stores were closed and all goods removed from the villages. All trade, including that in bread, was banned. Warehouses containing food grain were sealed and even seed grain was seized. All credits and advances, including bread, had to be repaid immediately. The kolkhozes were threatened with disso-lution if they still failed to deliver their quotas. Collective farms and state appa-ratuses were purged of those who argued that failure to meet quotas was a con-sequence of famine and urged the retention of seed grain to ensure spring sowing from collective farms. A special system of local prosecutors was established to im-pose criminal penalties for nonfulfillment of quotas.[71]

Agricultural Disaster: The Winter of 1932–1933

By the end of 1932, it was clear that Ukraine and North Caucasus, the lower and middle Volga region, the southern Urals, and Kazakhstan were in the grip of a cat-astrophic famine. The famine was not restricted to only these areas, however. Fainsod reports that the food crisis in the Western Oblast "reached a climax of desperation during the bitter Winter of 1932–1933."[72] Peasants left their villages in search of food, but roadblocks and military cordons prevented movement. Peasants had been in the habit of finding temporary work in towns in the winter, but this was now forbidden. Collective farmers were not allowed to leave their villages. Although some peasants managed to reach the towns, this failed to alleviate their desperate situation since all food was rationed and they lacked ration cards. Corpses lay in the streets of cities and towns until collected by special trucks.[73]

Once the true dimensions of the famine were evident, the regime realized that the lack of seed grain for spring sowing could endanger the next year's harvest. Some grain quotas were lowered and some grain reserves were opened. On February 25, 1933, a Central Committee decree allotted 320,000 tons of seed to Ukraine and 240,000 to the North Caucasus.[74] Minimal food rations were distributed to peasants who actually worked in the fields. The planting took place under the direct supervision of political departments of the MTS. In many places, the army guarded the seed grain from hungry peasants.[75] On May 8, 1933, Stalin and Molotov sent secret instructions to halt the "saturnalia of arrests" and curtail the scale of repression in the countryside. Maximum deportation quotas were established. Arrests and deportation could still occur on an individual basis against those who carried on active struggle against collective farms or organized refusals to sow and deliver produce.[76]

Impact on Ukraine

The agricultural disaster put Stalin's entire plan at risk. He could not accept the fact that the famine was the culmination of previous policies; scapegoats had to be found. Stalin attributed the catastrophe to recalcitrance on the part of peasants and disloyalty on the part of local leaders, especially in Ukraine. The Ukrainian party organization was assailed for failure to meet production quotas. Pavel Postyshev, a non-Ukrainian member of the All-Union Party Secretariat and close associate of Stalin, was sent to Ukraine as second secretary of the Ukrainian Communist Party with broad authority to reorganize and purge the party. Party personnel from outside Ukraine were transferred in, and urban cadres were transferred to rural areas. In February, a new OGPU chief was sent to Ukraine. On February 28, announcement was made of the uncovering of an alleged major anti-Soviet conspiracy to undermine agriculture. Seventy members of the agricultural commissariat were put on trial. Others lost their posts and were deported or imprisoned.[77]

Mykola Skrypnyk, a strong supporter of Ukrainization and boss of Ukraine since 1927, was demoted from his post as commissar of education and assigned to a less sensitive post in charge of the Ukrainian Gosplan. Orchestrated attacks against Skrypnyk followed, leading to his suicide on July 6, 1933. After Skrypnyk's death, the party campaign against Ukrainian nationalism accelerated. Henceforth, Russification would be imposed in politics, economics, and culture throughout the non-Russian areas of the Soviet Union. Decisions would be made in Moscow. Robert Sullivant contends that the pressures of collectivization and industrialization led the central leaders to regard any expression of independence in culture as an attack on the party. Their suspicions were exacerbated by the rebirth of German militarism, since Germany had earlier been the sponsor of Ukrainian nationalism. This led them to regard all nationalist manifestations as signs of subversion. He states that, therefore, it was not unreasonable for party leaders to conclude that, for both security reasons and the success of Soviet programs, Ukrainian nationalists had to be restricted or destroyed.[78]

In support of the conclusion that the famine resulted from the regime's determination to use grain procurements as an instrument to crush the Ukrainian people, Mace and Conquest point to the fact that the famine stopped at the Byelorussian-Ukrainian border in the north and the Russo-Ukrainian border in the northeast. The Russo-Ukrainian border was closed by security troops to prevent Ukrainian peasants from getting out to find food. If they did manage to leave, they were not allowed to return with food. However, the border with Byelorussia apparently was not closed. Many Ukrainians went there seeking food since the famine was much less severe.[79] Fitzpatrick writes that the flight of starving peasants toward the towns in the winter led to a crisis. The towns were already overcrowded from the influx of previous years and were unable to cope. The urban rationing and supply systems threatened to break down. Steps were therefore taken to cordon off the towns. Those not engaged in productive work were given ten days to leave. About 300,000 were deported from Moscow alone.[80]

On April 22, 1933, Stalin and Molotov circulated a directive in response to mass exodus from the North Caucasus and Ukraine to the central regions of Russia and Byelorussia. The directive insisted that the exodus was organized by Polish agents and enemies of the Soviet regime in order to agitate against collective farms and the Soviet system. Local authorities and the OGPU were ordered to prevent mass departures and to immediately arrest the "peasants" of the Ukraine and North Caucasus who made their way north and, after the counter-revolutionary elements had been separated, to return the remainder to their place of residence.[81] An order banned the sale of railroad tickets in the Ukrainian countryside to anyone without travel authorization from local authorities. OGPU guards inspected all trains at the border to search for peasant stowaways. About 220,000 fleeing peasants were caught and returned to their villages in the spring of 1933.[82]

Conclusion

The government could have relaxed procurement, eliminated grain exports, and even imported grain and encouraged famine relief; but its failure to take these measures does not justify the charge of Ukrainian genocide. J. Arch Getty stresses that objective effect is not the same as subjective intent.[83] Similarly, David R.

Marples, after reviewing recent publications by the Institute of History of the Ukrainian Academy of Sciences, concludes:

> It is more logical to perceive Stalinist agricultural policies, for example, as motivated by a desire for the acquisition of grain rather than by an aversion to Ukrainians as an ethnic or national group. . . . Because the effects of Soviet policies have been so tragic, the worst motives on the part of the perpetrators are often assumed.[84]

Unlike the Holocaust, the Great Famine was not an intentional act of genocide. The purpose was not to exterminate Ukrainians as a people simply because they were Ukrainians. Extermination was not an end in itself. The famine was the result of Stalin's effort to totally reconstruct Soviet society through rapid industrialization. The burden of industrialization, of necessity, fell most heavily on peasants. Since Ukrainians were overwhelmingly a peasant people, they suffered disproportionately. The deaths of millions of Ukrainians and other Soviet peoples in the famine were not the intent but rather the consequence of a ruthless economic policy. When the famine put Stalin's plans at risk, Stalin attributed the disaster to disloyalty, particularly in Ukraine, where resistance to forced procurement was strongest. Ukrainian nationalism was attacked because it was perceived as a threat to Stalin's procurement policies, thus endangering rapid industrialization.

A multitude of interconnected factors contributed to the Great Famine. An unrealistic procurement and pricing policy eliminated incentives for peasants to produce more than they and their families consumed. When their surpluses were taken away at low, state-imposed prices, they sowed less the next year. Kulaks, the hardest-working and most ambitious peasants, were eliminated, and middle peasants were discouraged from producing more, lest they be labeled kulaks. To ensure control over grain collection, the regime introduced forced collectivization when adequate machinery and management were not available. In protest, peasants slaughtered draft animals. Grain confiscation efforts took seed grain, fodder, and even the necessary minimal food from peasants. Increasing urbanization meant that grain-producing regions could not keep all they produced, even in a famine, lest the cities starve. The world economic depression lowered agricultural prices in relation to industrial prices, meaning that the country had to increase exports to obtain the same amount of imports. The most important factor, the one that overrode all other considerations, was Stalin's determination that nothing would stand in the way of forced, rapid industrialization.

After the famine, peasants no longer had the will to resist. By 1936, over 90 percent of peasant households were collectivized. Almost 250,000 kolkhozes replaced the 25 million inefficient, primitive, small individual peasant farms tying up labor needed for industrialization. The peasant was eliminated as an independent force standing in the way of modernization. The average rate of increase in large-scale industrial output from 1928 to 1937 was about 15–16 percent per year. The gross national product rose 6.5–7 percent annually. In 1926, more than 80 percent of the Soviet Union's workers were in the agricultural sector. During the next thirteen years, 25 million people moved to cities, doubling the urban population.[85]

The Soviet Union, through forced collectivization and the relentless struggle for industrialization, created a powerful industrial state; but Stalinism ultimately left the Soviet Union with an inefficient and distorted system of production. Heavy industry, especially defense, had absolute priority. The planning process itself distorted production, as industries strove to meet production targets rather than producing what the economy needed. Consumer goods were sacrificed. There was a housing shortage as more workers poured into the cities. The chaos of collectivization, peasant resistance, the lack of incentives for the individual peasant, and the low investment in agriculture continued to plague the Soviet economy. Ultimately the Soviet people discovered that their enormous sacrifices produced an economy that no longer worked.

NOTES

1. See Aleksandr M. Nekrich, *The Punished Peoples*, trans. George Saunders (New York: W. W. Norton, 1978); Bohdan Nahaylo and Victor Swoboda, *Soviet Disunion: A History of the Nationalities Problem in the USSR* (New York: Free Press, 1989), pp. 79–106; Helene Carrere d'Encausse, "When the 'Prison of Peoples' Was Opened," in *The Soviet Nationality Reader*, ed. Rachel Denber (Boulder: Westview Press, 1992), pp. 88–91; Shirin Akiner, *Islamic Peoples of the Soviet Union* (Boston: Kegan Paul International, 1983). For an account of the Kazakh tragedy, see Robert Conquest, *The Harvest of Sorrow: Soviet Collectivization and the Terror-Famine* (New York: Oxford University Press, 1986), pp. 189–198.

2. Marco Carynnyk, "The Famine the 'Times' Couldn't Find," *Commentary* 76 (November 1983):32–40; Marco Carynnyk, "Making the News Fit to Print: Walter Duranty, the *New York Times*, and the Ukrainian Famine of 1933," in *Famine in Ukraine, 1932–1933*, ed. Roman Serbyn and Bohdan Krawchenko (Edmonton: Canadian Institute of Ukrainian Studies, University of Alberta, 1986), pp. 67–95; Eugene Lyons, *Assignment in Utopia* (New York: Harcourt, Brace, 1937, republished, New Brunswick: Transaction Publishers, 1991), pp. 541–577; Conquest, *Harvest of Sorrow*, pp. 308–321.

3. Marco Carynnyk, "Blind Eye to Murder: Britain, the United States, and the Ukrainian Famine of 1933," in Serbyn and Krawchenko, *Famine in Ukraine*, pp. 109–138; the eighty-five documents collected in Marco Carynnyk, Lubomyr Y. Luciuk, and Bohdan S. Kordan, eds., *The Foreign Office and the Famine* (New York: Vestal, 1988), present contemporary descriptions of the famine sent to the West in British diplomatic pouches. These communications were largely ignored or suppressed at the time. See also Mark B. Tauger, "Reviews: The Foreign Office and the Famine/Investigation of the Ukrainian Famine, 1932–1933," *Slavic Review* 48 (Winter 1989):680.

4. James E. Mace, "Famine and Nationalism," *Problems of Communism* 33 (May-June 1984):37. See also Nahaylo and Swoboda, *Soviet Disunion*, p. 70; Conquest, *Harvest of Sorrow*; Commission on the Ukrainian Famine, *Investigation of the Ukrainian Famine*,

1932–1933: Report to Congress (Washington, D.C.: Government Printing Office, 1988). It should be noted that James E. Mace was the staff director for the congressional commission. For a sharp attack on Conquest's hypothesis, sources, and evidence, see J. Arch Getty, "Starving the Ukraine," *London Review of Books*, January 22, 1987.

5. See Robert C. Tucker, *Stalin in Power: The Revolution from Above, 1928–1941* (New York: W. W. Norton, 1990), as well as his "Stalinism as Revolution from Above," in *Stalinism: Essays in Historical Interpretation*, ed. Robert C. Tucker (New York: W. W. Norton, 1977); and Robert C. Tucker, *Political Culture and Leadership in Soviet Russia* (New York: W. W. Norton, 1987); Adam Ulam, *Stalin: The Man and His Era* (New York: Viking, 1973); Martin Malia, *The Soviet Tragedy: A History of Socialism in Russia, 1917–1991* (New York: Free Press, 1994), pp. 139–227.

6. Hannah Arendt, *The Origins of Totalitarianism*, 2d ed. (New York: Meridian Books, 1958), p. 320.

7. Stephen Wheatcraft, "Correspondence: Ukrainian Famine," *Problems of Communism* 33 (March-April 1985):134.

8. Nahaylo and Swoboda, *Soviet Disunion*, pp. 60–65.

9. Michael Ignatieff, *Blood and Belonging: Journeys into the New Nationalism* (New York: Farrar, Straus, and Giroux, 1993), pp. 194–195.

10. *Economist*, January 28, 1995, p. 18.

11. M. Maksudov, "Ukraine's Demographic Losses, 1927–1938," in Serbyn and Krawchenko, *Famine in Ukraine*, pp. 34–37.

12. James E. Mace, "The Famine of 1933: A Survey of Sources," in Serbyn and Krawchenko, *Famine in Ukraine*, p. 50. In "Famine and Nationalism in Soviet Ukraine," *Problems of Communism* 33 (May-June 1984):39, Mace concludes that 7.5 million people in Ukraine died prematurely from famine.

13. Robert Conquest, *Harvest of Sorrow*, pp. 299–307.

14. Robert E. Johnson, "Introduction," *Russian Studies in History* 31 (Summer 1992):2–7; Iurii Aleksandrov Poliakov, Valentina Borisovna Zhiromshaia, and Igor' Nikolaevich Kiselev, "A Half-Century of Silence: The 1937 Census," *Russian Studies in History* 31 (Summer 1992):53.

15. Elena Aleksandrovna Osokin, "The Victims of the Famine of 1933: How Many?" *Russian Studies in History* 31 (Fall 1992):5–18.

16. Stephen Wheatcraft, "More Light on the Scale of Repression and Excess Mortality in the Soviet Union in the 1930's," *Soviet Studies* 42 (April 1990):355–367.

17. Alec Nove, "How Many Victims in the 1930's?" in *Soviet Studies* 42 (April 1990):369–373. "Research Materials," *Journal of Soviet Nationalities* 1 (Winter 1990–1991):158–159, argues that data from the 1937 census indicate that more than 5 million Ukrainians died in the famine and that millions more were not born or died in collectivization and the Great Purge between 1926 and 1937. It suggests a total population loss for this period of about 10 million.

18. James E. Mace, "The Man-Made Famine of 1933 in Soviet Ukraine," in Serbyn and Krawchenko, *Famine in Ukraine*, p. 11.

19. For an analysis of the 1921 famine, see Roman Serbyn, "The Famine of 1921–1923: A Model for 1932–1933?" in Serbyn and Krawchenko, *Famine in Ukraine*, pp. 147–178. Serbyn argues that whereas the 1921 famine in Russia was a result of natural calamities, in Ukraine it was caused "primarily by excessive taxation and outright plunder" and served as an effective means to crush Ukrainian peasant resistance to the Soviet regime.

20. Malia, *The Soviet Tragedy*, p. 146.

21. Ulam, *Stalin: The Man and His Era*, p. 295.

22. Tucker, *Stalin in Power*, p. 72.

23. Ulam, *Stalin: The Man and His Era*, pp. 294, 249.

24. R. W. Davies, *The Socialist Offensive: The Collectivization of Soviet Agriculture, 1929–1930* (Cambridge, Mass.: Harvard University Press, 1980), p. 39; Roy A. Medvedev, *Let History Judge: The Origins and Consequences of Stalinism*, trans. Colleen Taylor (New York: Alfred A. Knopf, 1972), p. 77; Moshe Lewin, *Russian Peasants and Soviet Power* (New York: W. W. Norton, 1967), p. 216.

25. Ulam, *Stalin: The Man and His Era*, p. 355.

26. Lewin, *Russian Peasants and Soviet Power*, pp. 217–230.

27. Fedor Belov, *The History of a Soviet Collective Farm* (New York: Praeger, 1955), p. 6.

28. Lewin, *Russian Peasants and Soviet Power*, pp. 239–244; Davies, *Socialist Offensive*, pp. 46–56.

29. James Hughes, "Capturing the Russian Peasantry: Stalinist Grain Procurement Policy and the 'Ural-Siberian Method,'" *Slavic Review* 53 (Spring 1994):76–78.

30. Lewin, *Russian Peasants and Soviet Power*, pp. 344–352.

31. Roy Medvedev, *Let History Judge*, p. 83; Lewin, *Russian Peasants and Soviet Power*, pp. 353–354.

32. Ulam, *Stalin: The Man and His Era*, pp. 322–323.

33. Hughes, "Capturing the Russian Peasantry," pp. 81–102; Davies, *Socialist Offensive*, pp. 63–76; Lewin, *Russian Peasants and Soviet Power*, pp. 382–87; Tucker, *Stalin in Power*, pp. 131–132.

34. Merle Fainsod, *Smolensk Under Soviet Rule* (Cambridge, Mass.: Harvard University Press, 1958), pp. 239–241.

35. Davies, *Socialist Offensive*, pp. 82–103.

36. Roy Medvedev, *Let History Judge*, pp. 80–81.

37. Ibid., p. 83.

38. Ulam, *Stalin: The Man and His Era*, pp. 324–325; Tucker, *Stalin in Power*, pp. 130–132, 138–141.

39. Davies, *Socialist Offensive*, p. 133.

40. Tucker, *Stalin in Power*, pp. 134–135; Davies, *Socialist Offensive*, pp. 105–107.

41. Davies, *Socialist Offensive*, pp. 172–173.

42. Sheila Fitzpatrick, *Stalin's Peasants: Resistance and Survival in the Russian Village After Collectivization* (New York: Oxford University Press, 1994), p. 6.

43. Lewin, *Russian Peasants and Soviet Power*, p. 514.

44. Davies, *Socialist Offensive*, pp. 204–230.

45. Ulam, *Stalin: The Man and His Era*, pp. 327–329.

46. Fainsod, *Smolensk*, pp. 242–244; Roy Medvedev, *Let History Judge*, p. 98.

47. Fainsod, *Smolensk*, pp. 245–247.

48. Davies, *Socialist Offensive*, pp. 246–251; Malia, *The Soviet Tragedy*, p. 197; Tucker, *Stalin in Power*, pp. 176–182; Roy Medvedev, *Let History Judge*, pp. 85–87; Lewin, *Russian Peasants and Soviet Power*, pp. 494–505.

49. Tucker, *Stalin in Power*, pp. 138, 173–175, 180–181.

50. Davies, *Socialist Offensive*, p. 107.

51. Ibid., pp. 350–371.

52. Malia, *The Soviet Tragedy*, p. 198.

53. Conquest, *Harvest of Sorrow*, p. 168.

54. Fitzpatrick, *Stalin's Peasants*, p. 72; Zhores A. Medvedev, *Soviet Agriculture* (New York: W. W. Norton, 1987), pp. 87–88.

55. Sergei Tsikora, "The Truth About the 1930's Famine," *Izvestia*, February 8, 1990, in *Current Digest of the Soviet Press* 42 (March 14, 1990):30–31.

56. Mark B. Tauger, "The 1932 Harvest and the Famine of 1933," *Slavic Review* 50 (Spring 1991):70–84. The quotation is on page 71. See also Mark B. Tauger, "Reviews: The Foreign Office and the Famine/Investigation of the Ukrainian Famine, 1932–1933," *Slavic Review* 48 (Winter 1989):678–679. He cites the Soviet publication *Istoriia krest'ianstva SSSR: Istoriia sovetskogo krest'ianstva* t.2, *1927–1937* (Moscow: Nauka, 1986) for his statistical information.

57. Fitzpatrick, *Stalin's Peasants*, pp. 70–71; Zhores Medvedev, *Soviet Agriculture*, p. 87.

58. Fainsod, *Smolensk*, pp. 259–260.

59. Fitzpatrick, *Stalin's Peasants*, p. 72.

60. Tsikora, "The Truth About the 1930's Famine," pp. 30–31.

61. The reports of Andrew Cairns, a Canadian wheat expert, provide contemporary graphic descriptions of conditions at this time. See "*Mr. Cairns' Investigations in Soviet Union*: William Strang (Moscow) to Sir John Simon, 12 August 1932, and John Cairns to E.M.H. Lloyd, 3 August 1932," in Carynnyk, Luciuk, and Kordan, *The Foreign Office and the Famine*, pp. 104–165, and "*Description of a Tour in the Volga Region*: Report by Andrew Cairns (Moscow)," p. 22, August 1932 in ibid., pp. 174–194.

62. "*Conditions in Ukraine*: Sir Esmond Ovey (Moscow) to Sir John Simon, 18 July 1932," in Carynnyk, Luciuk, and Kordan, *The Foreign Office and the Famine*, pp. 79–81.

63. Hryhory Kostiuk, *Stalinist Rule in the Ukraine* (New York: Praeger, 1960), pp. 22–23.

64. Zhores Medvedev, *Soviet Agriculture*, pp. 89–90.

65. Tauger, *The 1932 Harvest*, pp. 88–89.

66. Ulam, *Stalin: The Man and His Era*, pp. 345–349.

67. Nikita Khrushchev, *Khrushchev Remembers*, trans. Strobe Talbott (Boston: Little, Brown, 1970), p. 73.

68. Zhores Medvedev, *Soviet Agriculture*, pp. 90–91.

69. Fitzpatrick, *Stalin's Peasants*, p. 74.

70. Belov, *History of a Soviet Collective*, p. 28.

71. Fitzpatrick, *Stalin's Peasants*, pp. 76–77; Mace, *Famine and Nationalism*, p. 46.

72. Fainsod, *Smolensk*, p. 262.

73. Zhores Medvedev, *Soviet Agriculture*, pp. 91–92.

74. "Sir Esmond Ovey to Sir John Simon, 27 February 1933," in *The Foreign Office and the Famine*, p. 214. See also "*Conditions in Northern Caucasus in Spring of 1933*: Report by Otto Schiller, German Agricultural Attache in Moscow, 23 May 1933, Forwarded to Anthony Eden by the Duchess of Atholl, July 1933," in ibid., pp. 258–268.

75. Lyons, *Assignment in Utopia*, p. 577.

76. Leonard Schapiro, *The Communist Party of the Soviet Union* (New York: Vintage Books, 1964), pp. 386–387; V. P. Danilov and N. V. Teptsov, "Kollektivizatiia: Kak eto bylo," *Pravda*, September 16, 1988, in *The Stalin Revolution*, 3d ed., ed. Robert V. Daniels (Lexington, Mass.: D. C. Heath, 1990), p. 122.

77. Robert S. Sullivant, *Soviet Politics and the Ukraine, 1917–1957* (New York: Columbia University Press, 1962), pp. 192–194.

78. Ibid., pp. 195–203; for a contemporary report, see "William Strang (Moscow) to Sir John Simon on the Suicide of Mykola Skrypnyk, 10 July 1933," in *The British Foreign Office and the Famine*, pp. 253–254.

79. James E. Mace, "Correspondence," *Problems of Communism* 34 (March-April 1985):137; Nahaylo and Swoboda, *Soviet Disunion,* p. 70.

80. Fitzpatrick, *Stalin's Peasants,* pp. 92–95.

81. The directive is cited in Nikolai Ivnitsky's June 18, 1993, article in *Moscow News,* in which he includes excerpts of recently declassified documents from the archives of the Politburo of the Soviet Communist Party.

82. Fitzpatrick, *Stalin's Peasants,* p. 95.

83. Getty, *Starving the Ukraine*, pp. 7–8.

84. David R. Marples, "New Interpretations of Ukrainian History," *RFE/RL Research Report* 2 (March 12, 1993):60.

85. A. F. K. Organski, *The Stages of Political Development* (New York: Alfred A. Knopf, 1965), pp. 103–105.

❈ 8 ❈

Uniqueness as Denial: The Politics of Genocide Scholarship

DAVID E. STANNARD

Forgetting the extermination is part of the extermination itself.
—*Jean Baudrillard*

I have tried to keep memory alive, I have tried to fight those who would forget. Because if we forget, we are guilty, we are accomplices.
—*Elie Wiesel*

I

Recently, the world marked the fiftieth anniversary of the end of World War II. Not a week passed in 1995 without the commemoration of some significant event that happened somewhere on the planet five decades earlier—from the fire-bombings of Dresden and Tokyo to the Yalta Conference and the death of Franklin Roosevelt, from the atomic bombings of Hiroshima and Nagasaki to the opening days of the Nuremberg trials—and much more.

But in the minds of many people the most hideous and stirring images of 1945 are those associated with the opening up of the Nazi confinement and extermination centers. With the evacuation of Auschwitz-Birkenau and the liberations of Mauthausen, Buchenwald, Dachau, and Bergen-Belsen, the world finally got to see up close what many Allied leaders had long denied or appeared indifferent to: the almost unimaginable magnitude and hideousness of the Nazi genocide campaign.[1]

No one will ever know with precision how many people died in the Second World War. The estimates of Chinese deaths, for example, have ranged from 2.5

million to 13.5 million. But, overall, the numbers total in the neighborhood of 50 million people—of whom more than 5 million were Jews. Put another way, by the time the war was over, almost two out of every three Jews in Europe (and one out of three worldwide) had died either in the concentration and death camps, in the ghettoes, or at the hands of mobile killing squads, the *Einsatzgruppen*.[2]

So huge was the carnage that even today it defies comprehension. But it was all too real. And in response to that reality—and to the possibility that something similar could conceivably happen again—many nations both within Europe and beyond have made it illegal to disseminate the hateful idea that the Germans' attempted destruction of European Jewry is an exaggeration or a myth.

Such malignant ideas have, of course, been propagated for many years by extremist groups and individuals. Some have argued that the whole story of the Holocaust is a fabrication. Others admit that it happened but claim that the number killed has been greatly exaggerated. Still more acknowledge that large numbers of deaths occurred but deny that they constitute genocide by claiming that the Jewish deaths, like all others at the time, were merely wartime casualties. Some claim that it was diseases such as typhus, along with the natural deprivations occasioned by war and forced relocation, that killed the Jews—that their deaths were real yet unintentional. Even the genocidal intent of Hitler has never been fully documented, claim others; and without hard proof of his intent the *Führer*, at least, cannot be implicated in whatever extermination effort may have occurred.

Recognizing that these assaults via the pages of history constitute forms of antisemitic cultural violence against Jews in the present, and portend serious danger for the future, the nations of the world have mounted a variety of defensive responses. Some European governments have forcibly prohibited anti-Zionists from speaking in public. A California court has awarded $100,000 to a survivor of Auschwitz for the pain and suffering he endured in an effort to prove untrue the claims of an antisemitic organization that the Nazis did not kill Jews in gas chambers. In Austria the publishers of magazines attempting to minimize Jewish deaths during the Holocaust have been indicted and convicted for their efforts. A professional antisemite who publicly denied the reality of the Holocaust has been sent to prison in Canada. German law states that "denial of the Holocaust" is punishable by up to five years in jail. And the United States has prohibited people who have expressed similar beliefs from entering the country. Other examples abound.[3]

One can imagine, then, the world's reaction if, in 1995, in a sudden eruption of outspoken antisemitism, the most prominent political figures in Germany, including leaders of the German parliament, had publicly ridiculed the Holocaust commemoration ceremonies. Or if they had denied that the Holocaust even happened and threatened to cut off government funds for a film project on World War II unless the word "genocide" was deleted from any references to the Nazis' treatment of the Jews. One can also imagine what the reaction might have been if, throughout that year of somber remembrance, Germany's most important and established newspapers and magazines—across the political spectrum from right to left—had repeatedly mocked the Jews and either denied that the Holocaust ever happened or, conversely, celebrated it as a beneficent event.

Now, clearly, although antisemitism remains far from stamped out in Germany, or anywhere else in the world, such events did not and are not happening in that country. Indeed, they would be illegal there. But they *did* happen in the United States only a few years earlier, when the native peoples of the Americas attempted to commemorate the ghastly destruction that had been visited upon them by European and, later, by white settler military invasions—invasions that brought in their wake wanton slaughter and massive population collapse on a scale and of a duration that dwarf anything that happened in Europe under Nazi rule.

It wasn't *German* politicians who insisted that the word "genocide" not be used in reference to the mass killing of Jews but members of the *U.S. Senate* who threatened to cut funds to the Smithsonian Institution if a film it was partially funding used that word, even in passing, to describe the destruction of the Western Hemisphere's indigenous peoples. And it wasn't German newspapers and magazines that either doubted the reality of the Nazi assault on European Jews or, conversely, admitted and celebrated that genocide. No, it was American publications that routinely denied, or even applauded, the genocide that was carried out against the New World's native inhabitants.

Consider just three examples that represent the "respectable" political spectrum. Scores of other writings—and radio and television presentations—could just as easily be called upon to make the same point.

First, Charles Krauthammer, one of *Time* magazine's regular political columnists, used an entire column to lambaste as "politically correct" opportunists anyone who dared express regret over the killing of millions of innocent people and the destruction of entire ancient cultures in the Americas. What happened in the wake of the European invasion was only what has always characterized human history, Krauthammer claimed, citing the Norman conquest of Britain as an apt (though actually absurd) comparison. "The real question is," he noted, "what eventually grew on this bloodied soil?" For, regardless of the level of destruction and mass murder that was visited upon the indigenous peoples of the Western Hemisphere, it was, in retrospect, entirely justified because in the process it wiped out such alleged barbarisms as the communally based Inca society (which really was only a "beehive," Krauthammer said) and gave the world "a culture of liberty that endowed the individual human being with dignity and sovereignty."[4]

Krauthammer, of course, is a conservative political pundit. But his approach to apologizing for mass murder was not limited to those on the right. Soon after, for example, historian and cold war liberal Arthur Schlesinger Jr. weighed in with much the same argument. Schlesinger, however, was not content to build his case on the purported shortcomings of the *ancient* indigenous societies of the Americas. No, he gazed into his crystal ball and asserted, in *The Atlantic*, that without the European conquests and slaughter at least some New World societies

166 David E. Stannard

today might be sufficiently unpleasant places to live so as to make eminently acceptable the centuries of genocide that were carried out against the native peoples of the entire Western Hemisphere.[5]

And in the person of Christopher Hitchens, writing in *The Nation,* the political left then sounded its voice. To Hitchens, anyone who refused to join him in celebrating with "great vim and gusto" the annihilation of the native peoples of the Americas was (in his words) self-hating, ridiculous, ignorant, and sinister. People who regard critically the genocide that was carried out in America's past, Hitchens continued, are simply reactionary, since such grossly inhuman atrocities "happen to be the way history is made." And thus "to complain about [them] is as empty as complaint about climatic, geological or tectonic shift." Moreover, he added, such violence is worth glorifying since it more often than not has been for the long-term betterment of humankind—as in the United States today, where the extermination of the Native Americans—the American Indians—has brought about "a nearly boundless epoch of opportunity and innovation."[6]

One possible exception Hitchens allowed to his vulgar social Darwinism, with its quasi-Hitlerian view of the proper role of power in history, was the Euro-American enslavement of tens of millions of Africans.[7] But even then, Hitchens contended, those centuries of massive brutality only "*probably* left Africa worse off than they found it." Clearly, however—as with Krauthammer's and Schlesinger's moral codes—if it could be shown to Hitchens's personal satisfaction that Africa was in fact "better off" following the enslavement and simultaneous mass killing of 40 million to 60 million of its people, he would celebrate the abominations of the slave trade with the same vim and gusto that he did the genocide against the native peoples of the Americas.[8]

These are, of course, precisely the same sort of retrospective justifications for genocide that would have been offered by the descendants of Nazi storm troopers and SS doctors had the Third Reich ultimately had its way: that is, however distasteful the means, the extermination of the Jews was thoroughly warranted given the beneficial ends that were accomplished. In this light it is worth considering again what the reaction would be in Europe and elsewhere if the equivalent of the *actual* views of Krauthammer and Schlesinger and Hitchens were expressed today by the respectable press in Germany—but with Jews, not Native Americans, as the people whose historical near-extermination was being celebrated. And there is no doubt whatsoever that if that were to happen, alarm bells announcing a frightening and unparalleled postwar resurgence of German neo-Nazism would, quite justifiably, be going off immediately throughout the world.

Of course, nothing of the sort happened when those three writers—and the countless others for whom they here stand as establishment representatives—proclaimed their delight in the historical destruction of millions of *non*-Europeans. And therein lies an apparent paradox: How can we account for this extraordinary difference?

Several answers to this question come immediately to mind, the most obvious of which is the deeply embedded Euro-American ideology of white supremacy. White supremacy of the same everyday sort that some years earlier led prominent British commentators to deride as a topic of inconsequence a detailed published account of genocide against the Brazilian Indians—who have been liquidated into near nonexistence, from a population of at least 2.5 million to barely 100,000 at last count. Such human carnage is unimportant and not worthy of serious attention, one critic put it, because "the tragedy of a civilisation's demise is commensurate with the value of what it achieved" and "the Brazilian Indians created nothing durable in building or in art." Not only unimportant, added another writer, but genocide in this instance was wholly justified, because "the money garnered from the lands, and the unwilling labours, of several million bewildered Indians" had made possible the creation of so much fine European culture—including even an admittedly "modest" Portuguese opera he said he recently had "greatly enjoyed."[9] Presumably, men of such refinement (like their American counterparts) would reject the appropriateness of this same criterion in evaluating the justness of enslaving and killing millions of *white* people—say, those Jews who may not have created much that was durable in the way of building or art but who certainly brought benefit and comfort to the citizens of Nazi Germany with their slave labor and consequent mass deaths in the I. G. Farben chemical plant at Auschwitz or in the coal mines located nearby.

For those who might find such overt racial distinctions distasteful and preferably avoided, however, a more "reasonable" explanation exists for the grossly differential responses that are so commonplace regarding the American and the Nazi holocausts. This explanation simply denies that there is any comparability between the Nazi violence against the Jews and the Euro-American violence against the Western Hemisphere's native peoples. In fact, in most quarters it is held as beyond dispute that the attempted destruction of the Jews in Nazi-controlled Europe was unique, unprecedented, and categorically incommensurable—not only with the torment endured by the indigenous peoples of North and South America, but also with the sufferings of any people at any time in any place during the entire history of humanity.

This rarely examined, taken-for-granted assumption on the part of so many did not appear out of thin air. On the contrary, it is the hegemonic product of many years of strenuous intellectual labor by a handful of Jewish scholars and writers who have dedicated much if not all of their professional lives to the advancement of this exclusivist idea. And it is the work of these people that I shall be addressing in most of the rest of this chapter. For not only is the essence of their argument demonstrably erroneous, the larger thesis that it fraudulently advances is fundamentally racist and violence-provoking. At the same time, moreover, it willingly provides a screen behind which opportunistic governments today attempt to conceal their own past and ongoing genocidal actions.

Before turning to the specific arguments of the Jewish uniqueness proponents, however, something must be said about the ad hominem impugning of motives that almost inevitably is encountered by those who choose to dispute the so-called uniqueness assertion. Indeed, anyone who even raises questions about the alleged uniqueness of the Jewish experience in the Holocaust is, by virtue of that fact alone, immediately in danger of being labeled an antisemite. For example, when President Jimmy Carter once gave a speech commemorating the victims of the Holocaust he mentioned the fact that others besides Jews had died. Because Carter did not limit his commemorative statement to the deaths of Jews, Yehuda Bauer, a professor of Jewish history at Jerusalem's Hebrew University, accused him of attempting to "de-Judaize" the Holocaust, an action, Bauer wrote, that was nothing less than "an unconscious reflection of antisemitic attitudes."[10] To Bauer, the simple acknowledgment of the suffering of others constituted Jew-hating.

But on this matter, Deborah Lipstadt, professor of modern Jewish and Holocaust studies at Emory University and the author of what probably is the most popular book on this topic, holds a place of particular distinction. Lipstadt regards as her enemy anyone who expresses doubt about the utter singularity in all of human history of Jewish suffering at the hands of the Nazis, an enemy situated intellectually and ideologically at one place or another along a posited antisemitic continuum stretching from those she calls Holocaust "deniers" to those she labels Holocaust "relativists." In Professor Lipstadt's considered opinion, a "denier" is someone who flatly rejects the very historical existence of the Holocaust, whereas a "relativist" is someone who recognizes that the mass killing of Jews in Hitler's Germany occurred and was a hideous act of genocide yet who also considers the Holocaust to be, in her words, one among "an array of other conflagrations in which innocents were massacred."[11]

In other words, you are to be considered in the same general category—as an antisemite, as a creator of "immoral equivalencies," as someone trying "to help the Germans embrace their past"—if you are either a neo-Nazi or a comparative historian. For, to Lipstadt, even someone who has no doubt regarding the ghastly horrors of Jewish suffering and death under Hitler—but who has the temerity to dissent from her insistence regarding the unquestionable uniqueness of the Jewish experience—is, in her phrase, merely a *not yet* denier. And "not yet" denial, she writes, is "the equivalent of David Duke without his robes." In short, if you disagree with Deborah Lipstadt that the Jewish suffering in the Holocaust was unique, you are, by definition—and like David Duke—a crypto-Nazi.[12] Needless to say, such intellectual thuggery usually has its intended chilling effect on further discussion.

Mention should also be made of another preliminary difficulty encountered by anyone who takes on the argument regarding the uniqueness of Jews as victims of suffering: locating the actual components of the uniqueness argument itself. Not only do different advocates of the uniqueness thesis disagree among themselves over the bases for their belief, but the general trend of the argument has shifted over the years and likely will continue transforming itself as new criticisms of specific assertions (such as those contained in this chapter) are raised. This is because, rather than proceeding along a path of open inquiry, virtually all proponents of the uniqueness argument have for years sought out and put forward only those data that appeared to support their own *preexisting* conviction regarding the uniqueness of Jewish suffering—a conviction that in large measure was and is itself an outgrowth not of true scholarly analysis but of straightforward religious dogma. I shall return to this later. But first let us take a look at the arguments themselves; then we can consider the likely motives for advancing them, along with the damage to others that they do.

II

For years it was assumed in many quarters that the sheer size and scope of the mass killing of Jews in Nazi-controlled Europe were unprecedented, and that alone was sufficient to mark Jewish suffering during the Holocaust as unique. As time passed, however, an accumulating body of research began to show that this assumption was false. For example, within the Holocaust itself the Romani people—Gypsies—suffered the same inhuman death camp conditions and probably lost a proportion of their prewar European population equal to that taken from the Jews, a conclusion that now has been accepted by many Jewish students of the Holocaust, including Simon Wiesenthal.[13]

In addition, in just two years between 1915 and 1917, the Armenian population of the Ottoman empire suffered near-obliteration from a Turkish genocide campaign, only two decades after suffering an earlier pogrom in which at least 100,000 Armenians, and probably closer to 200,000, were killed. No one knows for certain how many Armenians died in the second and far larger of these storms of mass killing, but estimates of the pre-genocide population of Armenians have ranged from 1.5 million to 3 million; the actual number of those killed has been put by some writers at under 1 million and by others as high as 2 million, with most serious scholars content to say that at least 1 million and probably closer to 1.5 million people died.[14]

Whether those numbers constitute a proportionate death rate equal to that of Jews in the Holocaust will remain an open question until better statistics become available, but there is little doubt that at least half of the pre-genocide Armenian population was destroyed, and it may have been substantially higher than that. The estimate in one recent analysis—between 50 and 70 percent—is roughly commensurate with the 60 to 65 percent rate of destruction suffered by European Jews during World War II. Moreover, contrary to the assertions of Jewish uniqueness advocates such as Lucy Dawidowicz who claim that "no other people anywhere lost the main body of its population and the fountainhead of its cultural resources," in fact the very hearts of both the Armenian and Gypsy populations were cut out by the genocides waged against them. In the process, the Armenians were also ruthlessly uprooted from 3,000 years of deep cultural relationship with the traditional land of their ancestors. And even today Gypsies remain the targets of ever-mounting racist discrimination wherever they live—including Germany, which recently deported 20,000 Gypsies to Romania, where they predictably have been met with terrorism, violence, and murder.[15]

Yet even if the field of genocide studies must necessarily remain one in which many questions will always go unanswered, there is no question at all regarding at least one matter: that the pre-twentieth-century destruction of native peoples at the hands of European invaders—from Australia to the Americas and elsewhere—frequently resulted in population collapses proportionately much higher than those experienced by any group, including Jews, during the Holocaust. Moreover, not only were *proportionate* losses routinely much higher among indigenous peoples (up to 100 percent in many cases—that is, total extermination—and between 90 and 95 percent generally), but the *gross number* of people destroyed by what I have elsewhere called the "American Holocaust" exceeded by many times over the number of Jews who died under the Nazis and, indeed, was even greater than the number of people of all nations killed worldwide during the entire duration of the Second World War. Even in specific locales—central Mexico and the Andes in particular—the deaths of culturally and ethnically distinct indigenous people in the wake of the European invasions vastly exceeded the mortality figures for Jews during the Holocaust, both in terms of proportional population loss and overall numbers killed.[16]

Most of these facts had become well known by the early 1980s, and thus quantitative criteria quietly began disappearing from the writings of proponents of the Jewish uniqueness argument. To be sure, they did not go away easily. Although acknowledging that, in general, mortality rates or counts could no longer be used as sufficient measures unto themselves to establish uniqueness, some proponents of the uniqueness argument continued to resort to quantification, but only selectively, when it worked to their advantage in establishing differences between the sufferings of Jews and others. Thus, for instance, Lucy Dawidowicz, in *The Holocaust and the Historians,* used the numerical difference between the deaths of Jews in the Holocaust and the deaths of Japanese civilians following the atomic bombings of Hiroshima and Nagasaki as one way of dismissing the possibility that the nuclear destruction of hundreds of thousands of Japanese lives might be termed genocide.[17] When the subjects of comparison are different, however—that is, when discussing other populations that experienced a numerically and proportionately larger loss of life, such as certain huge communities in sixteenth-century Mesoamerica—Jewish uniqueness proponents, of course, now reject any use of quantitative criteria.[18]

Other writers have used the absence of *complete* extermination among a comparison group, such as Armenians, Gypsies, and Native Americans, as a way of denying that genocide was actually perpetrated against the respective non-Jewish group. Michael R. Marrus, for example, distinguishes the suffering of the

Armenians from that of the Jews as arising in part from the fact that "however extensive the murder of Armenians . . . killing was far from universal." And, he notes, "the fact is that many thousands of Armenians survived within Turkey during the period of the massacres." Yehuda Bauer concurs, noting that neither the Armenian nor the Gypsy genocides were comparable to the experience of the Jews because "in neither case was the destruction complete." Adds Steven T. Katz: though the mass killing of New England's Pequot Indians was no doubt lamentable (and it is true, he concedes, that their government-sanctioned white killers did act "with unnecessary severity"), at most the destruction of the Pequots can be described as "*cultural* genocide" since, after all, "the number killed probably totaled less than half the entire tribe."[19]

This, to say the least, is a peculiar bit of historical reasoning—since Europe's Jews themselves were far from totally exterminated by the Nazis, with at least 80,000 Jews surviving in Germany alone; since the worldwide population of Jews was "only" reduced by about one-third during the Holocaust; and since the deaths of Jews in Germany, Romania, Hungary, and the USSR, though totaling about 1.3 million people, represented less than 30 percent of those countries' prewar Jewish populations.[20] But it does at least demonstrate the eagerness of some uniqueness advocates to make their case at any cost to logic or probity. In fact, one prominent writer on this topic occasionally defies all connection with reality by proclaiming that "total physical annihilation . . . is what *happened* to the Jews," contending, in a breathtaking somersault of deduction, that the complete extermination of the Jews by the Nazis is a historical *fact*—the survival of one-third of Europe's Jewish population notwithstanding—because those Jews who survived did so despite the "desire" of the Nazis to kill them.[21]

With the exception of this sort of inanity, however, even the most determined uniqueness proponent is today forced to admit, as Steven Katz has acknowledged, that "what might be thought the most acutely self-evident, the most blatantly incontestable grounds for establishing the novelty of Hitler's Judeocide"—that is, the proportions of population destroyed and/or the total numbers killed—do not in fact support the case for Jewish uniqueness.[22]

❀ ❀ ❀

If the quantitative criterion does not establish the uniqueness of Jewish suffering, particularly when compared with the far more destructive experiences of numerous indigenous peoples, some have then argued that it was the *way* in which the Jews died—that is, the relative speed with which the killing was accomplished—that makes their experience unique. This contention holds that whereas Jews were slaughtered in death camps by the most modern and expeditious methods of mass destruction available at the time, previous and subsequent victims of genocide have been destroyed by far cruder and more prolonged means. The Holocaust, it is said by proponents of this standard, "was unique in quantitive terms" because it destroyed more innocent people "per unit of time" than has any other mass killing event. Even uniqueness advocate Katz now rejects this claim, however, noting the counterexamples of the Soviets under Stalin and other twentieth-century genocides in such places as Bangladesh and Cambodia. More recently, between April and July 1994, as many as 850,000 Tutsi people were slaughtered in Rwanda, primarily with handguns and machetes. This is a rate of about 10,000 per day, a figure equal to the maximum ever achieved during a single 24-hour period at Auschwitz.[23] Surely, though, if speed is to be a criterion, no one has come close to matching the achievements of the United States in killing at least 100,000 people in a matter of hours with the firebombing of Tokyo and the subsequent vaporizing, in virtually a single nuclear instant, of more than 200,000 innocent Japanese civilians in Hiroshima and Nagasaki.

Moreover, beyond the clear factual incorrectness of the assertion that no people have ever been killed in large numbers as efficiently or as quickly as were the Jews under Nazi rule, there is the question of whether the claim itself—correct or not—is especially meaningful or noteworthy. Why, after all, is a genocide campaign that lasts for, say, three years (the approximate duration of the Final Solution) more momentous than one that proceeds at a slower pace but lasts twenty or fifty or a hundred times as long? Might it not just as cogently be argued that the very opposite is the case—that the quantitatively lower level (in the short term) but far more enduring suffering and extinction fear of many generations intrinsically is worse for its victims than the more acute but far briefer agony experienced by only a single historical generation? Who is to say? Who, really, has the *right* to say? Indeed, as Phillip Lopate observes, the very making of the so-called efficiency claim reveals more than anything else its authors' own "narcissistic preoccupations" with Western technology. As he puts it:

> Does it really matter so much if millions are gassed according to Eichmann's timetables, rather than slowly, crudely starved to death as in Stalin's regime, or marched around by ragged teenage Khmer Rouge soldiers and then beheaded or clubbed? Does the family mourning the loved one hacked to pieces by a spontaneous mob of Indonesian vigilantes care that much about abuses of science and technology? Does neatness count, finally, so damn much?[24]

In addition to the claim for distinctiveness based on the *rate* of extermination, uniqueness advocates often point to differences in the *means* of destruction. This is a nuance that appears to take on particular force when Jewish deaths during the Holocaust are contrasted with the historical eradication of the world's indigenous peoples. For native societies fell victim, so the customary argument goes, largely to unintentionally introduced diseases that were simply a by-product of Western imperialism. Steven Katz goes even further than this, contending that not only was the mass destruction of the Western Hemisphere's native peoples by disease "an *unintended* tragedy," it actually, he claims, was "a tragedy that occurred despite the sincere and indisputable desire of the Europeans to keep the Indian population alive." Thus, not only are the Jewish and Native American experiences not comparable, but the alleged good-heartedness of the European conquerors eliminates altogether the charge that the destruction of the aboriginal peoples of the Americas and elsewhere constituted genocide.[25]

Actually, though, the purported means-of-extermination distinction between the deaths of Jews in Nazi-controlled Europe and the deaths of indigenous peoples in their European-invaded homelands is nonsense. Despite frequent undocumented assertions that disease was responsible for the great majority of indigenous deaths in the Americas, there does not exist a single scholarly work that even pretends to demonstrate this claim on the basis of solid evidence. And that is because there *is* no such evidence, anywhere. The supposed truism that more native people died from disease than from direct face-to-face killing or from gross mistreatment or other concomitant derivatives of that brutality such as starvation, exposure, exhaustion, or despair is nothing more than a scholarly article of faith. It seems quite possible that deaths from disease *may* have exceeded those deriving from any other *single* cause, but the plain fact of the matter is that we have no way of ever determining individual degrees of responsibility for the many and various and overlapping factors that were involved in the native peoples' destruction. Because the devastation was so enormous and so complete, few technical demographic details of this sort exist in the historical record. Indeed, if anything is certain regarding this matter it is that most of those tens of millions of deaths— from the islands of the Caribbean to the high country of Mexico, then north and south throughout two huge continents—were in fact caused by intertwined and interacting *combinations* of lethal agents, combinations that took different forms in different locales.

Throughout the Americas, military invasions resulted in the direct massacres of huge numbers of people and the unleashing of bacteria and viruses for which the natives had little or no acquired resistance. In most of what is now the United States—excluding California and the Southwest—the dynamic interaction between military and microbial destruction (in different combinations from time to time and from place to place) was sufficient to lay waste almost an entire continent's indigenous inhabitants. In California and the Southwest, however, as in the Caribbean and Meso- and South America (where at least 90 percent of the Western Hemisphere's population lived) another deadly factor was added. There, survivors of the mass murders and the epidemics commonly were herded together into densely populated *congregacións* where they either starved in squalor or were worked to death as hired-out slaves in labor camps, in mines, or on plantations—all of which, of course, were hothouses of pestilence and fatal violence. It was under these constantly *interacting* conditions of direct slaughter, disease, and forced labor—combined, as in the Nazi concentration and death camps, with the consequential reduction of live birth rates to far below replacement levels— that the indigenous populations of what are now Chile and Peru, for example, were reduced collectively by 95 percent or more, from somewhere between 9 million and 14 million people to barely 500,000, before the holocaust subsided.[26]

But perhaps the best way to recognize the bankruptcy of this component of the Jewish uniqueness claim—the outright denial that genocide is an appropriate term to describe what happened to the indigenous people of the Western Hemisphere because of the *way* in which the devastation occurred—is simply to imagine how people like Yehuda Bauer and Steven Katz and Deborah Lipstadt and other advocates of this position would describe the centuries-long experience of the Americas' native peoples if that experience instead had been endured by Jews. Consider, then, the following highly compressed but fully documented historical chronicle, drawn from my book, *American Holocaust*, in which the only departure from reality is the substitution of "Jews" for "native peoples."[27]

At the end of the fifteenth century a huge island in the Caribbean, twice the size of Switzerland and inhabited by at least a million and perhaps as many as 8 million Jews, was invaded by Spanish military men in search of gold. The Spaniards also were carriers of deadly diseases that the Jews had never encountered before, diseases that killed them en masse. But in their hunt for gold the Spaniards also rounded up and, under force of arms, enslaved whole communities of Jews, beating and torturing and working them in mines and on plantations with barely enough food to survive until they dropped. And all the while that this was happening (and the Jewish population was plummeting toward zero), the Spaniards' own documents today reveal that their soldiers took great delight in skewering Jewish babies on yard-long rapiers; of hacking off the breasts of Jewish women just for fun; of burning to death entire towns full of Jews. And more.

After the total population of Jews on this immense island—plus the hundreds of thousands of Jews on neighboring islands in the Caribbean—had finally been exterminated in a matter of decades, the horrifying violence then spread to an entire continent. And now still more Jews, numbering by this time in the *tens* of millions, died from the Spanish onslaught. Scores of Jewish cities were reduced to rubble. Synagogues beyond counting were crushed. All the religious books that could be found were burned. Jewish women and children were enslaved and branded on the face with their owners' initials. Armies of Jews were force-marched to labor in mountain-top silver mines where they could consider themselves lucky to survive for six months—while other whole communities of Jews were driven to toil on plantations in tropical forests where the life expectancy was even shorter. In central Mexico more than 20 million Jews died before it was over. And there, as elsewhere in Meso- and South America, those huge numbers of deaths from violence, disease, starvation, and slave labor represented the destruction of fully 90 to 95 percent of the Jewish population.

Everywhere, entire Jewish towns were obliterated—their residents hacked to death or burned at the stake—because their leaders did not renounce their religious traditions quickly enough. And all of this was justified by the common and often expressed belief of the murderers—including the wisest and holiest men in the Spanish realm—that the Jews were semi-human beasts created by God to be the slaves of Christians; that it was the divine right of Christians to hunt Jews down as animals of the forest for no other purpose than to feed their carcasses to dogs.

But the bloodbath didn't stop there—and didn't end with the Spanish. Rather, it was taken up by other Europeans, and with particular delight by the British. Jews were also the original inhabitants of North America in this scenario, and English adventurers and settlers, having decided that Jews were too beast-like to deserve the land that they had cultivated for centuries, launched full-scale extermination campaigns against them—campaigns that, over and over and over again, resulted in the deaths of 19 out of every 20 Jews who happened to live where the English wanted to live. And as the English hunted down and shot and chopped and burned to death every Jew who could not escape into the forest, pious Christian ministers celebrated what they believed to be the imminent extinction of the Jewish people, routinely exclaiming (to quote just one of the most esteemed such leaders) that "it was a fearful sight to see the Jews thus frying in the fire and the streams of blood quenching the same, and horrible was the stink and scent thereof; but the victory seemed a sweet sacrifice, and we gave the praise thereof to God, who had wrought so wonderfully for us."

And, again, it didn't stop there. For years and decades and centuries, Jews were stalked and killed like the animals that the British—and later the Americans—said they were. All the residents of certain Jewish communities, each one numbering in the thousands of people, were herded together and forced to embark on refugee death marches that commonly killed half of their victims—leading at least one hardened veteran and death march overseer to remark that "I fought through the Civil War and have seen men shot to pieces and slaughtered by the thousands, but the Jewish removal was the cruelest work I ever knew." And even after the death marches were over typically another 50 percent and more of such violently dispossessed Jews perished in the concentration camps that were the death marches' established destination points.

During the nineteenth century, meanwhile, the governors of individual states, such as Colorado and California, officially urged the citizenry to exterminate all the Jews they could find, using state funds to finance the actions of mobile killing squads; Jewish children could be—and routinely were—legally taken from their parents and enslaved; and Jews had no legal standing in court to protest against any horrors that were perpetrated against them or against their children. It was during this time as well that a man who was to become President of the United States proudly boasted of personally killing Jews and mutilating their bodies, of supervising the slicing off of Jewish noses and the stripping of flesh from Jewish bodies to be tanned and turned into bridle reins. He also gave specific instructions to kill all the Jewish babies that could be found, pointing out that true extermination could not be accomplished unless all the children as well as the adults were butchered.

Another President of the United States during this era referred to Jews as "beasts of prey," and ordered his military commanders to attack and "lay waste" all the Jewish communities they could find, demanding "that they not be merely overrun but destroyed." Still a third President of the United States instructed his Secretary of War that any Jews who resisted the seizure of their land should be met with the "hatchet" and "exterminated" if necessary. And as time wore on other Presidents over the course of an entire century expressed similar genocidal attitudes, and ordered similar genocidal actions against the Jews.

Even a twentieth-century American President and winner of a Nobel Peace Prize joined the fray, describing one of the many government-launched mass murders of

Jewish men and women and children that had occurred during his lifetime (this particular massacre including the clubbing and shooting to death of infants and the proud public display of mutilated Jewish male and female genitals) as a "righteous and beneficial deed," because, after all, as he laughingly put it, "I don't go so far as to think that the *only* good Jews are dead Jews, but I believe nine out of ten are, and I shouldn't like to inquire too closely into the case of the tenth."

When all the dust had settled, throughout the entire North American continent approximately 95 percent of the original Jewish population had been exterminated—from the combined violence, torture, removal, disease, exhaustion, exposure, and other factors that snatched their lives away. The remaining 5 percent were then forcibly driven away to live in abject poverty and squalor on segregated encampments set up by the American government in the most inhospitable environments that could be found.

This description, of course, is far too benign, as it leaves out volumes of ghastly but true accounts. Still, however truncated and thus necessarily understated it is, there can be little doubt that the likes of Yehuda Bauer and Steven Katz and Deborah Lipstadt would describe as "genocide" the account I have just rendered if the tens of millions of victims had indeed been Jews and not the native peoples of the Americas. There also is no doubt that if this were a chronicle of Jewish suffering and a non-Jew referred to it the way Katz has in fact summarized the experience of its *actual* victims—as "an *unintended* tragedy, a tragedy that occurred despite the sincere and indisputable desire of the Europeans to keep the [Jewish] population alive"—he would quite properly be pilloried as a Holocaust denier and a blatant antisemite.

But in fact we needn't have gone to all this trouble. For even if it were accurate to say with assurance that the massive destruction of the native people in the Americas was in large measure the immediate consequence of disease, starvation, and related causes—that is, what the U.S. government now calls the "collateral damage" that follows in the wake of direct violence—*precisely the same thing is true regarding Jewish deaths during the Holocaust.* According to the most authoritative tabulation that exists, the work of Raul Hilberg, Jewish deaths outside of the concentration and death camps during the Holocaust totaled just over 2 million. Of that number, nearly half did not die from direct Nazi violence but rather from what Hilberg describes as "ghettoization and general privation," a category that of course includes very high levels of death from disease. Moreover, within the camps themselves, where more than 3 million Jews died, the mortality rate from disease was even greater. As one recent account, published by the United States Holocaust Memorial Museum and focused on Auschwitz-Birkenau, notes:

Epidemics of lice, typhus, dysentery, and common phlegmon, particularly in Birkenau, resulted in skyrocketing mortality rates in the period from July 1942 [when, under pressure of the Final Solution, the population of the camps had begun to climb sharply] to March 1943; according to available data, they ranged from 19 percent to 25 percent per month. The decline that followed can be attributed to some improvement in the camp conditions in general and in hospitals in particular. In May 1943, the monthly mortality rate dropped to 5.2 percent, and in the main Auschwitz camp it dropped even more.[28]

A death rate of between 19 percent and 25 percent per month, of course, translates into a projected annual mortality rate of between 228 percent and 300 percent. That means the equivalent of the entire camp population was at this time dying from *disease* every four to five months. Moreover, without minimizing the deaths by gassing and other direct means of hundreds of thousands of others, even the subsequent drop to a maximum disease-caused death rate of 5.2 percent per month at Birkenau, once medical conditions improved, still represented a projected mortality rate solely attributable to illness of more than 60 percent per year.

And what was true of Auschwitz was more than equally true in other camps. In Buchenwald, for instance, of the nearly 239,000 persons who were incarcerated there between 1937 and 1945, more than 55,000 (about 23 percent) died in the camp. However, more than 33,000 of those deaths—or approximately 60 percent—were hospital-registered mortalities resulting from disease and related causes.[29] Thus, during the entire time of Buchenwald's existence as a concentration camp, the single greatest cause of death was illness and malnutrition. (These two seemingly separable factors constitute a singular "cause" since, in situations of high disease prevalence and severe nutritional deficiency, it generally is impossible to determine retrospectively which of the two was the principal agent of death.)[30]

Indeed, so extreme were the conditions of illness and deprivation in the camps that more than *half* the nearly 137,000 prisoners brought into *all* the German concentration camps between June and November of 1942 quickly died of disease and/or starvation. Even the SS was alarmed at this degree of mortality, causing the SS Main Economic and Administrative Office to issue a directive to all camp doctors, ordering them to better supervise the care and feeding of prisoners and to "work with all means at their disposal to substantially lower mortality figures," since, "with such a high death toll, the number of prisoners can never be brought to the level that the Reich SS leader has ordered."[31]

A so-called historical revisionist could, of course, use this document (and others like it) to contend, as Katz has done with regard to the destruction of the indigenous peoples of the Americas, that mass death in the Nazi concentration camps was "an unintended tragedy" and a "tragedy that occurred despite the sincere and indisputable desire of the [Nazis] to keep the [concentration camp] population alive." That, of course, would be an assessment equal to Katz's in historical falsity. But all these documents, and many others, do provide powerful support to the assertion of Princeton historian Arno J. Mayer that "from 1942 to 1945, certainly at Auschwitz, but probably overall, more Jews were killed by so-called 'natural' causes than by 'unnatural' ones"—"natural" causes being "sickness, disease, undernourishment, [and] hyperexploitation," as opposed to "unnatural" causes such as "shooting, hanging, phenol injection, or gassing."[32]

There is little doubt that Mayer is correct here regarding Auschwitz, and in his overall claim as well. Even Deborah Lipstadt admits that such "is the case in every war." And on this, at least, she is largely correct. The Japanese ordeal in World War II, during which fully two-thirds of Japan's *military* deaths were the result of illness and starvation, was far from atypical. Indeed, throughout the world today—from Sudan to Angola to Rwanda to Cambodia to Bosnia to Somalia and beyond—literally tens of millions of people who are trapped in the midst of wilfully genocidal warfare are at risk or have died from starvation or disease that is a secondary consequence of the outright killing, a number that often far exceeds the death toll from direct violence itself.[33]

According to the most minimal quantitative translation of Mayer's highly credible claim, then, of the 3.1 million Jewish deaths that took place in the concentration and death camps, at least 1.6 million resulted from "natural" causes, including disease, added to the more than 800,000 Jews outside the camps who died of Hilberg's "ghettoization and general privation." That makes a total of more than 2.4 million of the 5.1 million Jewish deaths during the Holocaust, at a bare minimum, directly attributable to the same so-called natural phenomena—disease, exploitation, malnutrition, and the like—that also were the immediate cause of death for many of the Americas' indigenous people.

Katz and others find that if a significant number of native deaths in the Americas were the result of such causes, then the destruction of the Western Hemisphere's indigenous people was "unintentional" and non-genocidal. The same conclusion should then hold regarding the destruction of Jews during the Holocaust. But does it? Of course not. And why not? The obvious reply is that the so-called natural causes responsible for the deaths of those two and a half million innocent Jews occurred as a corollary to other, more direct, killings during the period that the Jewish people of Europe were either under assault outside the camps or were trapped helplessly within them. But, again, the same thing is true regarding the conditions under which most of the indigenous inhabitants of the Americas contracted the diseases or succumbed to the general privations that led to so many of *their* premature deaths during four long centuries of conquest.

What, then, do Katz and his supporters and like-thinkers propose to *do* about those millions of Jews, fully half the Jewish victims of the Holocaust, who died from disease and destitution? Deny that their deaths were an intrinsic part of the genocide? To do so would be a monumental act of immorality; yet that is precisely the judgment they render when the victims are *not* Jews. As I have written elsewhere, on this point Holocaust scholar Michael R. Marrus has said it as well as anyone:

> It is clearly wrong to separate from the essence of the Holocaust those Jews who never survived long enough to reach the camps, or who were shot down by the Einsatzgruppen in the Soviet Union, or who starved in the ghettos of eastern Europe, or who were wasted by disease because of malnutrition and neglect, or who were

The Politics of Genocide Scholarship   179

killed in reprisal in the west, or who died in any of the countless other, terrible ways—no less a part of the Holocaust because their final agonies do not meet some artificial standard of uniqueness.[34]

Of course, Marrus is correct: Jews who died during the Holocaust of disease and malnutrition and neglect or in "countless other, terrible ways" would not have been exposed to those deadly forces if not for the direct violence that was all about them—thus certainly making their deaths part of the genocide that is called the Holocaust. But so too with the native people of the Americas, who died in precisely those same ways, but in vastly higher numbers and proportions, directly as a result of the larger genocidal conditions created by violent European invasions of their communities.

Much has often been made, for example—and rightly so—of the ghastly physical condition of most concentration camp survivors at the moment that they were liberated. In Buchenwald it has been estimated that in the time immediately leading up to liberation most prisoners existed on a greatly restricted diet providing only 600–700 calories per day.[35] That is fewer calories than are provided by a pint of milk and a cup of dry cornmeal and is barely one-quarter the caloric requirement needed simply to maintain the weight of an average adult.

In contrast, much less has ever been made of the fact that during the late eighteenth and early nineteenth centuries (to select just one example among many) the Spanish military in California and the Southwest used the same system of *congregación/reducción* that had been tested with such lethal success in the Andes to imprison tens of thousands of native people in concentration camps euphemistically called missions, forcing inmates to produce the foodstuffs and other goods necessary to sustain the garrisons. In some of these prison workhouses, such as those at San Antonio and San Miguel, the indigenous inmates *routinely*—over the course of half a century—struggled to survive on rations of approximately 640–780 calories per day, roughly the same minuscule caloric intake as that endured by the Buchenwald prisoners on the eve of liberation. Moreover, on average, Indians in all missions in the region lived and worked at slave labor year in and year out, generation after generation, on hardly more than 1,000 calories per day.[36]

Under the prevailing labor requirements these were literally starvation diets, as is apparent in the records of such missions as San Francisco, Santa Clara, and San Jose, where mortality rates regularly exceeded birthrates by ratios of four- and five-to-one. These are life-table statistics that guarantee extremely rapid and wholesale extermination. Nor did the mere fact of being born matter much in these internment camps, since conditions were so abysmal—with individual living space measuring about seven feet by two feet, or about the size of a coffin—that projected life expectancy at birth could *average* from only eight months to two years—year after year after year.[37]

It should come as no surprise to discover, in light of these circumstances, that by the time the mission camps were shut down starvation, disease, torture, and outright murder had killed a proportion of the native inmate population more

than *three times larger* than that ultimately destroyed at Buchenwald a century or
so later. Yet, the victims of Buchenwald, quite properly, are memorialized universally as appalling reminders of the Holocaust, while the proportionally far more
damaged mission-incarcerated Indians of California rarely are even mentioned in
discussions of genocide. Instead, like most native peoples, they are relegated to
the status of "unintended" victims of progress—as people, in the words of one
writer, who simply "did not wear well."[38]

❁ ❁ ❁

The identical double-standard regarding deaths from disease and privation is
evident in other areas as well. For instance, it sometimes is asserted that the deaths
of many native people, particularly in North America, do not "count" as genocide
because they occurred in the midst of physical resistance to conquest. Thus, it is
said, these must be regarded as wartime deaths rather than genocide. This is an
argument similar to one used to downplay the Armenian genocide: The
Armenians, it is claimed, "provoked" the Turks to try to exterminate them.[39]

But, of course, if by resisting oppression a group defines itself out of the category of genocide victim, then once again a great many Jewish deaths during the
Holocaust cannot qualify as genocide either. Literally tens of thousands of Jews,
after all, fought heroically against Nazi repression—from the Warsaw ghetto to
the forests of Poland and beyond—most of them dying in the process. According
to Yehuda Bauer, Jews mounted armed resistance against the Nazis in more than
a hundred ghettoes throughout Poland, and even within death camps there were
major uprisings, invariably followed by Nazi massacres of the resistance leaders
and others.[40] Are these peoples' brave deaths—like those that were the result of
disease and deprivation in the camps or the ghettoes—not to be counted as part
of the Holocaust? And if they are to be counted (as surely they must), what kind
of perverse logic is it that at the same time *denies* the category of genocide victim
to Native American men and women and children who fought valiantly to resist
the murderous depredations of invading armies that ultimately overran and
obliterated whole Indian nations?

In this regard—that is, the wholesale eradication of many entire Native
American communities, peoples, and nations—an important but simple fact must
be noted, one that is far too rarely recognized in discussions on this topic. And that
is: There were many—indeed, at least 2,000—*distinct* peoples, with deep and complex communal roots, living in the pre-Columbian Americas. Even today, after
near total annihilation of the overall indigenous population, the U.S. government
officially recognizes more than 500 separate and discrete native nations residing
within its political borders. In many cases those peoples differed (and continue to
differ) among one another in terms of religion, language, culture, and ethnicity to
a much greater extent than do the far fewer separate peoples of Europe, and that
includes the differences within Europe between Jews and non-Jews.[41]

Because of the unprecedented immensity of the disaster that befell the people of the Americas as a collectivity, resulting in a population collapse of somewhere between 50 and 100 million—that is, in the annihilation of 90 to 95 percent of the entire hemisphere's indigenous human inhabitants—it has become conventional to speak of genocide in the Americas as a long-term but singular event. On one level, of course, that is apt. But it is much more correct, and much more supportable within the finer points of conventionally accepted genocide terminology, to recognize that even though some (albeit a relative few) ancestrally distinctive groups of people in the Western Hemisphere did not fall victim to genocide, many others most certainly did.

There is a plainly racist "all-of-them-look-alike" bias in the Euro-American tendency to lump the native peoples of North and South America into one or a handful of large and nondistinctive categories of "Indians" (as often is done as well with Africans and Asians), while insisting on fine points of differentiation among European religious, cultural, ethnic, and national groups. One consequence of this lack of discrimination is the failure to recognize that numerous entirely distinct and separate native peoples (some of them now long since completely exterminated) met, or meet, all the strictest criteria for categorization as genocide victims.

In fact, if this all-too-common failure to discriminate ethnically, culturally, and religiously among indigenous peoples was applied to the study of internal violence in Europe during the 1940s, it might be difficult to sustain the argument—solely in quantitative terms—that the killing of Jews that did occur during the Nazis' reign was of sufficient *proportional* magnitude to be historically significant. This is because the comparable group in Europe to "Indians," or to "Africans" or "Asians" on other continents, is "Caucasians"—that is, all 400 million or so "Native Europeans" at the time of the Nazi rise to power. Among this number, Jews, at less than 3 percent of the overall population, would constitute only a small and *invisible because undifferentiated* collectivity whose loss of life under the Third Reich reduced the population of Europe by hardly more than 1 percent between 1939 and 1945. Again, focusing only on quantitative concerns, such a death rate, during a comparable six-year period, is barely one-half of that caused by heart disease in the United States today. Although this admittedly represents an unpleasant number of deaths, as a percentage of the overall population—again, in this unfair and undiscriminating context—it is hardly worthy by itself of being called historically important, let alone "unique." Yet that is precisely the same misleadingly aggregative numerical context that, in calculating death rates, is *routinely* imposed on *non*-European victims of genocide.

Indeed, had the collective and undifferentiated indigenous populations of the Americas been reduced in number by only the same 1 percent that Europe's overall population was reduced by the deaths of Jews in the Holocaust, few people would even think of describing what happened in the Americas as genocide. Conversely, for the European experience to equal that of North and South America in proportional terms, between 360 million and 380 million people—

that is, 90 to 95 percent of Europe's pre-Nazi population—would have to have been annihilated by Nazi violence and related causes, a figure that is nearly *ten times* the number of Europeans, including Russians, who actually did die in the war from all causes. If this all begins to seem like a recondite numbers game, it is—but one that conventionally is played only in reverse, and more guilefully, to advance the Jewish uniqueness agenda and to diminish the significance of every other people's historical suffering.

It is of particular irony, moreover, that some of the points used to establish the alleged uniqueness of the Jewish genocide experience, especially those pertaining to the dehumanizing language used by the Nazis to describe their victims, are in fact *derivative* of expressed Euro-American attitudes toward Native Americans— who, characteristically, never have claimed uniqueness for their own sufferings. Yehuda Bauer, for example, makes much of the fact that in their antisemitic descriptions of Jews the Nazis often used the imagery of "a virus, parasite, or a pest of some sort . . . that had to be destroyed, as vermin would be." And indeed, SS Chief Heinrich Himmler was not alone among Nazis who thought that antisemitism "is exactly the same as delousing."[42] But decades before Hitler or Himmler were even born it had become a cliché in the United States to refer to Indians as vermin, particularly as lice, often as prelude to launching a new wave of annihilative violence against them. The function of this parasitic terminology can best be seen by examining the full phrase within which it most commonly was used: "Nits make lice," the killers would say, as justification for killing all the children, as well as the adults, in an Indian group slated for extermination. For to fail to destroy the nits—the eggs of the lice—was to invite reinfestation.[43]

Similarly, in a discussion of the uniqueness of the Holocaust in contrast to earlier genocides, Zygmunt Bauman sees one aspect of the singularity of "modern" genocide in what he describes as the Nazis' image of the world as a garden in which the Jews were weeds. "And weeds," he writes, "are to be exterminated." It's really quite an unemotional business, he notes, a coldly calculating implementation of the perverse demands of instrumental reason—for weeds are pests, and "modern genocide, like modern culture in general, is a gardener's job."[44] "Modern" though such consciousness may or may not be, however, there is nothing unique about Jews or any other victims of the Holocaust being viewed in this way. For it was G. Stanley Hall, often regarded as the founder of American psychology, who at the turn of the twentieth century described Native Americans and the other indigenous peoples who made up "nearly one-third of the human race, occupying two-fifths of the land surface of the globe" as "weeds in the human garden" that are in the process of being "extirpated . . . both by conscious and organic processes," adding that "in many minds this is inevitable and not without justification" since "the world will soon be overcrowded, and we must begin to take selective agencies into our own hands."[45]

Bauer certainly is correct when he observes that the repeated Nazi descriptions of Jews as germs and as other lower forms of life served the function of dehumanization, of establishing that the Jew was "not really a human being at all." And once such imagery is internalized by an oppressor it greatly facilitates the psychological distancing, as Christopher Browning puts it, "in which 'the enemy' is easily objectified and removed from the community of human obligation," thus making mass killing and extermination "acceptable" behavior.[46] But Bauer is equally *incorrect* in thinking that the Jewish experience in this regard is unique or even especially distinctive.

For the native peoples of the Americas such dehumanization began more than 400 years before the rise of Hitler, with published descriptions of the inhabitants of the Caribbean and Central America (while they were being enslaved and annihilated) as "beasts in human form," as "*homunculi* in whom you will scarcely find even vestiges of humanity," as "a third species of animal between man and monkey," and much more. In addition, these and other comparable terms, describing Indian peoples as subhuman creatures deserving of liquidation, became commonplace among the Euro-American conquerors throughout the Western Hemisphere for the next few centuries—as they fed native babies to their dogs for food, as they hung native carcasses on their porches like sides of beef, as they sliced off native women's breasts and native men's scrotums for use as exotic change purses, as they decorated their hats with excised female genitals, as they skinned Indian bodies from the hips down to make boot tops and leggings from human flesh. And as, in general, they deliberately erased entire peoples from the face of the earth.[47]

❀ ❀ ❀

Finally there is the matter of what has become not only a central claim of the Jewish uniqueness argument but actually the very core of that position, now that other, earlier assertions have withered under scrutiny: The Jewish experience is unique among other genocides throughout history, it is now said, because of the Nazis' unrestrained *intent* to destroy all Jewish people, not only those residing in Europe, but throughout the entire world. And though Jewish uniqueness proponents have begun to back away from most other traditional uniqueness criteria in the face of telling criticism, here they seem determined to make their stand.

Both Yehuda Bauer and Steven Katz, probably the leading and certainly the most prolific advocates of the uniqueness of the Jewish Holocaust, have now admitted that on every other significant point previously asserted as grounds for proclaiming the uniqueness of Jews as victims one or more other groups have at least an equal claim to recognition. But no other group, they assert, can claim that their tormentors were seized with what Bauer calls the Nazis' "pseudo-religious, pseudo-messianic" obsession with not allowing a single Jew on the face of the earth to escape. "To date," says Bauer, "this has happened once, to the Jews under Nazism." What was and remains unprecedented about the Jewish experience, Katz adds in concurrence, was "the Nazi racial imperative that *all* Jews must die, and that they must die here and now."[48]

Confronted with this claim, one might easily cite numerous sources attesting to the fact that throughout the course of the Holocaust Gypsies were slated to receive, and did receive, precisely the same murderous treatment as Jews.[49] But the historical record also reveals many pre-twentieth-century examples of unambiguous official calls by European or white American political leaders for the total annihilation of any number of individual Native American peoples. Such examples might begin (although in fact there were precedents) with the plan of William Berkeley, Virginia's colonial governor during the mid-seventeenth century, as conveyed to his military commander, "to Destroy *all* these Northern Indians," a scheme, incidentally, that was carried out successfully and with dispatch: By the time the century came to a close, 95 percent of the native population of Virginia that had been on hand to welcome the first English settlements had been killed off.[50]

We might then leap forward in time nearly two centuries, to witness the direct call from the first governor of the state of California to his legislature, that a war be waged upon the numerous individual native peoples of that region "until the Indian race becomes extinct." By this time, three-fourths of the original native population of California had already been killed off by the Spanish. Now, within the course of just eight bloody years following the gubernatorial death warrant, the state spent more than $1.5 million (subsequently reimbursed by the U.S. Congress) in determinedly destroying fully 60 percent of the remaining Indians. This is approximately the same rate of extermination, during roughly the same number of years, as that suffered by all of Europe's Jews in the Holocaust. And then 50 percent of that remnant group of Indians was *further* annihilated in the next few decades, leading to an overall rate of destruction, under combined Spanish and American rule, of more than 95 percent—far higher even than the hideous death rate, from all causes, endured by the inmates of Auschwitz during the time of that extermination camp's operation.[51]

Moreover, during the period between the Virginia and California exterminations there were numerous other genocidal proclamations and statements of intent—often as a part of the express plans of government officials, including state governors and U.S. presidents—to totally exterminate this or that group of native people, any one of which was as well recognized an independent cultural or religious or ethnic entity in its time and place as were the Jews of twentieth-century Europe. And lest anyone during those years have moral qualms about such savage behavior (as later did even many of Hitler's *Einsatzkommandos*), the popular President Andrew Jackson had words of reassurance. He, himself, had on more than one occasion supervised the mutilation of the corpses of Indians his troops had killed, so as to take home body parts as prizes—and he, himself, had urged the murder of Indian babies (referring to them as "wolves") in order to be certain that *no* one would survive his men's murderous depredations. Killing off entire peoples, after all, as he later advised the U.S. Congress, was only like causing "the extinction of one generation to make room for another."[52]

In addition to such overwhelming evidence, from one side of North America to the other, regarding the clear *non*-uniqueness of the alleged Nazi intent to kill all the Jews, there is the obvious (but rarely asked) built-in question of whether a *failed* intent to kill all the members of a given group—as in the case of the Nazis and the Jews—is truly a distinction more notable than the *successful* extermination of an entire people (for example, the Tasmanians of Oceania or the Beothuk people of Newfoundland, among many others), regardless of whether there is left behind any record of an ideology of extermination on the part of the perpetrators.[53] Thus, if one were to follow Bauer and Katz to their extreme but inevitable conclusions, a nation today that publicly announced its intent to kill all the members of an ethnically defined group of people—and then launched a failed campaign that succeeded in killing only, say, 10 percent of the targeted victims—*would* be guilty of genocide because of its stated and recorded intent. On the other hand, a different nation that actually killed 90 or even 100 percent of a defined population, however large, but left no evidence of clear intent, would *not* be found to have committed genocide. This is sophistry.

But finally, there is the most elementary question that must be asked of those who claim that the keystone of the argument in favor of Jewish uniqueness resides in the Nazi determination to kill all Jews everywhere: Is the very assertion regarding Nazi intent *itself* true? The answer is no.

Apart from the clear comparability—and more—of numerous other peoples who have been slated for (and sometimes suffered) complete extermination, the fundamental problem with the intent argument is its amateurish and simplistic understanding of historical process. Within the conventional range of explanations for the Holocaust, from the so-called intentionalist perspective (which views the unfolding of events in Nazi Germany as directed and controlled by a powerful, single-minded, and consistent core of ideologues) to the so-called functionalist interpretation (in which decisions of the Reich are seen as largely improvisational and even chaotic, in response to changing circumstances), the claim that Jews and only Jews have ever been singled out for total extermination emanates from the extreme intentionalist position.[54] This is the way of thinking that also undergirds most conspiracy theories on a variety of topics. Unable or unwilling to accept the fact that human history proceeds by compromise and accommodation among competing, complex, and ever-unfolding forces—in the case of the Holocaust, as Arno J. Mayer puts it, the "constant interplay of ideology and contingency in which both played their respective but also partially indeterminate roles"—intentionalists and conspiracy theorists seek out and interpret to suit their own unsubtle predispositions any pieces of data that can be made to smack of willful stratagem or intrigue.[55]

This is not, by any means, to say that historians should ignore such information, only to insist that materials of this sort—particularly as regards the Holocaust—are usually scattered and piecemeal, requiring a good deal of attention to nuance and context. For the fact of the matter is, as Holocaust scholar Christopher Browning notes:

There are no written records of what took place among Hitler, Himmler, and Heydrich concerning the Final Solution, and none of them survived to testify after the war. Therefore, the decision-making process at the center must be reconstructed by the historian, who extrapolates from events, documents, and testimony originating outside the inner circle. Like the man in Plato's cave, he sees only the reflection and shadows, but not reality.[56]

Thus, even the widely accepted belief in a Nazi plan to kill all the Jews of Europe (putting aside for the moment the alleged plot aimed at *worldwide* destruction) is based largely on a combination of hearsay recollection and the interpretation of nonexplicit language in such writings as the infamous Wannsee Protocol. This document consists of the minutes of a meeting held on January 20, 1942, attended by a number of high- and mid-level Nazi officials and convened by Reinhard Heydrich, chief of Security Police and the Security Service. At this meeting, which commonly is regarded as the "smoking gun" for those seeking solid evidence for the Nazi plan to kill all the Jews in Europe, Heydrich is recorded as discussing a proposed "final solution" that involved the forced evacuation "to the East" of all the Jews of Europe, including those in countries that were not yet under German military control, such as England and Spain and Switzerland. "Able-bodied Jews will be taken in large labor columns to these districts for work on roads, separated according to sexes, in the course of which action a great part will undoubtedly be eliminated by natural causes," read the minutes of that meeting—followed by this crucial sentence: "The possible final remnant will, as it must undoubtedly consist of the toughest, have to be treated accordingly, as it is the product of natural selection, and would, if liberated, act as a bud cell of a Jewish reconstruction (see historical experience)."[57]

Never, in this, the key document establishing the plan for a Final Solution, is the outright killing of Jews discussed. To reach the conclusion that this is what in fact was being described requires both an interpretation of the phrase "treated accordingly" and additional supporting documentation. Careful historians, recognizing this problem, have begun by analyzing the phrase in its larger context. Raul Hilberg, for instance, points out that although "Heydrich did not elaborate on the phrase 'treated accordingly' . . . we know from the language of the Einsatzgruppen reports that he meant killing." Others have connected the Wannsee Protocol to other documentary evidence, including Adolf Eichmann's postwar trial interrogation in which he recalls, as the recorder at the Wannsee meeting, that discussions at the conference actually took place "in very plain terms—not in the language that I had to use in the minutes, but in absolutely blunt terms . . . [and] the discussion covered killing, elimination, and annihilation."[58]

Based on this and other, more voluminous, evidence, there seems little doubt that by late 1941 or early 1942 a plan was being put into place that, if carried out, would eventuate in the extermination of most Jews residing "in the German sphere of influence in Europe" (to quote an earlier letter, which had been drafted by Eichmann and signed by Hermann Göring, authorizing the development of plans for a Final Solution), or in "the Lebensraum of the German people" or "Reich territory," to cite the Wannsee Protocol itself. Further, it is true that the inclusion in the Protocol of a statistical table listing estimated numbers of Jews residing in European countries that were at the time outside of German control clearly suggests that *if* those countries were to fall under German domination Heydrich wished to include those Jews as well in the Final Solution. However, it is an enormous and unjustified leap to take the *potential* inclusion of other *European* Jews in Heydrich's report to the furthest extreme possible and claim, as Yehuda Bauer has, that *therefore* the Nazis regarded "the so-called 'Jewish Problem' [as] not a German, or ultimately even European issue, but a *global, universal, even cosmic problem* of the greatest magnitude"—and that therein, with the Nazis' alleged "pseudo-religious" and "pseudo-messianic" plan to kill every Jew on the face of the earth, lies the central proof of Jewish suffering as historically unique.[59]

In the first place, there is no documentary evidence to suggest that any plan to kill even most of the Jews in Nazi-controlled Europe existed prior to the year 1941. As Christopher Browning, among many others, has demonstrated in detail, "The practice of Nazi Jewish policy until 1941 does not support the thesis of a long-held, fixed intention to murder the European Jews."[60] That is, unlike religious and messianic convictions that focus on "universal" and "cosmic" problems, the Final Solution—though certainly rooted in the deep history of German antisemitism and in Hitler's particularly pathological hatred of Jews—was not a long-premeditated and ideologically irresistible Nazi plan or doctrine, as the extreme intentionalist interpretation (and its "uniqueness" offshoot) would have it. Rather, the decision to exterminate the Jews of Europe emerged in the *midst* of the war because of specific mundane and intra-European historical circumstances. And it ended (following the appalling destruction of millions of innocent people) because of changes in those same thoroughly profane and materialist conditions.

This is demonstrable by a large and disparate body of evidence, but one particularly compelling series of incidents irrefutably makes the point. It has long been known that representatives from the highest levels of Nazi leadership, including Adolf Eichmann and *Reichsführer* Heinrich Himmler himself, offered in 1944—that is, two years following the initial implementation of the Final Solution and a year before the war ended—to *release* from Nazi captivity 1 million Jews. (One report says "all the European Jews.") In return, the Nazis wanted 10,000 trucks from the western Allies, to be used only in the Soviet Union, and an unspecified amount of money. (Himmler, at one point, was even supposed to have said that he "wanted to bury the hatchet between us and the Jews.") This was but one of several attempts made by Nazi authorities in 1944 to receive ransom in exchange for the freedom of incarcerated Jews and to begin the process of negotiating a separate peace with the western Allies. Some Jews in fact were freed by the Nazis in this way, though not in numbers close to those that Himmler was proposing. Indeed, as numerous Jewish scholars, including Yehuda Bauer, have long contended, the Nazis were willing to release Jews; the *Allies* were the ones who refused to negotiate. In Bauer's words: "It was the West that failed."[61]

In November 1944, without any major ransom agreements worked out and six months prior to the end of war in Europe, the *Reichsführer* called a halt to the Jewish exterminations and directed that the killing machinery at Auschwitz be dismantled, since "for practical purposes the Jewish question had been solved"— although at least one-third of Europe's Jews, and two-thirds of the world's Jewish population, remained alive.[62] This series of events, to say the least, hardly seems appropriate or consistent behavior for a group that allegedly is obsessed with a messianic, global, even cosmic racial imperative commanding (to quote Katz again) "that *all* Jews must die, and that they must die here and now." And this claimed imperative, it is important to remember, is the final criterion said to establish the uniqueness of the Jewish experience, now that all previous criteria have been found wanting.

That this is a serious problem for proponents of the Jewish uniqueness thesis has not gone unnoticed. Thus, in a recent book entitled *Jews for Sale?*, Bauer tackles head-on the dilemma posed by the Nazi leadership's willingness to trade Jewish lives for money and materiel. His answer:

> Is it not possible to argue that there was no inherent contradiction between the Nazi design to murder all the Jews everywhere and their willingness to compromise temporarily, to permit the flight of some Jews from their domain in return for real advantages to the Reich? If the Nazis expected to be in control, directly or indirectly, of the whole world, might they not have seen the flight of *some* Jews as purely temporary, because they would catch up with those escapees sooner or later?[63]

Following more than 200 pages of further discussion, Bauer not surprisingly answers his own rhetorical questions in the affirmative. While acknowledging the ransom efforts of the Nazis, he contends that this does not constitute contradictory behavior for a group bent on the utter destruction of world Jewry because "the Nazis expected to win the war, and if they did, they would finally 'solve' the 'Jewish question' by total annihilation; any Jews who might escape momentarily would in the end be caught and killed."[64]

Now, it must be said that this is a very imaginative attempt on Bauer's part to wriggle free from an otherwise unsolvable factual and logical dilemma. But it doesn't work. Indeed, it is founded on fantasy. This is so, first, because there is still no evidence whatsoever of any Nazi effort or "plan" (as distinct from bombastic public oratory) to kill every Jew on earth; and second, because the serious Nazi offers regarding the ransoming of Jews were first extended in the late spring and summer of 1944, by which time it was clear to any and all that Germany was in the throes of inevitable and increasingly imminent defeat. Thus, contrary to

Bauer's claim, the Nazis at this time did *not* "expect to be in control, directly or indirectly of the whole world," and they had no hope (or apparent desire) of ever "catching up" with those Jews whose liberation they were proposing.

To quote an earlier publication of Bauer's (evidently written before the contradiction had occurred to him): "Were they [the Nazis] willing to release Jews against such materials and in the process of talks regarding peace feelers? Yes, most probably. *They knew that the war was lost* and the hoped-for talks, as well as possible materials, were more important to them than the Jews, whether alive or dead." In fact, no other conclusion is possible. Even as early as the previous winter, with the devastating collapse of Germany's Sixth Army at Stalingrad, discussion of capitulation was being heard in Berlin. To note just one example of how German attitudes toward the war were changing: Whereas in 1941 the Nazis had issued sixty-five *Sondermeldungen,* or special propaganda announcements, to tell the nation how well the war was going, in all of 1943 there were only three *Sondermeldungen*—and one of them was a desperate effort to turn the most massive military defeat of the war into an exhortation on behalf of collapsing national pride. By late summer of 1944, as Himmler and others acting on his behalf were offering to free all the remaining Jews in exchange for money and supplies, a plot among German military leaders to kill Hitler had been attempted, German troops were suffering enormous losses in the field, their front lines collapsing everywhere, and Paris was in the process of being liberated. No Nazi leader, even probably Hitler, who by this time was almost totally withdrawn and speaking at all only rarely, thought that victory for the Germans was still possible.[65]

In short, the supposed Nazi pseudo-religious mania for pursuing and murdering every Jew on earth, thus distinguishing Jews as the victims to end all victims who had ever lived, melted rapidly away (to the largely imaginary extent that it ever truly existed) once defeat was apparent and the possibility occurred to Nazi leaders that living Jews might be more valuable to them than dead ones. Moreover, from the earliest years of Nazi rule until the collapse of the Reich and the liberation of the camps, the German government had always had a policy of excluding from imprisonment and destruction various categories of Jews, including different subdivisions of *Mischlinge,* or part-Jews. Even the Wannsee Protocol devoted as much space to discussing categories of Jews and part-Jews who would be included in or excluded from extermination (based on such matters as age, record of military service, degree of "mixed blood," and ethnicity of marriage partner) as it did to the Final Solution itself. And from the start those categories of exclusion from persecution, especially as they pertained to the matter of ancestry, were far more liberal for Jews than they were for Gypsies.[66]

Thus, the final justification for the contention that Jewish suffering during the Holocaust, stupendously evil and hideous as it was, was unique in human history—that it was a *novum,* something utterly new and unprecedented in all the world's experience—turns out, like its predecessor arguments, to be more rhetorically apparent than real.[67]

❀ ❀ ❀

In fact, the entire process of seeking grounds for Jewish victim uniqueness is one of smoke and mirrors. Uniqueness advocates *begin* by defining genocide (or the Holocaust or the Shoah) in terms of what they already believe to be experiences undergone only by Jews. After much laborious research it is then "discovered"—*mirabile dictu*—that the Jewish experience was unique. If, however, critics point out after a time that those experiences were not in fact unique, *other* allegedly unique experiences are invented and proclaimed. If not *numbers* killed, then how about *percentage* of population destroyed? If not *efficiency* or *method* of killing employed, how about perpetrator *intentionality*? Ultimately, as we have seen, such insistent efforts extend to the point of frivolousness, as one after another supposedly significant criterion is found to have been either nonexistent or shared by others.

Of course, those other groups could, if they so chose, do precisely the same thing. It might well and logically be asserted by American Indians, for instance, that for the word "genocide" to be properly applicable in describing mass destruction in which there were at least *some* survivors, a minimum of, say, 90 percent of the victim group would have to be wiped out. Is this an arbitrary criterion? Perhaps, although it could certainly be argued that short of total extermination (the only "pure" definition of genocide) 90 percent is a reasonable and round figure that identifies real genocide and prohibits the indiscriminate use of the word in comparatively "insignificant" cases of mass killing—say, the roughly 65 percent mortality rate suffered by European Jews during the Holocaust.

Were it pointed out that this figure is self-serving, since by its standard only American Indians and some other indigenous peoples would be characterized as victims of genocide, it would be easy to demonstrate that the 90 percent criterion is no more self-serving—and no more arbitrary—than those criteria put forward over the years (and time after time found wanting) by advocates of Jewish uniqueness. But in fact both cases are examples of cultural egotism driving scholarship before it. As Stephen Jay Gould has described its equivalent in the work of would-be scholars on another topic: "They began with conclusions, peered through their facts, and came back in a circle to the same conclusions," a matter of "advocacy masquerading as objectivity."[68] The fact that Gould was writing of nineteenth-century scientists bent on proving the superiority of their race over others just makes the citation more apt, as we shall see momentarily.

And, finally, as for restricting use of the word "holocaust" to references having to do with the experience of Jews under the Nazis, that copyright was filed at least three centuries too late. Although "The Holocaust," in what has become conventional usage, clearly applies exclusively to the genocide that was perpetrated by the Nazis against their various victims, "holocaust" in more general parlance, as a term to describe mass destruction or slaughter, belongs to anyone who cares to use it. It is a very old word, after all, and as the *Oxford English Dictionary* points out, apart from previous uses that may have been applied to violent assaults on specific peoples, it was used in this way by Milton in the seventeenth century as well as by Ireland's Bishop George Berkeley in 1732—to describe the Druids' brutal treatment of free-thinkers.

III

And yet, the Jewish experience in the Holocaust *was* unique. In certain ways. Just as the Armenian genocide was. Just as the genocide against the Gypsies was. Just as the many genocides against the native peoples of the New World were. And just as, more recently, the genocides in Cambodia, East Timor, Bosnia, Rwanda, and elsewhere have been—despite the fact that Steven Katz, ever obsessed with his Jewish uniqueness *idée fixe*, crassly has dismissed the killing in Bosnia as a mere "population transfer supported by violence" and has described the massive slaughter of up to a million people in Rwanda as "not genocidal" but simply a struggle for "tribal domination."[69]

Some of these horrendous purges killed more people than others. Some killed higher percentages of people than others. Some were carried out with highly advanced death technology harnessed to coldly bureaucratic planning. Others resulted from crude weapons of war, purposeful mass starvation, enslavement, and forced labor. Some were proudly announced by their perpetrators. The intentions of other mass killers were never publicly made known or have been lost to history. There are, of course, numerous other ways in which individual genocides differed, and on this or that specific point many of them no doubt have been "unique." For no two events, even though they commonly may be acknowledged to fall within a single large classification, are ever precisely alike.

The same thing is true with other major historical phenomena that, however different in particular respects, are conceded by historians to fall within certain general categories of definition. Take political revolution, for instance. Consider, for purposes of discussion, the revolutions in colonial America, France, Russia, and China. In an extraordinary variety of ways—including motivation, duration, and outcome—these revolutions greatly differed from one another. That is, there were certain circumstances and occurrences that were unique to each of them. Yet all of them are agreed to have *been* revolutions. That is why, as serious scholars sift through the data and analyze this or that or another characteristic that marks as particular the American or the French or the Russian or the Chinese revolutions, none among them has ever attempted to proclaim any one of these to be the "unique" revolution—the revolution so different from all others, not only in degree but in fundamental essence, that a special capitalized word must be used to identify it. This has not been done, because to do so would be to depart from the world of scholarship and enter the world of propaganda and group hagiography—which in fact quite clearly is what Holocaust uniqueness proponents are up to: elevating the Jewish experience to a singular and exclusive hierarchical category, thereby reducing all other genocides to a thoroughly lesser and wholly separate substratum of classification.

Uniqueness advocates do not, of course, represent, by any means, the whole of Jewish scholarship on the Holocaust or on genocide. Indeed, if anything, they are something of a cult within that scholarly community—though a cult quite skilled at calling attention to itself and one with powerful friends in high places. In contrast, for example, Princeton historian Arno J. Mayer, a self-described "unbelieving yet unflinching Jew whose maternal grandfather died in the Theresienstadt concentration camp," writes critically of "the dogmatists who seek to reify and sacralize the Holocaust" and of "the exaggerated self-centeredness" of the uniqueness proponents, "which entails the egregious forgetting of the larger whole and of all other victims."[70] Similarly, Israel W. Charny, executive director of the Institute on the Holocaust and Genocide in Jerusalem, rebukes what he calls the "leaders and 'high priests' of different cultures who insist on the uniqueness, exclusivity, primacy, superiority, or greater significance of the specific genocide of their people," adding elsewhere:

> I object very strongly to the efforts to name the genocide of any one people as the single, ultimate event, or as the most important event against which all other tragedies of genocidal mass death are to be tested and found wanting. . . . For me, the passion to exclude this or that mass killing from the universe of genocide, as well as the intense competition to establish the exclusive "superiority" or unique form of any one genocide, ends up creating a fetishistic atmosphere in which the masses of bodies that are not to be qualified for the definition of genocide are dumped into a conceptual black hole, where they are forgotten.

Indeed, it is partly in response to these lamentable tendencies of the uniqueness "high priests" that Charny recently has constructed a sophisticated, and inclusive rather than exclusive, generic typology of genocides.[71]

The thoughtful efforts of such scholars are a welcome and important contribution to understanding in this highly charged and contested field of study. But neither the basic and obvious recognition of certain aspects of uniqueness in all genocidal events, nor Charny's carefully worked out scholarly model, is of interest to Jewish uniqueness advocates. On the contrary, so intense in some quarters is the insistence on the a priori and unchallengeable status of Jews as the most damaged people in the history of the world—what Phillip Lopate calls "extermination pride" affording Jews "a sort of privileged nation status in the moral honor roll"—that any effort to place the admittedly horrifying Jewish experience at the hands of the Nazis within the context of comparative genocide analysis is described by some as "stealing the Holocaust."[72]

According to uniqueness advocate Edward Alexander, for instance, the experience of the Holocaust provided "a Jewish claim to a specific suffering that was of the 'highest,' the most distinguished grade available." Even to mention the genocidal agonies suffered by others, either during the Holocaust or at other times and places, is, Alexander says, "to plunder the moral capital which the Jewish people, through its unparalleled suffering in World War II, had unwittingly accumulated."[73] One of the most ghastly amassments of genocidal suffering ever experienced is thereby made the literal equivalent for its victims of a great bounty of jealously guarded "capital" or wealth. It is unlikely that there exists any more forthright expression than this of what Irving Louis Horowitz calls Holocaust "moral bookkeeping," nor any clearer indication of how obstinate, even in the face of overwhelming evidence to the contrary, true believers in the Jewish uniqueness orthodoxy are certain to remain.[74]

But why? To be sure, as psychologist Charny points out, on one level subjective expressions of belief in the uniqueness of one's own particular suffering, or that of one's compatriots, are a natural and quite common accompaniment to an "outpouring of grief, disbelief, horror and rage at the tragedy and infamy done to one's people."[75] But we are not addressing that phenomenon here. Rather, we are concerned with a small industry of Holocaust hagiographers arguing for the uniqueness of the Jewish experience with all the energy and ingenuity of theological zealots. For that is what they are: zealots who believe literally that they and their religious fellows are, in the words of Deuteronomy 7:6, "a special people . . . above all people that are on the face of the earth," interpreting in the only way thus possible their own community's recent encounter with mass death.

Jews, of course, are not the only people who consider themselves Chosen. The Afrikaners also view themselves as a people of the Covenant, as do the Ulster-Scots of Northern Ireland, and as did America's New England Puritan settlers, among others.[76] In each of these cases the corporate self-identity of Chosenness may, on a day-to-day level, be no more harmful to others than the commonplace ethnocentrism displayed by most of the world's religions or cultures. But with its special emphasis on the maintenance of blood purity (e.g., Deuteronomy 7:3; Joshua 23:12–13), and on the either tacit or expressed pollution fear of corrupting that purity with the defiling blood of others, the ideology of the Covenant intrinsically is but a step away from full-blown racism and, if the means are available, often violent oppression of the purportedly threatening non-Chosen.

Thus, the Afrikaners' self-identification with the ancient Hebrews, and with their own Great Trek regarded by them as a second Exodus—combined with their explication of the biblical story of Ham as meaning that black Africans were divinely ordained to be their servants—formed the theologically legitimizing core of the reprehensible doctrine of apartheid. Thus, the covenantal belief of the Ulster-Scots in their self-defined status as one of God's predestined "elect" peoples has served to justify their occupation of the "promised land" of Northern Ireland, along with their historical persecution of that land's native Irish people. And thus, on one occasion (among many) that the Puritan settlers of New England laid waste an entire neighboring Indian nation with barely a pretext of provocation—shooting and stabbing and burning to death every man, woman, and child that they could find—they wrote in justification that "sometimes the Scripture declareth women and children must perish with their parents," and noted that as Chosen People (alluding to Deuteronomy 20:16) the Lord had given them the Indians' "Land for an Inheritance." Citing the rest of the scriptural passage—"thou shalt save alive nothing that breatheth"—was unnecessary as it would have been redundant.[77]

Justifications for Israel's territorial expansionism and suppression of the Palestinian people, when it has been admitted that the Palestinians *are* a people, of course have long followed this same path of Chosen People self-righteousness. Moreover, it is a self-righteousness that commonly is yoked to the Holocaust's role as part of the founding myth of the Israeli state. That is why an Israeli government official confidently can expect a favorable hearing when he defends his nation's policy of expansionism by saying that to move back from the pre-1967 frontier would be equivalent to returning to the "borders of Auschwitz." And it is why an Israeli military leader can anticipate widespread support for assertions that it is "the holy martyrs of the Holocaust" from whom Israel's army "draws its power and strength" and that the Holocaust is nothing less than "the root and legitimation of our enterprise." As Zygmunt Bauman has observed, Israel uses the Holocaust "as the certificate of its political legitimacy, a safe-conduct pass for its past and future policies, and above all as the advance payment for the injustices it might itself commit."[78]

If, then, the claimed historical uniqueness of Jewish suffering during the Holocaust serves an important function in a theocratic state that perceives itself as under siege—the function served by all "life-sustaining lies," in Karl Jaspers's phrase—it is a falsehood for which others have had to pay a very high price.[79] For implicit in—indeed, *essential* to—the notion of the uniqueness and incomparability of the Jews' genocidal suffering is the concomitant trivialization or even outright denial of the genocidal suffering of *others*, since those others (Armenians, Gypsies, Native Americans, Cambodians, Rwandans, and more) by plain and unavoidable definition are *un*-Chosen beings whose deaths, in the larger scale of things, simply don't matter as much. And this is racist, just as the diminution or denial of Jewish suffering during the Holocaust is antisemitic.

This, of course, is a grave and solemn matter despite the fact that on occasion the transparent superficiality of uniqueness supporters in dealing with non-Jewish peoples is almost comical. Yehuda Bauer, for example, is fond of pretending to be a scholar who has studied the claim that genocide was carried out against the native peoples of the Americas, specifically, he says, "the Pierce Nez" Indians—when in fact there are not now and never have been any such people. Presumably he means the Nez Percé people of the American Northwest, whose noses, incidentally, were not pierced and whose Westernized name apparently is a corruption of the French *nez près*.[80] In any case, the Nez Percé people never have been known by anyone, save Professor Bauer, as "Pierce Nez," and to refer to them as such demonstrates the same level of serious scholarly concern for and knowledge of the topic at hand as would someone, say, claiming to be writing Jewish history who couldn't spell the word "Jew." Clearly, one should avoid declaiming in feigned seriousness on the historical experiences of people whose very name one does not know. For to treat the Nez Percé and others in this way is only to confirm Jean Baudrillard's insight that "the deepest racist avatar is to think that an error about earlier societies is politically or theoretically less serious than a misinterpretation of our own world. Just as a people that oppresses another cannot be free, so a culture that is mistaken about another must also be mistaken about itself."[81]

Deborah Lipstadt provides another variant on this sort of thing when she decries a statement by a Holocaust denier who makes claims for moral comparability between the United States internment of Japanese-American citizens during the Second World War and the Nazi "internment" of Jews. She is quite correct in rejecting this comparison, of course (Manzanar and Tule Lake were outrages, to be sure, but they were not Treblinka or Sobibór), but in doing so she contends that, however improper it was to intern the Japanese, the attempted comparison breaks down because "the Jews had not bombed Nazi cities or attacked German forces in 1939."[82] No, but neither did those Americans of Japanese ancestry who were interned by the U.S. government bomb American cities or attack American forces. Indeed, by equating Japanese-American citizens with the armed forces of the nation of Japan, Lipstadt betrays in herself the very same racist sentiment that led the United States to intern Americans of Japanese ancestry in the first place.

And then there is the case of Rabbi Seymour Siegel, former professor of ethics at the Jewish Theological Seminary and executive director of the U.S. Holocaust Memorial Council. When asked if room might be made on the council for a representative of the Romani, or Gypsy, people who had suffered so horrendously under the Nazis—side by side, in the same death camps and gas chambers and ovens as the Jews—Siegel described such a proposal as "cockamamie" and expressed doubt that the Gypsies even existed as a people.[83]

If such examples of intellectual or moral malfeasance, demonstrating at best wilful ignorance and racist disdain for the non-Jewish group whose sufferings allegedly are being compared with the Jewish experience, are legion among upholders of the Jewish uniqueness persuasion—and they are—further evidence of callous scorn for and *organized* denial of the sufferings of others are even more insidious. For example, for many years now the Turkish government has employed an extraordinary range of strong-arm tactics to prevent international recognition of the Armenian genocide. It is understandable, if still detestable, that perpetrator governments would deny their own complicity in mass murder. It is quite another thing, however, for a group that itself has been terribly victimized by an extermination campaign to collaborate with a historically murderous state in denying that state's documented participation in genocide.

Yet that is precisely what happened only a few years ago when Turkish and Israeli government officials together pressured the White House, which was then involved in planning for the United States Holocaust Memorial Museum, to reject any mention of the Armenian genocide in the museum's exhibits. It is what happened on another occasion when the head of the Jewish community in Turkey, Jewish lobbyists in the United States, and Israeli officials of the Foreign Office conspired with the Turkish government to prevent the United States from holding an official Armenian day of remembrance. And it is what continues to happen today, when, among many other examples, a documentary film on the Armenian genocide remains banned on Israeli television, and when an effort by people in Israel's Education Ministry to produce high school curricula on the Armenian and Gypsy genocides recently was quashed by an oversight committee of government-paid historians.[84]

All this, of course, did not happen without some quid pro quo. So the Turkish government has repaid these generous efforts on its behalf by publicly stating not only that (as their Jewish friends obligingly have confirmed for them) there never was an Armenian genocide but that the Nazi assault on the Jews was indeed historically unique. This is the process, aided in the current instance by the complicity of Holocaust uniqueness proponents and the Israeli government, that Roger W. Smith has called "denying genocide by acknowledging the Holocaust."[85]

For a government with the blood of genocide on its hands—such as Turkey or the United States—to deny the presence of that blood is disgraceful enough. But in certain ways it is worse, because it is so gratuitous, for former *victims* of genocide to befriend such nations and promote their lies purely in the interest of preserving one's own fabricated self-image as history's Victim of victims. For whether it is Israeli government officials conspiring with the Turkish government to conceal the Armenian genocide or Jewish-American Holocaust scholars ridiculing the idea that Native Americans were or are victims of genocide, the damage and the dangers are the same.

The damage done by such actions is what international peace scholar Johan Galtung has called "cultural violence": the systematic degradation and denial of a group's sense of dignity or self-worth and the concealment (by "normalization" of their reduced status) of past and ongoing direct and structural violence that they have suffered. Building on a previously elaborated typology of "direct violence" (straightforward maiming and killing) and "structural violence" (the institutionalization of gross inequality), Galtung demonstrates some of the ways in which cultural violence resides and operates in the intellectual and symbolic infrastructures of certain societies. (For instance, in their manufactured and self-serving but subsequently taken-for-granted history and ideology that use the socially constructed notion of a group's allegedly inborn degeneracy to legitimize continuing direct and structural violence against it.) As Galtung puts it: "Cultural violence makes direct and structural violence look, even feel, right—or at least not wrong."[86]

Jews, of course, have long suffered from all three types of violence, and few better examples exist of attempted cultural violence than the ongoing actions today of neo-Nazi Holocaust deniers. "The general public tends to accord victims of genocide a certain moral authority," observes Deborah Lipstadt, adding, in a good capsule description of one of the things that cultural violence does: "If you devictimize a people you strip them of their moral authority"—and you thereby make more acceptable whatever the amount of their past or present suffering that you cannot simply conceal.[87] Lipstadt understands this quite well, of course, precisely because she sees discussion of genocide as a competitive endeavor and devotes much of her work to devictimizing and thus stripping of their possible moral authority any and all victim groups other than Jews.

In addition to the damage that is inherent in the cultural violence of genocide denial, there is the matter of the future dangers that it promotes. As Roger Smith, Eric Markusen, and Robert Jay Lifton recently have written regarding the continuing denial of the Armenian holocaust:

> Where scholars deny genocide, in the face of decisive evidence that it has occurred, they contribute to a false consciousness that can have the most dire reverberations. Their message, in effect, is: murderers did not really murder; victims were not really killed; mass murder requires no confrontation, no reflection, but should be ignored, glossed over. In this way scholars lend their considerable authority to the acceptance of this ultimate human crime. More than that, they encourage—indeed invite—a repetition of that crime from virtually any source in the immediate or distant future. By closing their minds to truth, that is, such scholars contribute to the deadly psychohistorical dynamic in which unopposed genocide begets new genocides.[88]

This, of course, is one of the great and justified fears that Jews long have harbored regarding the threat of Holocaust denial—that it invites repetition of anti-Jewish mass violence and killing. But when advocates of the allegedly unique suffering of Jews during the Holocaust *themselves* participate in denial of *other* historical genocides—*and such denial is inextricably interwoven with the very claim of uniqueness*—they thereby actively participate in making it much easier for those other genocides to be repeated. And, in the case of genocides against the native peoples of the Americas, not to be repeated but to continue. As, indeed, they are at this very moment. For never, really, have they stopped.

Elie Wiesel is one of the few proponents of the Jewish uniqueness idea who has ever examined with care and seriousness any documents on genocide in the Americas. Those materials, which he studied in the 1970s, related to the Paraguayan government's then ongoing effort to exterminate the Aché Indians. Wiesel was stunned, horrified, and overwhelmed; he said: "Until now, I always forbade myself to compare the Holocaust of European Judaism to events which are foreign to it." Yet, he now conceded, "there are here indications, facts which cannot be denied: it is indeed a matter of a Final Solution. It simply aims at exterminating this tribe. Morally and physically. So that nothing will remain, not even a cry or a tear. Efficient technique, tested elsewhere."[89]

But why hadn't this acclaimed student of genocide spoken out on these ghastly events earlier? "I didn't know," was all he could say. "But is that only an excuse? I

can't think of any other." Of course he was not alone in his ignorance, as he was
more than ready to point out. After listing some of the horrors he now knew that
the Aché people were experiencing—"men hunted, humiliated, murdered for the
sake of pleasure . . . young girls raped and sold . . . children killed in front of their
parents reduced to silence by pain . . . ghettos, collective murders, manhunts, tortures, and agonies"—he concluded:

> Our society prefers not to know anything of all that. Silence everywhere. Hardly a few
> words in the press. Nothing is discussed in the U.N., nor among the politicized in-
> tellectuals or the moralists. The great consciences kept quiet. Of course, we had an
> excuse! We didn't know. But now, after having read these testimonies, we know.
> Henceforth we shall be responsible. And accomplices.[90]

That was written twenty years ago in a book that has long been out of print.
How many Americans today have heard of the Aché Indians? Or of the scores of
other separate and independent indigenous peoples of Central and South
America who have been totally exterminated, under equally ghastly conditions,
during our lifetimes? Or of those who are being destroyed in the same way even
now? Who knows of the many more still—tens of millions of people from Alaska
in the far north to Tierra del Fuego in the far south, and on the 16 million square
miles of land between—who were liquidated by outside invaders and settlers during past centuries? There is nothing left of most of them. Not a trace. Others cling
on to existence, their numbers tiny fractions of what they were before the waves
of violence swept over them.

The willful maintenance of public ignorance regarding the genocidal and racist
horrors against indigenous peoples that have been and are being perpetrated by
many nations of the Western Hemisphere, including the United States—which
contributes to the construction of a museum to commemorate genocide only if
the killing occurred half a world away—is consciously aided and abetted and le-
gitimized by the actions of the Jewish uniqueness advocates we have been discussing. Their manufactured claims of uniqueness for their own people are, after
all, synonymous with dismissal and denial of the experience of others—others
much weaker, more oppressed, and in far more immediate danger than they.
Further—and this would be ironic were it not so tragic—in their denial of genocide victim status to other groups, Jewish uniqueness advocates almost invariably
mimic *exactly* the same pattern of assertions laid out by the antisemitic historical
revisionists who deny Jewish suffering in the Holocaust: The number of people
killed is said to be exaggerated, the deaths that did occur are labeled as provoked
or wartime casualties, most of the victims are claimed to have succumbed to natural causes such as disease, there is alleged to be no evidence of official intent to
commit genocide, and so on. In this way, narcissistic, false claims of uniqueness
are joined with brutal, racist denials of the sufferings of others, becoming two
sides of the same debased coin.

But as uniqueness proponents never tire of reminding anyone who will listen, denial encourages more violence against those who truly are its victims. Jews suffered horrendously during the reign of the Third Reich—to say nothing of the millennium of oppression and exile and pogrom that led inexorably toward the Holocaust—and so all people of conscience must be on guard against Holocaust deniers who, in many cases, would like nothing better than to see mass violence against Jews start again.

By that same token, however, as we consider the terrible history and the ongoing campaigns of genocide against the indigenous inhabitants of the Western Hemisphere and other peoples elsewhere, there no longer is any excuse for maintaining the self-serving masquerade of Jewish genocide uniqueness—the endlessly refined and revised deception that serves equally to deny the sufferings of others, and thus, in murderous complicity with both past and present genocidal regimes, to place those terribly damaged others even closer to harm's way. It is a moral issue. And a serious one. As Elie Wiesel has said: "Now we know. Henceforth we shall be responsible. And accomplices."

NOTES

This essay is a revised and expanded version of a lecture given on May 2, 1995, at the University of Colorado, Boulder. I am grateful to the consortium of organizations and academic departments at the university that invited me to speak—particularly the Center for Studies of Ethnicity and Race in America—and for the spirited and enlightening post-lecture discussion that ensued.

1. See, among other discussions of the Allies' wartime denial and indifference, David S. Wyman, *The Abandonment of the Jews: America and the Holocaust, 1941–1945* (New York: Pantheon Books, 1984); and Christopher Simpson, *The Splendid Blond Beast: Money, Law, and Genocide in the Twentieth Century* (Monroe, Maine: Common Courage Press, 1995).
2. The overall death toll of the war, including the range of figures for China, is summarized in Peter Calvocoressi, Guy Wint, and John Pritchard, *Total War: Causes and Courses of the Second World War*, rev. 2d ed. (New York: Pantheon, 1989), pp. 576–578. The most exhaustive quantitative study of Jewish deaths during the Holocaust, putting the total figure at 5.1 million, is Raul Hilberg, *The Destruction of the European Jews*, rev. and definitive ed. (New York: Holmes and Meier, 1985), three volumes; for the cited total and percentages of Jewish deaths, see especially volume 3, pp. 1047–1048 and 1201–1220. Hilberg's figures have, of course, been criticized (ineffectively) by neo-Nazis and so-called historical revisionists as being far too high. Conversely, others have claimed that they are too low, some even arguing that in Auschwitz alone as many as 4 million people—including 2 million Jews—perished. Hilberg's estimate of 1.1 million as the number of Jewish deaths at Auschwitz has received confirmation in subsequent research, however, lending further credence to his widely accepted overall figure as well. For recent and authoritative discussion of the death toll at Auschwitz, see Franciszek Piper, "The Number of Victims," in *Anatomy of the Auschwitz Death Camp*, ed. Yisreal Gutman and Michael Berenbaum (Bloomington:

Indiana University Press in association with the United States Holocaust Memorial Museum, 1994), pp. 61–76.

3. For discussion of some of the more prominent of these cases, see Deborah Lipstadt, *Denying the Holocaust: The Growing Assault on Truth and Memory* (New York: Free Press, 1993), pp. 11–12, 14, 141, 157–170, 219–222. See also Erich Kulka, "Denial of the Holocaust," in *Genocide: A Critical Bibliographic Review*, vol. 2, ed. Israel Charny (London: Mansell, 1991), pp. 38–62. It should be noted that following the case of Ernst Zundel, who was twice sentenced to prison terms in Canada for disseminating hate literature denying the existence of the Holocaust, the Canadian Supreme Court found the statute in question to be unconstitutional. One of the more infamous cases of a Holocaust denier being hailed before the bar of justice involves the French academic Robert Faurisson, discussed most fully in Pierre Vidal-Naquet, *Assassins of Memory: Essays on the Denial of the Holocaust* (New York: Columbia University Press, 1992). Such prosecutions continue today. Thus, during the summer of 1995, a young man named Bela Ewald Althans was sentenced by a Berlin court to three and one-half years in prison for telling tourists at Auschwitz that the Holocaust "is a giant farce." Centre for Comparative Genocide Studies (Macquarie University, Australia), *Newsletter* 2(1) (1995):14. The term "cultural violence" in this paragraph is borrowed from Johan Galtung, whose work on the topic is discussed later in this chapter.

4. *Time,* 27 May 1991, p. 74.

5. *The Atlantic,* September 1992, pp. 16–30.

6. *The Nation,* 19 October 1992, p. 422. That people on the left can be as racist as their partners on the right, especially regarding indigenous peoples, is a matter too often overlooked. For another example, see the exchanges in Ward Churchill, ed., *Marxism and Native Americans* (Boston: South End Press, 1983).

7. Here I do not use the term "quasi-Hitlerian" lightly. For example, compare Hitchens's expressed sentiments in his essay in praise of power and historical inevitability with those of Hitler in a speech he delivered in Munich in April of 1923: "The whole work of Nature is a mighty struggle between strength and weakness—an eternal victory of the strong over the weak. There would be nothing but decay in the whole of Nature if this were not so. States which offend against this elementary law fall into decay.... History proves: He who has not the strength—him the 'right in itself' profits not a whit." Quoted in Alan Bullock, *Hitler: A Study in Tyranny,* rev. ed. (New York: Harper and Row, 1962), pp. 398–399.

8. Emphasis added in Hitchens quote. Traditional estimates suggest that about 10 million captured Africans survived the ordeal of forced migration to become plantation laborers in North or South America or the Caribbean. Recent research puts the figure at closer to 12 million or 15 million. However, for every African who survived to become a working slave, between three and four died during the enslavement process. With a total of 10–15 million Africans surviving to become slaves, this makes for an overall death rate directly attributable to enslavement of anywhere from 40 million to 60 million—and this was *prior* to the surviving Africans' beginning to labor under further horrendous and life-diminishing conditions as New World bondsmen and bondswomen. For a brief bibliographical discussion of this matter, see David E. Stannard, *American Holocaust: Columbus and the Conquest of the New World* (New York: Oxford University Press, 1992), pp. 317–318.

9. Quoted and discussed in Desmond C. Derbyshire and Geoffrey K. Pullum, eds., *Handbook of Amazonian Languages,* vol. 1 (Berlin: Mouton de Gruyter, 1986), pp. 4–8. I am grateful to Professor Pullum for calling these writings to my attention.

10. Yehuda Bauer, "Whose Holocaust?" *Midstream* 26(9) (November 1980):42, 45.

11. Lipstadt, *Denying the Holocaust*, pp. 20, 74.

12. Ibid., pp. 212–215. Although Lipstadt's technique of preemptively villifying anyone who might disagree with her is especially egregious, she is far from alone in employing it. And for such ire to be raised the issue at hand does not have to be limited to the uniqueness question. For many years now, for instance, even the most eminent Jewish scholars who have failed to follow the established historical line regarding the causes and conduct of the Nazi campaign against the Jews have thereby courted withering ad hominem criticism from within certain segments of the Jewish intellectual community. Prominent examples, among many, include the attacks on Hannah Arendt for writing *Eichmann in Jerusalem* more than thirty years ago, critical responses to which included the *New York Times Book Review* calling it a defense of the Nazis and an attack on their Jewish victims and the *Intermountain Jewish News* headlining its report on the book while it was being serialized in the *New Yorker*: "Self-Hating Jewess Writes Pro-Eichmann Series." At about that same time, Raul Hilberg was "showered with criticism" (to use Michael R. Marrus's words) for making some remarks about limited Jewish resistance to the Nazis at the end of his monumental study, *The Destruction of the European Jews*. More recently some Jewish students organized a boycott of classes conducted by distinguished Princeton scholar Arno J. Mayer, because in his book *Why Did the Heavens Not Darken?* he wrote critically both of "'revisionists' who categorically deny the Judeocide *and* of "dogmatists who seek to reify and sacralize the Holocaust." For a contemporary discussion of the response to Arendt's book, see Dwight Macdonald, "Hannah Arendt and the Jewish Establishment," *Partisan Review* (spring 1964), reprinted in Macdonald's *Discriminations: Essays and Afterthoughts, 1938–1974* (New York: Grossman, 1974), pp. 308–317. The harsh treatment accorded Hilberg is discussed in Michael R. Marrus, "Jewish Resistance to the Holocaust," *Journal of Contemporary History* 30 (1995):83–110. On the Princeton students and Professor Mayer, see his "Memory and History: On the Poverty of Remembering and Forgetting the Judeocide," *Radical History Review* 56 (1993):5–20. Mayer is also included in a rogues' gallery of "Hitler apologists" compiled by the Anti-Defamation League because he does not toe the line on the uniqueness question. See *Hitler's Apologists: The Anti-Semitic Propaganda of Holocaust "Revisionism"* (New York: Anti-Defamation League, 1993), pp. 3–4, 48–49.

13. Ian Hancock, "'Uniqueness' of the Victims: Gypsies, Jews, and the Holocaust," *Without Prejudice* 1 (1988):55; and the same author's "Uniqueness, Gypsies, and Jews," in *Remembering for the Future: Working Papers and Addenda*, ed. Yehuda Bauer et al. (Oxford: Pergamon Press, 1989), vol. 2, pp. 2017–2025. For an excellent bibliography of writings on the Gypsies as Holocaust victims, see Michael Burleigh and Wolfgang Wippermann, *The Racial State: Germany, 1933–1945* (Cambridge: Cambridge University Press, 1991), pp. 364–367.

14. A good recent summary discussion of the Armenian genocide, including bibliographical suggestions, is Richard G. Hovannisian, "Etiology and Sequelae of the Armenian Genocide," in *Genocide: Conceptual and Historical Dimensions*, ed. George J. Andreopoulos (Philadelphia: University of Pennsylvania Press, 1994), pp. 111–140. For discussion of a variety of issues on this matter, see also Richard G. Hovannisian, ed., *The Armenian Genocide in Perspective* (New Brunswick, N.J.: Transaction Books, 1986); and Florence Mazian, *Why Genocide? The Armenian and Jewish Experiences in Perspective* (Ames: Iowa State University Press, 1990). On the legitimacy of these numbers it is worth noting that decades ago even

Bernard Lewis, regarded by many as an apologist for the Turks, put the Armenian death toll at 1.5 million and described it as a "terrible holocaust." Bernard Lewis, *The Emergence of Modern Turkey* (Oxford: Oxford University Press, 1961), p. 356.

15. Gerard J. Libaridian, "The Ultimate Repression: The Genocide of the Armenians, 1915–1917," in *Genocide and the Modern Age: Etiology and Case Studies of Mass Death,* ed. Isidor Wallimann and Michael N. Dobkowski (Westport, Conn.: Greenwood Press, 1987), pp. 203–235. The Dawidowicz reference is from Lucy S. Dawidowicz, *The Holocaust and the Historians* (Cambridge: Harvard University Press, 1981), p. 13.

16. Stannard, *American Holocaust,* part 2.

17. Dawidowicz, *The Holocaust and the Historians*, pp. 15, 17. Considering that there has been some controversy on the number of Japanese deaths in Hiroshima and Nagasaki following the bombings, note that the most thorough review of the topic remains that by the Committee for the Compilation of Materials on Damage Caused by the Atomic Bombs in Hiroshima and Nagasaki, *Hiroshima and Nagasaki: The Physical, Medical, and Social Effects of the Atomic Bombings,* trans. Eisei Ishikawa and David L. Swain (New York: Basic Books, 1981), pp. 363–369.

18. See note 22.

19. Michael R. Marrus, *The Holocaust in History* (Hanover, N.H.: Brandeis University Press and University Press of New England, 1987), pp. 21–22 (emphasis in original); Bauer, "Whose Holocaust?" p. 45; and Steven T. Katz, "The Pequot War Reconsidered," *New England Quarterly* 64 (1991):206–224 (emphasis in original). (In this essay Katz also recommends that "we hold our charges of racism in reserve" if we are adequately to understand the white colonists' slaughter of the Indians—a suggestion as obtuse as saying that we should hold our charges of antisemitism in reserve if we wish to understand the Nazi destruction of the Jews. I previously commented on this article in *American Holocaust*, p. 318, note 11.)

20. Hilberg, *Destruction of the European Jews*, vol. 3, pp. 1047–1048 and 1220.

21. Yehuda Bauer, "Holocaust and Genocide: Some Comparisons," in *Lessons and Legacies: The Meaning of the Holocaust in a Changing World,* ed. Peter Hayes (Evanston, Ill.: Northwestern University Press, 1991), p. 40 (emphasis added).

22. Steven T. Katz, *The Holocaust in Historical Context, Volume I: The Holocaust and Mass Death Before the Modern Age* (New York: Oxford University Press, 1994), pp. 97–98. As of this writing only the first volume of Katz's proposed multivolume study has been published. Both Marrus and Bauer are among those who also now explicitly make this concession. See Marrus, *The Holocaust in History*, pp. 23–24; and Yehuda Bauer, "Is the Holocaust Explicable?" in Bauer et al., *Remembering for the Future*, pp. 1969–1970.

23. George M. Kren and Leon Rappoport, *The Holocaust and the Crisis of Human Behavior* (New York: Holmes and Meier, 1980), p. 2. Katz, *Holocaust in Historical Context*, p. 98, note 128. Gérard Prunier, *The Rwanda Crisis: History of a Genocide* (New York: Columbia University Press, 1995), pp. 264–265. For the maximum rate of killing ever achieved at Auschwitz, see the statement by the camp's commandant, Rudolf Hoess, quoted in Burleigh and Grimes, *The Racial State*, p. 106.

24. Phillip Lopate, "Resistance to the Holocaust," in *Testimony: Contemporary Writers Make the Holocaust Personal,* ed. David Rosenberg (New York: Times Books, 1989), p. 292.

25. Katz, *Holocaust in Historical Context*, p. 20 (emphasis in original).

26. For convenient overviews, see Noble David Cook, *Demographic Collapse: Indian Peru, 1520–1620* (Cambridge: Cambridge University Press, 1981); and John Hemming, *The*

Conquest of the Incas (New York: Harcourt Brace Jovanovich, 1970). On sexual inactivity and infertility in the Nazi camps, see Terrence Des Pres, *The Survivor: An Anatomy of Life in the Death Camps* (New York: Oxford University Press, 1976), pp. 189–191.

27. All of the accounts and information that follow are documented in detail—along with much else for which there is no room here—in my *American Holocaust*, especially part 2.

28. Yisrael Gutman, "Auschwitz—An Overview," in Gutman and Berenbaum, *Anatomy of the Auschwitz Death Camp*, p. 27.

29. David A. Hackett, ed., *The Buchenwald Report* (Boulder: Westview Press, 1995), pp. 109–115.

30. For examples of efforts to deal with this problem in historical analysis, see Andrew B. Appleby, "Disease or Famine? Mortality in Cumberland and Westmorland, 1580–1640," *Economic History Review*, 2d ser., 26 (1973):403–431; and John D. Post, "The Mortality Crises of the Early 1770s and European Demographic Trends," *Journal of Interdisciplinary History* 21 (1990):29–62.

31. Hilberg, *Destruction of the European Jews*, vol. 3, p. 1220, table B-3; Hackett, *Buchenwald Report*, pp. 226–227.

32. Arno J. Mayer, *Why Did the Heavens Not Darken? The "Final Solution" in History*, with a new foreword by the author (New York: Pantheon, 1990), pp. 365, 462.

33. Lipstadt, *Denying the Holocaust*, p. 215; John W. Dower, *War Without Mercy: Race and Power in the Pacific War* (New York: Pantheon, 1986), p. 298. For a concise summary of the situation in the world today, see Laurie Garrett, *The Coming Plague: Newly Emerging Diseases in a World Out of Balance* (New York: Farrar, Straus, and Giroux, 1994), pp. 607–608.

34. Marrus, *The Holocaust in History*, p. 20. See also Des Pres, *The Survivor*, p. 114, where he wonders at the notion of a hierarchy of death, depending on whether one was confined to a death camp or a concentration camp: "What, really, is the difference," Des Pres asks, "if Buchenwald was not classified as an extermination camp and had no gas chamber, but had special rooms for mass shooting and a level of privation so severe that prisoners died in hundreds every day?"

35. Hackett, *Buchenwald Report*, p. 7.

36. On the calories provided in the diets supplied to California's mission-concentration camp Indians, see Sherburne F. Cook, *The Conflict Between the California Indian and White Civilization* (Berkeley: University of California Press, 1976), p. 37, table 2, and pp. 42–43, where a downward adjustment of at least 10 percent of the table 2 figures is discussed.

37. For the ghastly statistics of life and death in the northern California missions, see Robert H. Jackson, "The Dynamic of Indian Demographic Collapse in the San Francisco Bay Missions, Alta, California, 1776–1840," *American Indian Quarterly* 16 (1992):141–156. For a still more recent analysis of a wide variety of lethal life conditions in the California missions that provides strong support for Cook's pioneering statistical computations, see Robert H. Jackson, *Indian Population Decline: The Missions of Northwestern New Spain, 1687–1840* (Albuquerque: University of New Mexico Press, 1995). For discussion of inmate living space in the missions, see Cook, *Conflict Between the California Indian and White Civilization*, pp. 89–90. Modern osteological analysis of native skeletal remains from California mission burials has confirmed the devastating impact of malnutrition in these death camps—in marked contrast to the skeletal remains at preinvasion burial sites. See, for example, Phillip L. Walker et al., "The Effects of European Contact on the Health of

Alta California Indians, in *Columbian Consequences, Volume 1: Archeological and Historical Perspectives on the Spanish Borderlands West,* ed. David Hurst Thomas (Washington, D.C.: Smithsonian Institution Press, 1989), p. 351.

38. Despite constant infusions of new inmates to replace those who were perishing in the mission compounds, by the time the missions closed they had killed off at least 72 percent of their native prisoners—including up to one-third of the imprisoned children each year—compared with the previously cited 23 percent at Buchenwald. See Cook, *Conflict Between the California Indian and White Civilization,* p. 346. While the idea is commonplace that the destruction of the native peoples of the Americas was, as Katz has put it, "an *unintended* tragedy" (see note 25), the specific reference to them as people who "did not wear well" comes from Alfred W. Crosby, "Infectious Disease and the Demography of the Atlantic Peoples," *Journal of World History* 2 (1991): 124.

39. For a brief discussion, see Robert Melson, "Revolution and Genocide: On the Causes of the Armenian Genocide and the Holocaust," in *The Armenian Genocide: History, Politics, Ethics,* ed. Richard G. Hovannisian (New York: St. Martin's Press, 1992), esp. pp. 86–87.

40. See the recent discussion in Marrus, "Jewish Resistance to the Holocaust."

41. Putting aside religion and ethnicity—which in themselves were greatly varied—in linguistic terms alone the native peoples of the Western Hemisphere were astonishingly diverse, speaking at least 1,500 to 2,000 different and mutually unintelligible languages. These have been traced to a cluster of more than 150 highly distinct language families, each one as different from the others as Indo-European is from Sino-Tibetan. In contrast, there are hardly more than forty comparably distinct language families that are ancestral to the entirety of Europe and the Middle East. For discussion, see, among many sources, L. Campbell and M. Mithun, eds., *The Languages of Native America: Historical and Comparative Assessment* (Austin: University of Texas Press, 1979), and an early but still valuable overview, Harold E. Driver, *Indians of North America,* 2d rev. ed. (Chicago: University of Chicago Press, 1969), ch. 3. For more recent discussion of certain specific points of controversy, cf. Joseph H. Greenberg, *Language in the Americas* (Stanford: Stanford University Press, 1988), and James Matisoff, "On Megalocomparison," *Language* 66 (1990):106–120.

42. Yehuda Bauer, *The Holocaust in Historical Perspective* (Seattle: University of Washington Press, 1978), pp. 8–9, 32–33; and Bauer, "Whose Holocaust?" pp. 44–45. Himmler is quoted in Robert Jay Lifton, *The Nazi Doctors: Medical Killing and the Psychology of Genocide* (New York: Basic Books, 1986), p. 477.

43. See, for example, David Svaldi, *Sand Creek and the Rhetoric of Extermination: A Case Study in Indian-White Relations* (New York: University Press of America, 1989), p. 291; and Lynwood Carranco and Estle Beard, *Genocide and Vendetta: The Round Valley Wars of Northern California* (Norman: University of Oklahoma Press, 1981), ch. 4.

44. Zygmunt Bauman, *Modernity and the Holocaust* (Cambridge: Polity Press, 1989), pp. 91–92, 98.

45. G. Stanley Hall, *Adolescence: Its Psychology,* vol. 2 (New York: D. Appleton, 1904), pp. 648, 651.

46. Bauer, *Holocaust in Historical Perspective,* p. 8; Christopher R. Browning, *Ordinary Men: Reserve Police Battalion 101 and the Final Solution in Poland* (New York: HarperCollins, 1992), p. 162.

47. Stannard, *American Holocaust,* pp. 83, 88, 120, 133, 204, 210–212, 240–246.

48. Bauer, "Is the Holocaust Explicable?" p. 1970; Bauer, *Holocaust in Historical Perspective,* p. 38; Katz, *Holocaust in Historical Context,* vol. 1, p. 580.

49. For example, Benno Müller-Hill, *Murderous Science: Elimination by Scientific Selection of Jews, Gypsies, and Others, 1933–1945* (Oxford: Oxford University Press, 1988); Burleigh and Wippermann, *The Racial State*, pp. 113–135; and Hancock, "'Uniqueness' of the Victims," pp. 53–54. See also Brenda Davis Lutz and James M. Lutz, "Gypsies as Victims of the Holocaust," *Holocaust and Genocide Studies* 9 (1995):346–359, who contend that the proportion of Gypsies killed during the Holocaust was lower than the Jewish figure, but who demonstrate that the Nazi *intent* was identical for Gypsies and Jews.

50. Edmund S, Morgan, *American Slavery—American Freedom: The Ordeal of Colonial Virginia* (New York: W. W. Norton, 1975), p. 233 (emphasis added); Stannard, *American Holocaust*, p. 107.

51. Albert L. Hurtado, *Indian Survival on the California Frontier* (New Haven: Yale University Press, 1988), p. 135; Edward D. Castillo, "The Impact of Euro-American Exploration and Settlement," in *Handbook of North American Indians,* vol. 8, ed. William C. Sturtevant (Washington: Smithsonian Institution Press, 1978), p. 108; Stannard, *American Holocaust*, pp. 107, 142–145, 240–246. In Auschwitz 1.1 million of the 1.3 million prisoners died—a rate of 84.6 percent (Piper, "The Number of Victims," p. 71); the 95 percent rate of destruction for California Indians is the most conservative of the current scholarly estimates—that of Douglas H. Ubelaker, "North American Indian Population Size: Changing Perspectives," in *Disease and Demography in the Americas,* ed. John W. Verano and Douglas H. Ubelaker (Washington: Smithsonian Institution Press, 1992), p. 174, table 5. It is based on a pre-European contact population estimate that most scholars would increase by at least 50 percent—for example, Russell Thornton, *American Indian Holocaust and Survival: A Population History Since 1492* (Norman: University of Oklahoma Press, 1987), p. 109, table 5-4—and likely much more. Similarly, whereas Ubelaker's total population decline estimates for the native peoples of North America (excluding Mexico) result in a continent-wide collapse of 73 percent—compared with about 65 percent among European Jews during the Holocaust—the estimates of other scholars, based on projections of much higher pre-Columbian population figures, result in an overall reduction of 95 percent of the indigenous population in the aftermath of the European invasion. Ubelaker's 73 percent figure is based on a pre-Columbian population estimate of less than 2 million people for the area of what is now the United States, a figure that most contemporary scholars would at least double and more likely multiply by a factor of at least five. For a range of such figures, from roughly 4 million to 12 million or more, compare William M. Denevan, *The Native Population of the Americas in 1492*, 2d ed. (Madison: University of Wisconsin Press, 1992), p. xxviii, table 1, and Ann F. Ramenofsky, *Vectors of Death: The Archaeology of European Contact* (Albuquerque: University of New Mexico Press, 1987), p. 162.

52. On the psychological resistance of *Einsatzkommandos* to their massive killing assignments, see Lifton, *The Nazi Doctors*, pp. 159–162. Jackson is quoted in Ronald T. Takaki, *Iron Cages: Race and Culture in 19th-Century America* (New York: Alfred A. Knopf, 1979), pp. 96, 102–103.

53. Lyndall Ryan, *The Aboriginal Tasmanians* (St. Lucia: University of Queensland Press, 1981); L.F.S. Upton, "The Extermination of the Beothuks of Newfoundland," *Canadian Historical Review* 58 (1977):133–153.

54. Originally developed by Tim Mason in his essay, "Intention and Explanation: A Current Controversy About the Interpretation of National Socialism," in *Der Führerstaat: Mythos und Realität*, ed. Gerhard Hirschfeld and Lothar Kettenacker (Stuttgart, 1981), pp.

21–40, these terms are discussed insightfully in Christopher R. Browning, *Fateful Months: Essays on the Emergence of the Final Solution* (New York: Holmes and Meier, 1985), pp. 8–38.

55. Mayer, *Why Did the Heavens Not Darken?* p. 459.

56. Browning, *Fateful Months*, pp. 13–14.

57. John Mendelsohn and Donald S. Detwiler, eds., *The Holocaust: Selected Documents in Eighteen Volumes* (New York: Garland, 1982), pp. 22–25. This is a reproduction and translation of the only known extant copy of the Wannsee Protocol.

58. Hilberg, *Destruction of the European Jews*, vol. 2, p. 405; Gerald Fleming, *Hitler and the Final Solution* (Berkeley: University of California Press, 1982), pp. 91–92.

59. Hilberg, *Destruction of the European Jews*, vol. 2, p. 401; Mendelsohn and Detwiler, *The Holocaust*, p. 20; Bauer, "Is the Holocaust Explicable?" p. 1970. Much is sometimes made of the fact that the Wannsee Protocol refers to "the Reich Fuehrer-SS and the Chief of the German Police"—namely, Heinrich Himmler—being "entrusted with the official handling of the final solution of the Jewish problem centrally *without regard to geographic borders*" as if this suggests a worldwide plan (emphasis added). See, for instance, Leni Yahil, *The Holocaust: The Fate of European Jewry, 1932–1945* (New York: Oxford University Press, 1990), p. 313. Clearly, however, this phrase must be read in context—and that context is unambiguously provided by the immediately preceding two sentences that twice refer to "the final solution of the Jewish problem *in Europe*" (emphasis added). The geographic borders in question, then, plainly were European borders.

60. On the absence of evidence (or even grounds for logical deduction) concerning a pre-1941 plan for the Final Solution, see the thoughtful and evenhanded discussion in Browning, *Fateful Months*, pp. 8–38.

61. For general discussion of this topic, see Arthur D. Morse, *While Six Million Died: Chronicle of American Apathy* (New York: Random House, 1967), pp. 353–361; Wyman, *Abandonment of the Jews*, pp. 243–249; and Bauer, *The Holocaust in Historical Perspective*, pp. 94–155. For recent interpretations, see also Paul L. Rose, "Joel Brand's 'Interim Agreement' and the Course of Nazi-Jewish Negotiations, 1944–1945," *Historical Journal* 34 (1991):909–929; and Richard Breitman and Shlomo Aronson, "The End of the 'Final Solution'? Nazi Plans to Ransom Jews in 1944," *Central European History* 25 (1993): 177–203. The reprehensibly cynical "bury the hatchet" quotation attributed to Himmler appears in Monty Noam Penkower, *The Jews Were Expendable: Free World Diplomacy and the Holocaust* (Urbana: University of Illinois Press, 1983), p. 281. The quotation from Bauer is on p. 155 of *The Holocaust in Historical Perspective*.

62. Hilberg, *Destruction of the European Jews*, vol. 3, pp. 980–981.

63. Yehuda Bauer, *Jews for Sale? Nazi-Jewish Negotiations, 1933–1945* (New Haven: Yale University Press, 1994), p. 2.

64. Ibid., p. 252.

65. Bauer, *The Holocaust in Historical Perspective*, p. 154 (emphasis added). For a convenient summary of Germany's military situation at this time, see Calvocoressi, Wint, and Pritchard, *Total War*, esp. pp. 512–54.

66. On the grotesque Nazi efforts to create a "third race" between Aryans and Jews, see Hilberg, *Destruction of the European Jews*, vol. 1, pp. 65–80. The substantive portions of the Wannsee Protocol, in translation, cover thirteen pages, of which more than six are concerned with the proposed treatment of various categories of "mixed blood" persons, and of elderly Jews and Jews with distinguished war records, who might be exempt from evac-

uation—and thus from extermination. On the more stringent categorization of Gypsies than Jews—from 50 to 100 percent stricter in terms of "desirable blood quantum" sufficient to exclude one from persecution—see Donald Kenrick and Grattan Puxon, *The Destiny of Europe's Gypsies* (New York: Basic Books, 1972), pp. 67, 85; and Angus Fraser, *The Gypsies* (Oxford: Blackwell, 1992), p. 260.

67. The term *novum* in this context is derived from Katz's claim at the beginning of the recently published first volume of his Holocaust study that the *Endlösung*—the Final Solution—was a *novum*—a "singularity as a historical phenomenon." Katz, *Holocaust in Historical Context*, vol. 1, p. 3.

68. Stephen Jay Gould, *The Mismeasure of Man* (New York: W. W. Norton, 1981), p. 85.

69. Liz McMillen, "The Uniqueness of the Holocaust," *Chronicle of Higher Education* 40(42) (June 22, 1994):A13.

70. Mayer, "Memory and History," pp. 6 and 17.

71. Israel W. Charny, "Introduction" to Charny, *Genocide*, p. xxiv; and Israel W. Charny, "Toward a Generic Definition of Genocide," in Andreopoulos, *Genocide*, pp. 72, 91–92.

72. Lopate, "Resistance to the Holocaust," pp. 299, 300.

73. Edward Alexander, *The Holocaust and the War of Ideas* (New Brunswick, N.J.: Transaction Publishers, 1994), p. 195; Edward Alexander, "Stealing the Holocaust," *Midstream* 26(9) (November 1980):47.

74. Irving Louis Horowitz, "Genocide and the Reconstruction of Social Theory: Observations on the Exclusivity of Collective Death," in Wallimann and Dobkowski, *Genocide and the Modern Age*, p. 62.

75. Charny, "Toward a Generic Definition of Genocide," p. 72.

76. Donald Harman Akenson, *God's Peoples: Covenant and Land in South Africa, Israel, and Ulster* (Ithaca, N.Y.: Cornell University Press, 1992).

77. On the Afrikaners and the Ulster-Scots, see ibid., esp. pp. 72–77, 94–95, and 119–122; on the Ulster-Scots also see Steve Bruce, *God Save Ulster: The Religion and Politics of Paisleyism* (Oxford: Clarendon Press, 1986). The quotation from a Puritan writer is from John Mason, *A Brief History of the Pequot War* (Boston: Kneeland and Green, 1736 [reprint]), p. 21, discussed in Stannard, *American Holocaust*, pp. 111–115.

78. Israeli officials quoted in Mayer, "Memory and History," p. 13; Bauman, *Modernity and the Holocaust*, p. ix.

79. Jaspers is quoted by Gordon Craig in his review of the Hannah Arendt–Karl Jaspers correspondence, *New York Review of Books*, May 13, 1993, p. 12.

80. Bauer, "Is the Holocaust Explicable?" p. 1969; Robert H. Ruby and John A. Brown, *Indians of the Pacific Northwest: A History* (Norman: University of Oklahoma Press, 1981), p. 16.

81. Jean Baudrillard, *The Mirror of Production* (St. Louis: Telos Press, 1975), p. 107.

82. Lipstadt, *Denying the Holocaust*, pp. 213–214.

83. Edward T. Linenthal, *Preserving Memory: The Struggle to Create America's Holocaust Museum* (New York: Viking Press, 1995), pp. 242–243.

84. Judith Miller, *One, by One, by One: Facing the Holocaust* (New York: Simon and Schuster, 1990), p. 259; Linenthal, *Preserving Memory*, pp. 238–239; and Yossi Klein Halevi, "The Forgotten Genocide," *Jerusalem Report* 6(2) (June 1995):20–21. For good discussion of the relentless Turkish campaign to conceal the Armenian holocaust, see Roger W. Smith, "Denial of the Armenian Genocide," in Charny, *Genocide*, vol. 2, pp. 63–85. See also the in-

credible tale of political manipulation and scholarly dishonesty on this subject in Roger W. Smith, Eric Markusen, and Robert Jay Lifton, "Professional Ethics and the Denial of Armenian Genocide," *Holocaust and Genocide Studies* 9 (1995):1–22.

85. Smith, "Denial of the Armenian Genocide," p. 71.

86. Johan Galtung, "Cultural Violence," *Journal of Peace Research* 27 (1990):291–305.

87. Lipstadt, *Denying the Holocaust*, pp. 7–8.

88. Smith, Markusen, and Lifton, "Professional Ethics and the Denial of Armenian Genocide," p. 16.

89. Elie Wiesel, "Now We Know," in *Genocide in Paraguay,* ed. Richard Arens (Philadelphia: Temple University Press, 1976), pp. 165–166.

90. Ibid., pp. 166–167.

About the Book

*E*valuating the Jewish Holocaust is by no means a simple matter, and one of the most controversial questions for academics is whether there have been any historical parallels for it. Have Armenians, Gypsies, American Indians, or others undergone a comparable genocide? In this fiercely controversial volume, distinguished scholars offer new discussions of this question. Presenting a wide range of strongly held views, they provide no easy consensus.

Some critics contend that if the Holocaust is seen as fundamentally different in kind from other genocides or mass deaths, the suffering of other persecuted groups will be diminished. Others argue that denying the uniqueness of the Holocaust will trivialize it. Alan Rosenbaum's introduction provides a much-needed context for readers to come to terms with this multi-dimensional dispute, to help them understand why it has recently intensified, and to enable them to appreciate what universal lessons might be gleaned from studying the Holocaust.

This volume makes an important contribution to our comprehension of one of the defining events of modern history. It should be essential reading for scholars, students, and general readers interested in the Holocaust and its relationship to other instances of politically inspired mass murder.

About the Contributors

Israel W. Charny is Professor of Psychology and Family Therapy at the Hebrew University of Jerusalem, Israel, and is executive director of the Institute on the Holocaust and Genocide (Jerusalem). He is the author of How Can We Commit the Unthinkable? Genocide, The Human Cancer (1982), and the editor of Toward the Understanding and Prevention of Genocide (1980), and three volumes in the series, Genocide: A Critical Bibliographic Review (1988, 1991, 1994). His writings have appeared as chapters in other edited works and in professional journals.

Vahakn N. Dadrian is former professor of sociology at the State University of New York at Geneseo (1970–1991) and is currently director of a major genocide studies project supported by the H. F. Guggenheim Foundation. He is the author of two monographs on Armenian genocide in the issues of *International Journal of Middle Eastern Studies* (1986, 1991). His monograph entitled "Genocide as a Problem of National and International Law: The World War I Armenian Case and Its Contemporary Legal Ramifications," first appeared in the *Yale Journal of International Law* (1989) and has now been published as a book in Turkish and French. His articles have appeared in many professional publications. He recently published a comprehensive study on the Armenian genocide entitled *History of the Armenian Genocide: Ethnic Conflict from the Balkans to Anatolia to the Caucasus* (1995, with French translation to come).

Seymour Drescher is professor of history at the University of Pittsburgh, Pennsylvania. His books include: *The Meaning of Freedom: Economics, Politics and Culture After Slavery* (with Frank McGlynn, 1992); *Capitalism and Anti-Slavery: British Mobilization in Comparative Perspective* (1986); *Econocide: British Slavery in the Era of Abolition* (1977); and many other writings in professional journals.

Barbara B. Green is professor of political science (and former associate provost and vice president) at Cleveland State University, Ohio. She is the author of *The Dynamics of Russian Politics: A Short History* (1994). Her other writings have appeared in many professional journals. In a recent issue of *Wellesley* magazine (Winter 1994), First Lady Hillary Rodham Clinton cited Green as among the best and most brilliant teachers she ever had.

Ian Hancock is professor of linguistics and English at the University of Texas at Austin. He is United Nations representative for the International Romani Union. He is the author of *The Pariah Syndrome: An Account of Gypsy Slavery and Persecution* (1988), and many articles in professional journals.

Steven T. Katz is professor of Jewish history and thought at Cornell University in Ithaca, New York, and editor of *Modern Judaism*. His latest books include: *The Holocaust in Historical Context*, vol. 1 (1994); *Mysticism and Philosophical Analysis* (1978); *Mysticism* *and Religious Traditions* (1983); and *Mysticism and Language* (1992). His writings have also appeared as chapters in other edited works and in professional journals.

Robert F. Melson is professor of political science at Purdue University and co-director of the Jewish Studies Program. His books include: *Nigeria: Modernization and the Politics of Communalism* (1971); and *Revolution and Genocide* (1992), and his writings have appeared in numerous professional journals.

Alan S. Rosenbaum is professor of philosophy at Cleveland State University, Ohio. He is the author and/or editor of four books: *The Philosophy of Human Rights: International Perspectives* (ed.) (1980); *Coercion and Autonomy: Foundations, Issues and Practices* (1986); *Constitutionalism: The Philosophical Dimension* (ed.) (1988); and *Prosecuting Nazi War Criminals* (1993). His articles have appeared in numerous professional journals.

Richard L. Rubenstein is currently president of the University of Bridgeport. He is the former Robert O. Lawton Distinguished Professor of Religion at Florida State University. His books include: *After Auschwitz* (1966); *The Cunning of History* (1975); *Approaches to Auschwitz* (with John Roth) (1987); and many other books and articles.

David E. Stannard is professor of American studies at the University of Hawaii. His books include: *Death in America* (1975); *The Puritan Way of Death* (1977); *Shrinking History* (1980); *Before the Horror: The Population of Hawai'i on the Eve of Western Contact* (1989); and *American Holocaust: The Conquest of the New World* (1992). He has published in numerous professional journals.

Index